COSY TASTES of POLAND

HEIRLOOM RECIPES
VOLUME 2

COSY TASTES of POLAND

Wacław Jankiewicz

HEIRLOOM RECIPES

VOLUME 2

CONTENTS

Introduction   *8*
How to use this book   *11*

6. Party Food   13

Oscypek with Cranberries and Boczek......15
Barbecued Kiełbaski.................................17
Zapiekanka..21
Tuna Salad...23
Kebab Salad...27
Pickled Mushroom Salad..........................31
Spinach, Feta and Boczek Salad...............35
"Greek" Fish (Ryba po grecku)..................39
Chicken Jelly..43

7. Cakes and Desserts   47

Victoria Sponge..49
Walnut Sponge with Almond Cream.......53
Tiramisu...59
Rhubarb Cake..63
Chocolate Cake with Apples,
Dried Fruit and Nuts................................67
Apple Pie..71
Plum Pie...75
Cherry and Custard Pie............................79
Coconut Cream Pie with Plum Jam..........85
Dewdrop Cheesecake...............................89
Viennese Cheesecake...............................93
Apple and Twaróg Cake...........................97
Napoleon..103
Kocie Oczka..109
Walnut Pie...113
Easy Kremówka......................................117
Cream Horns..121
Marmalade Biscuits................................127
Sweet Twaróg Biscuits............................131
Karpatka...135
Kajmak Pischinger..................................139

8. Fat Thursday   143

Pączki...145
Oponki..151
Faworki...155

Faworki folding techniques   *158*

9. Easter — 161

Easter Żurek 163
Sałatka Jarzynowa
(Polish Vegetable Salad) 167
Stuffed Eggs
with Sundried Tomatoes,
Garlic and Feta Cheese 171
Stuffed Eggs with Mushrooms 174
Stuffed Eggs with Tuna 176
Stuffed Eggs with Ham and Cheese 178
Easter Babka 181
Easter Keks 185
Makowiec (Poppy Seed Roll) 189

10. Christmas — 195

Christmas Eve Red Borscht
with Uszka 197
    Beetroot Zakwas 199
    Soured Red Borscht 203
    Uszka Filling 207
    Uszka Dough 211
    Uszka 215
Christmas Eve Fried Fish 221
Christmas Eve Sauerkraut with
Mushrooms 225
Makowiec with Walnut Cream
and Chocolate Glaze 229
Christmas Gingerbread Cake 235
Traditional Christmas
Gingerbread Biscuits 241
Mulled Wine 245

11. Pantry — 249

Tea-Boiled Ham 251
Beef and Poultry Pasztet 255
Ogórki Kiszone (Sour Gherkins) 259
Ogórki Konserwowe
(Pickled Gherkins) 263
Tomato Purée 267
Pickled Beetroot 271
Pickled Peppers 275
Seasoned Red Cabbage 279
Cucumber and Carrot Salad 283
Pickled Vegetable Salad 287
Courgette Leczo 291
Raspberry Juice 295
Strawberry Syrup 299
Sweet Cherry Kompot 301
Pear Kompot 304
Preserved Apple Slices 307
Apple Sauce 309
Raspberry Jam 313
Powidła Śliwkowe (Plum Jam) 317
Candied Orange Peel 321

Weights and measures   326
About the products   328
About the accessories   340
Pasteurisation   342
Index   344
Good to know   355
Polish pronunciation   362

Find more delicious recipes in volume 1

MORE TASTY GOODNESS...

Thank you so much for buying *Cosy Tastes of Poland: Heirloom Recipes Volume 2*. This book will introduce you to Polish cuisine - both traditional and more modern recipes that have been passed down through generations in my family.

And if you're hungry for more, feel free to visit my website, www.cosytastes.com, where you'll find even more recipes in a simple, step-by-step format. With them, creating something delicious will be easy!

You're also warmly invited to follow me on social media @CosyTastes.

Thank you and *Smacznego*!
Wacław

INTRODUCTION

Food has always been an important part of our everyday lives and of all the special occasions we so gladly celebrate in Poland and in my family home. Celebrating important occasions brings people closer, and delicious meals prepared especially for a given holiday are a great addition. From the times of my childhood, I remember how my grandmother Emilia fried *pączki* for Fat Thursday, how she prepared *święconka* on Easter or the twelve dishes on Christmas Eve. My mother Krystyna keeps these traditions alive, capturing them here to cherish the memory of them within the pages of this book.

With my grandma; Emilia

In the second volume of *Cosy Tastes of Poland: Heirloom Recipes* I collected my mother's and my grandmother's recipes which are a guarantee that your parties, festivities and family gatherings will have amazing flavours to remember. A big part of the book is dedicated to dishes served during the most important holidays in Polish culture – Easter and Christmas. Dishes prepared for these occasions make them unforgettable and magical and are a vital part of communal celebration and creating a homely atmosphere. The recipes I included in this book cannot exhaust the multitude of festive dishes that vary depending on the region, instead they present the tradition of my home, where I would like to invite you. I hope that these recipes will inspire you to explore and experiment in the kitchen.

When gathering with loved ones, having something sweet is also a must. My mum's apple pie is very popular – guests will often ask in anticipation of it. Tiramisu is also a hit at parties and family gatherings - I brought the flavour from Italy and managed to recreate it using ingredients available here. With this book you will also find other popular desserts – homemade *pączki*, delicious cookies, cheesecakes and pies filled with seasonal fruit. I'm sure once you taste them, you won't be able to resist having more!

The final chapter of the book is all about the pantry – it's where you will find preserves that use up seasonal fruit and vegetables. Carefully prepared by my mum, they allowed the flavours of summer to return in the middle of winter. Prepare your own preserves and see for yourself how easy it is!

I hope the recipes I included in this volume of the book will put you in a joyful, festive mood. If you want to learn about dishes cooked in Poland on an everyday basis, I encourage you to check out the first volume. There you will find recipes for breakfasts, soups, main courses, sides, and *pierogi* which Polish cuisine is famous for!

I wanted the recipes to be as clear and straightforward as possible. I hope you're going to use them to prepare something for you or your loved ones. Please let me know how you get on with them or send a photo - my contact details and other interesting recipes can be found on my website www.cosytastes.com.

Finally, I wish you many wonderful moments spent with family and friends at the table together. Eat, drink and be merry! *Smacznego!*

With my mother; Krystyna

I'd like to thank all the people that this book would be impossible without.

Your advice, suggestions, support and cheering are invaluable!

I'd especially like to thank my mum, Jamie and Bartłomiej

as well as Maria, Madzia and Maja, Ania and Marcin, Zofia and Michał.

HOW TO USE THIS BOOK

1. Before making the dish, read the recipe and prepare all the ingredients and utensils.

2. The "~" symbol means "approximately" and refers to the amount of ingredients or time needed to prepare a given dish.

3. If you are not familiar with one of the ingredients or aren't sure what substitute to use, check the "About the products" chapter. This information might help you find a local substitute.

4. In the "Good to know" section you will find information on most common dietary restrictions and allergens, but not all of them. Read the recipe and modify it according to your diet. The "Good to know" section also provides information about ingredient substitutions.

5. When you finish your work, remember to clean the kitchen and wash all of the utensils. This is good practice and will help your kitchen equipment last longer.

6. Enjoy your time cooking. Dishes made with love taste better: they will bring joy to your guests and give you great satisfaction.

6. PARTY FOOD

Meetings with family and friends are usually accompanied by something to eat – we don't need big celebrations to sit together at a table and share some delicacies! In this chapter you can find recipes for party classics that are easy to share – on both formal occasions, such as birthdays or name days, and during relaxed social gatherings.

For my readers from outside Poland, name days are a customer in which each day of the year is assigned one or more names. The names are of saints from the Catholic calendar. Name days are especially popular in Poland and observed in other Central and Eastern European countries, such as Greece and Sweden. The celebration day is determined by the person's birthday. Usually falling on the closest name day after their birthday. My mother's birthday is in January and her name day is in March.

Mum celebrates her name day instead of her birthday (I do the opposite), so she always prepares something to eat for her guests – often her pickled mushroom salad and a pie. It's not a big celebration, but she's always prepared for a visit from a neighbour or aunty Mary. On Mary's name day mum returns the visit. My aunty Mary always prepares a delicious spinach, feta and *boczek* salad – I simply had to include the recipe in this book!

Very often people also meet on *Majówka*. In the beginning of May in Poland a couple of holidays are celebrated, which means there are a few non-working days – it often turns into a long weekend. It is therefore assumed that this is a great time to start the barbecue season with family and friends, when you can't miss barbecued *kiełbasa* and other delicacies.

I hope that you and your guests enjoy my culinary ideas for a joyful gathering!

OSCYPEK WITH CRANBERRIES AND BOCZEK

Smoked, grilled cheese made with sheep's milk wrapped in crispy boczek. When served with cranberry jam, it is a simple, delicious appetiser, perfect for every occasion.

Difficulty	Makes	Preparation	Frying	Total
SIMPLE	8	~20 MIN	~20 MIN	~40 MIN

INGREDIENTS

For the *oscypek*
- ☐ 1 *oscypek* (or 8 small ones) (~320g) *(Note 1)*
- ☐ 300g smoked *boczek* (or smoked back bacon)

To serve
- ☐ 150g cranberry jam

 Polish products differ from the ones available locally. You will find more information about oscypek and pork in the chapter "About the products" on page 328.

DIRECTIONS

Preparing the *boczek*
1. If using a block of *boczek*, slice finely. Eight slices are needed.
2. Put the hob on medium heat.
3. Put into a frying pan.
4. Fry the *boczek* until golden and the fat has been released. Each side can take around 5 minutes.
5. Put the fried *boczek* onto a plate lined with paper towel. *(Note 2)*
6. Set the pan with leftover fat aside.

Preparing the *oscypek*
1. Cut the *oscypek* into 7mm slices. Eight slices are needed. *(Note 3)*
2. Put the hob on medium heat.
3. Add the sliced *oscypek* to the pan with the *boczek* fat.
4. Fry on both sides until slightly melted.

Preparing to serve
1. Wrap the *oscypek* with a slice of *boczek*.
2. Put a toothpick in the *oscypek*, so the *boczek* doesn't unwrap.
3. Put the jam in a small bowl for dipping.

To serve
- Can also be served with <u>ogórki kiszone (sour gherkins)</u>, cut the *ogórki kiszone* into quarters lengthwise and serve with the *oscypek*.

NOTES

1. You can buy different sizes of *oscypek*. Usually you buy it in packages containing 4 little portions.
2. The paper towel will absorb excess fat.
3. If the *oscypek* is small, you don't have to slice it.

KITCHEN ACCESSORIES

☐ frying pan
☐ small bowl
☐ knife
☐ chopping board
☐ large plate
☐ teaspoon
☐ fork
☐ toothpicks
☐ paper towel

GOOD TO KNOW

vegetarian option
- use a vegetarian bacon alternative
- swap the fat needed to fry the *oscypek* for 1 tsp butter

gluten-free

contains dairy
- contains *oscypek*

contains pork
- contains *boczek*

pork-free option
- use turkey ham as an alternative

kcal
- 354 per *oscypek*, 2832 total

GOES WELL WITH

Ogórki Kiszone **(Sour Gherkins)**
11. Pantry, page 259

Party Food

BARBECUED KIEŁBASKI

You should always begin barbecue season with delicious, barbecued kiełbaski! Using this fantastic marinade will enrich the flavour of the kiełbasa, turning it into a real superstar.

Difficulty SIMPLE	Serves 4	Preparation 15 MIN	Resting ~30 MIN	Grilling ~15 MIN	Total ~1 H

INGREDIENTS

For the *kiełbasa*
- 1kg *kiełbasa śląska* (Silesian *kiełbasa*)
- 2 garlic cloves (or 1½ tsp garlic powder)
- 6 tbsp olive oil
- 1 tsp paprika
- 1 tsp marjoram
- 1 tsp ground black pepper
- ½ tsp tarragon
- ½ tsp hot paprika (or chilli flakes)
- ½ tsp smoked paprika
- ½ tsp herbes de Provence

To serve
- bread
- ketchup
- mustard

 Polish products differ from the ones available locally. You will find more information about ketchup and kiełbasa in the chapter "About the products" on page 328.

DIRECTIONS

Preparing the marinade
1. Add the oil to a bowl.
2. Peel the garlic.
3. Crush the garlic into the bowl.
4. Add the spices: mild, hot and smoked paprika, marjoram, pepper, tarragon and herbes de Provence.
5. Mix well.

Preparing the *kiełbasa*
1. Make a cut in the *kiełbasa* on both sides.
2. Transfer to a container.
3. Pour the marinade over the *kiełbasa* until completely covered.
4. Put into the fridge for around 30 minutes.

Barbecuing
1. Put the *kiełbasa* on the barbecue grill.
2. Barbecue until browned and piping hot.

To serve
- Serve the *kiełbasa* with bread, ketchup and mustard.
- The *kiełbasa* can also be served with tzatziki.

KITCHEN ACCESSORIES

- ☐ bowl
- ☐ knife
- ☐ chopping board
- ☐ tablespoon
- ☐ teaspoons
- ☐ garlic crusher (press)
- ☐ food container

GOOD TO KNOW

gluten-free option
- use gluten-free bread to serve

contains pork
- contains Silesian *kiełbasa*

contains beef
- contains Silesian *kiełbasa*

kalorie
- without bread, ketchup and mustard
  992 per serving, 3968 total

fridge
- after barbecuing, until the next day
- can be eaten hot or cold – to reheat, heat oil in a frying pan and fry on each side, until the *kiełbasa* is warm; you can also reheat in the oven or microwave

GOES WELL WITH

Tzatziki
vol 1, 4. Sides, page 249

ZAPIEKANKA

The iconic Polish toasted baguette topped with a variety of ingredients. You can add mushrooms, sweetcorn, tomatoes, cucumbers and cheese. It's delicious served with mayonnaise, ketchup and a sprinkling of chives.

Difficulty	Makes	Preparation	Frying	Baking	Total
SIMPLE	2	15 MIN	~10 MIN	~5 MIN	~30 MIN

INGREDIENTS

For the *zapiekanka*
- ☐ 1 baguette (~140g)
- ☐ 250g mushrooms
- ☐ 1 onion (~150g)
- ☐ 1 tbsp butter
- ☐ 100g cheddar cheese

To serve
- ☐ 1 tinned sweetcorn (~200g)
- ☐ 1 tomato (~170g)
- ☐ ½ bunch of chives (~10g)
- ☐ ¼ cucumber (~100g)
- ☐ mayonnaise
- ☐ ketchup

 Polish products differ from the ones available locally. You will find more information about ketchup in the chapter "About the products" on page 328.

DIRECTIONS

Preparing the mushrooms and onion
1. Rinse the mushrooms and peel if necessary.
2. Chop finely.
3. Peel the onion and chop finely.
4. Put the hob on medium heat.
5. Melt the butter in a frying pan.
6. Add the chopped onion.
7. Occasionally stir with a wooden spoon.
8. Fry until translucent.
9. Add the chopped mushrooms.
10. Fry long enough for the liquid from the mushrooms to evaporate.
11. Set the fried mushrooms and onion aside.

Preparing the oven
1. Preheat the oven to 180°C / 350°F or gas 4.

Preparing the rest of the ingredients
1. Cut the baguette in half lengthwise.
2. Open the tin of sweetcorn and strain the liquid.
3. Grate the cheese using a grater with large holes into a bowl.
4. Rinse the tomato and slice.
5. Rinse the cucumber and slice.
6. Rinse the chives and chop finely.

Preparing the *zapiekanka*
1. Spread the mushroom and onion mixture on the baguette.
2. Sprinkle with grated cheese.
3. Put the baguettes onto a baking tray.

Baking
1. Bake for around 4-5 minutes, until the cheese melts.

To serve
1. Put the slices of tomato and cucumber on the *zapiekanka*.
2. Serve with mayonnaise and ketchup.
3. Sprinkle with chopped chives and sweetcorn.

KITCHEN ACCESSORIES

☐ frying pan
☐ 2 bowls
☐ knife
☐ chopping board
☐ large plate
☐ tablespoon
☐ 2 teaspoons
☐ wooden spoon
☐ grater
☐ tin opener
☐ baking tray (measured inside 30x26cm)

GOOD TO KNOW

 **vegetarian**

 contains mushrooms
- contains fresh mushrooms

 **gluten-free option**
- use a gluten-free baguette

 kcal
- 845 per *zapiekanka*, 1690 total

 contains dairy
- contains butter
- contains cheddar cheese

TUNA SALAD

*A simple tuna salad, full of flavour, texture,
and colour thanks to the addition of a variety of vegetables.
Perfect for any celebration or as a tasty sandwich filling.*

Difficulty	Serves	Preparation	Cooking	Resting	Total
SIMPLE	6	~20 MIN	8 MIN	30 MIN	~1 H

INGREDIENTS

For the salad
- ☐ 150g cheddar cheese
- ☐ 4 pickled gherkins (~200g) *(Note 1)*
- ☐ 1 tinned sweetcorn (~200g)
- ☐ 1 tinned peas (200g)
- ☐ 1 tin of tuna in spring water (~150g)
- ☐ 1 tomato (~170g)
- ☐ 3 tbsp mayonnaise
- ☐ 2 tbsp ketchup
- ☐ 1 tbsp yellow mustard
- ☐ salt to taste
- ☐ pepper to taste

For the onions
- ☐ 1 onion (~100g) *(Note 2)*
- ☐ 250ml boiling water

For the eggs
- ☐ 2 large eggs
- ☐ ~1 litre water *(Note 3)*

To serve
- ☐ a slice of your favourite bread

 Polish products differ from the ones available locally. You will find more information about ketchup in the chapter "About the products" on page 328.

DIRECTIONS

Preparing the eggs – part 1
1. Put the hob on medium heat.
2. Pour the water into a medium saucepan and bring to a boil.

Preparing the salad – part 1
1. Open the tinned tuna and drain the liquid.
2. Put the tuna into a large bowl.
3. Mash the tuna with a fork.
4. Open the tin of sweetcorn, strain and add to the bowl.
5. Open the tin of peas, strain and add to the bowl.
6. Cube the pickled gherkins and tomato, add to the bowl.

Preparing the eggs – part 2
1. The water should already be boiling.
2. Using a spoon, carefully lower the eggs into the water.
3. Boil for 8 minutes.
4. Turn off the heat.

5. Pour the hot water out and cover the eggs with cold water to cool.
6. Set the saucepan aside.

Preparing the salad – part 2
1. Peel the onion and chop finely.
2. Put into a sieve and rinse with hot water. *(Note 4)*
3. Squeeze the water out.
4. Transfer to the bowl.
5. Peel the eggs.
6. Rinse the eggs to get rid of any shell.
7. Grate using a grater with large holes into the bowl.
8. Grate the cheese using a grater with large holes into the bowl.
9. Add the mayonnaise, ketchup and mustard.
10. Add salt and pepper to taste.
11. Mix well.
12. Put into the fridge for around 30 minutes.

To serve
- Spread on a slice of your bread of choice.

NOTES

1. You can buy pickled gherkins or make them yourself. You will find a recipe for *ogórki konserwowe* (pickled gherkins) in the "Pantry" chapter.
2. You can also use red onion.
3. The amount of water needed for cooking the eggs will depend on the size of the saucepan. There should be enough water to cover the eggs completely.
4. Pouring hot water over the onions takes away some of their sharpness. If you are using red onion, you can omit this step.

KITCHEN ACCESSORIES

- ☐ medium saucepan
- ☐ large bowl
- ☐ knife
- ☐ chopping board
- ☐ 3 tablespoons
- ☐ fork
- ☐ grater
- ☐ tin opener
- ☐ sieve

GOOD TO KNOW

gluten-free option
- use gluten-free bread to serve

contains dairy
- contains cheddar cheese

contains fish
- contains tuna

fridge
- for up to 2 days

kcal
- without bread
  318 per serving, 1908 total

GOES WELL WITH

Ogórki Konserwowe **(Pickled Gherkins)**
11. Pantry, page 263

Party Food

KEBAB SALAD

A colourful kebab salad with marinated chicken is a must on the party table!
Spices in the marinade penetrate all the ingredients
and enrich the flavour of the whole dish.

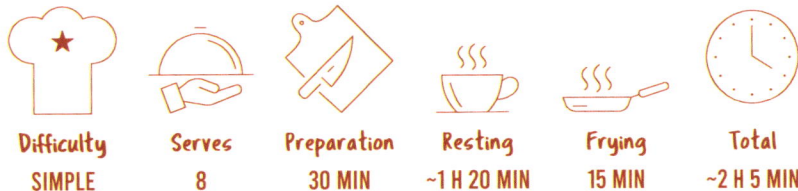

Difficulty	Serves	Preparation	Resting	Frying	Total
SIMPLE	8	30 MIN	~1 H 20 MIN	15 MIN	~2 H 5 MIN

INGREDIENTS

For the meat
- ☐ 500g chicken fillets
- ☐ 5 tbsp olive oil
- ☐ 15g kebab seasoning *(Note 1)*

For the kebab seasoning (optional) *(Note 2)*
- ☐ 3 tsp paprika
- ☐ 2 tsp ground coriander
- ☐ 1½ tsp mustard seeds
- ☐ 1½ tsp garlic powder
- ☐ 1½ tsp dried rosemary
- ☐ 1 tsp hot paprika (or chilli flakes) *(Note 3)*
- ☐ 1 tsp dried oregano
- ☐ 1 tsp salt
- ☐ ⅔ tsp ground black pepper
- ☐ ½ tsp dried thyme
- ☐ ½ tsp sugar
- ☐ ½ tsp ground turmeric
- ☐ ¼ tsp ground allspice
- ☐ 4 juniper berries
- ☐ 1 clove

For the salad
- ☐ 1 Chinese cabbage (~700g)
- ☐ 2 red onions (~220g)
- ☐ 4 sour gherkins (~200g) *(Note 4)*
- ☐ 4 pickled gherkins (~200g) *(Note 5)*
- ☐ 1 tinned sweetcorn (~200g)
- ☐ 2 garlic cloves (or 1½ tsp garlic powder) (optional)
- ☐ 100g natural yoghurt
- ☐ 3 tbsp mayonnaise
- ☐ 2 tbsp ketchup *(Note 6)*
- ☐ salt to taste (optional) *(Note 7)*
- ☐ pepper to taste

To serve
- ☐ a slice of your favourite bread

 Polish products differ from the ones available locally. You will find more information about ketchup and sour gherkins in the chapter "About the products" on page 328.

Party Food

DIRECTIONS

Preparing the kebab seasoning (optional)
1. Add all the ground spices to a bowl: paprika, spicy paprika, coriander, garlic powder, turmeric, allspice, salt and pepper.
2. Grind the mustard seeds and a clove in a pestle and mortar and add to the bowl with the rest of the spices.
3. Grind the juniper berries and sugar in the pestle and mortar and add to the bowl with the rest of the spices.
4. Grind the dried oregano, thyme and rosemary in the pestle and mortar and add to the bowl with the rest of the spices.
5. Mix well.

Preparing the meat – part 1
1. Cut the meat into small 1.5cm cubes.
2. Add 3 tbsp of oil to a bowl.
3. Add the kebab seasoning.
4. Mix well.
5. Add the pieces of meat.
6. Mix thoroughly so that the meat is covered with oil and spice.
7. Cover the bowl with cling film.
8. Put the meat in the fridge for around 30 minutes. *(Note 8)*
9. While waiting, prepare all the other ingredients.

Preparing the rest of the ingredients
1. Rinse the cabbage and chop finely.
2. Put into a large bowl.
3. Peel the onion and chop finely, then add to the bowl.
4. Cube the sour and pickled gherkins and add to the bowl.
5. Open the tin of sweetcorn, strain and add to the bowl.
6. Peel the garlic.
7. Crush the garlic into the bowl.
8. Mix well.
9. Set the bowl aside.

Preparing the meat – part 2
1. Put the hob on medium heat.
2. Heat 2 tbsp of oil in a frying pan.
3. Fry the meat until golden. This can take around 15 minutes.
4. Stir the meat frequently with a wooden spoon to prevent burning.
5. Transfer the meat to a separate bowl to cool. This can take around 20 minutes.

Preparing the salad
1. When the meat is cool, add to the bowl with the salad ingredients.
2. Mix well.
3. Add the yoghurt, mayonnaise and ketchup.
4. Add salt and pepper to taste.
5. Mix well.
6. Put into the fridge for around 30 minutes.

To serve
- Serve with a slice of your bread of choice.

NOTES

1. You can use a ready-made kebab seasoning or make your own according to the given recipe.
2. This amount of ingredients will give you 36g of kebab seasoning. You need 20 more minutes to make the seasoning, which you should add to the total time.
3. If you prefer a milder version, instead of 1 tsp hot paprika, use 1 tsp paprika.
4. You can buy sour gherkins or make them yourself. You will find a recipe for _ogórki kiszone (sour gherkins)_ in the "Pantry" chapter.
5. You can buy pickled gherkins or make them yourself. You will find a recipe for _ogórki konserwowe (pickled gherkins)_ in the "Pantry" chapter.
6. You can add mild or spicy ketchup, depending on what you prefer.
7. You'll only need the salt if the salad is not salty enough.
8. It would be best if you prepared the meat much earlier, so that it marinates for around 2 hours.

KITCHEN ACCESSORIES

- ☐ large bowl
- ☐ small bowl
- ☐ frying pan
- ☐ knife
- ☐ chopping board
- ☐ 3 tablespoons
- ☐ teaspoons

- ☐ wooden spoon
- ☐ garlic crusher (press)
- ☐ tin opener
- ☐ pestle and mortar (optional)
- ☐ cling film / plastic wrap
- ☐ paper towel

GOOD TO KNOW

gluten-free option
- use gluten-free bread to serve

contains dairy
- contains natural yoghurt

fridge
- for up to 2 days

kcal
- without bread
  180 per serving, 1440 total

GOES WELL WITH

Ogórki Kiszone **(Sour Gherkins)**
11. Pantry, page 259

Ogórki Konserwowe **(Pickled Gherkins)**
11. Pantry, page 263

PICKLED MUSHROOM SALAD

A delicious salad with pickled mushrooms, sour gherkins, eggs, cheese and sweetcorn.
A fantastic party dish also perfect for a picnic in the Polish forest.

Difficulty	Serves	Preparation	Cooking	Resting	Total
SIMPLE	6	30 MIN	8 MIN	30 MIN	~1 H 10 MIN

INGREDIENTS

For the salad
- [ ] 100g cheddar cheese
- [ ] 4 sour gherkins (or pickled) (~200g) *(Notes 1 and 2)*
- [ ] 1 jar pickled mushrooms (300g)
- [ ] 1 tinned sweetcorn (~200g)
- [ ] 4 tbsp mayonnaise
- [ ] 1½ tbsp yellow mustard
- [ ] salt to taste
- [ ] pepper to taste

For the eggs
- [ ] 5 large eggs
- [ ] ~1 litre water *(Note 3)*

To serve
- [ ] a slice of your favourite bread

 Polish products differ from the ones available locally. You will find more information about pickled mushrooms and sour gherkins in the chapter "About the products" on page 328.

DIRECTIONS

Preparing the eggs – part 1
1. Put the hob on medium heat.
2. Pour the water into a medium saucepan and bring to a boil.

Preparing the salad – part 1
1. Take the mushrooms out of the jar.
2. Put on a chopping board and cube finely.
3. Set a sieve over a bowl.
4. Put the mushrooms in the sieve and drain.
5. Put the drained mushrooms in a separate large bowl.
6. Set the bowl aside.

Preparing the eggs – part 2
1. The water should already be boiling.
2. Using a spoon, carefully lower the eggs into the water.
3. Boil for 8 minutes.
4. Turn off the heat.
5. Pour the hot water out and cover the eggs with cold water to cool.
6. Set the saucepan aside.

Party Food

Preparing the salad – part 2
1. Finely cube the sour gherkins.
2. Put the gherkins in a sieve and drain.
3. Put the drained gherkins in the bowl with the mushrooms.
4. Open the tin of sweetcorn, strain and add to the bowl.
5. Peel the eggs.
6. Rinse the eggs to get rid of any shell.
7. Grate using a grater with large holes into the bowl.
8. Grate the cheese using a grater with large holes into the bowl.
9. Add the mayonnaise and mustard.
10. Add salt and pepper to taste.
11. Mix well.
12. Put into the fridge for around 30 minutes.

To serve
- Spread on a slice of your bread of choice.
- Alternatively, cut a few slices of <u>tea-boiled ham</u> and place on the bread along with the salad.

NOTES

1. You can also use a mix of sour and pickled gherkins.
2. You can buy sour or pickled gherkins, or make them yourself. You will find a recipe for <u>*ogórki kiszone* (sour gherkins)</u> and for <u>*ogórki konserwowe* (pickled gherkins)</u> in the "Pantry" chapter.
3. The amount of water needed for cooking the eggs will depend on the size of the saucepan. There should be enough water to cover the eggs completely.

KITCHEN ACCESSORIES

- ☐ medium saucepan
- ☐ large bowl
- ☐ bowl
- ☐ knife
- ☐ chopping board
- ☐ 2 tablespoons
- ☐ grater
- ☐ tin opener
- ☐ sieve

GOOD TO KNOW

 vegetarian

 gluten-free option
- use gluten-free bread to serve

 contains dairy
- contains cheddar cheese

 contains mushrooms
- contains pickled mushrooms

 fridge
- for up to 2 days

 kcal
- without bread
  250 per serving, 1500 total

GOES WELL WITH

 **Tea-Boiled Ham**
11. Pantry, page 251

 ***Ogórki Konserwowe* (Pickled Gherkins)**
11. Pantry, page 263

 ***Ogórki Kiszone* (Sour Gherkins)**
11. Pantry, page 259

Party Food

SPINACH, FETA AND BOCZEK SALAD

A delicious salad which combines the flavours and textures of smoked boczek, feta and sunflower seeds. Crispy croutons are a great addition which adds even more texture to the salad.

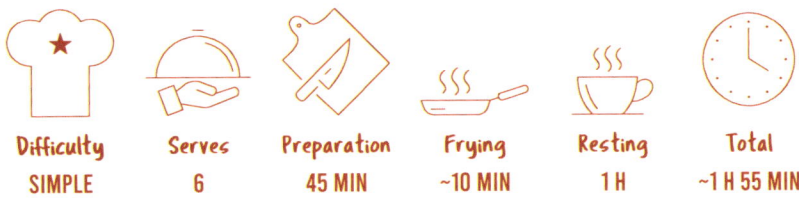

Difficulty	Serves	Preparation	Frying	Resting	Total
SIMPLE	6	45 MIN	~10 MIN	1 H	~1 H 55 MIN

INGREDIENTS

For the salad
- 300g smoked *boczek* (or smoked back bacon)
- 200g cherry tomatoes
- 200g feta cheese
- 170g fresh spinach
- 150g sunflower seeds
- 10 sundried tomato pieces
- 1 red onion (~130g)
- 1 avocado *(Note 1)*
- 4 tbsp sundried tomato oil
- pepper to taste

For the dressing
- 200ml natural yoghurt
- 1 garlic clove (or ¾ tsp garlic powder)
- 3 tbsp mayonnaise

For the croutons
- 2 bread slices

 Polish products differ from the ones available locally. You will find more information about pork in the chapter "About the products" on page 328.

DIRECTIONS

Preparing the sunflower seeds
1. Put the hob on low heat.
2. Pour the sunflower seeds into a frying pan and roast until golden. This can take around 3 minutes.
3. Shake the pan from time to time or stir the seeds with a wooden spoon.
4. Put the roasted seeds in a bowl and set aside.

Preparing the *boczek*
1. Chop the *boczek* into 1cm cubes.
2. Put into the frying pan.
3. Put the hob on medium heat.
4. Fry the *boczek* until golden and the fat has been released. This can take around 5 minutes.
5. Occasionally stir with a wooden spoon.
6. Put the fried *boczek* onto a plate lined with paper towel. *(Note 2)*

Party Food

Preparing the dressing
1. Put the yoghurt and mayonnaise together into a separate small bowl.
2. Peel the garlic.
3. Crush the garlic into the small bowl.
4. Mix well.
5. Set the bowl aside.

Preparing the salad
1. Rinse the spinach and pat dry with a paper towel.
2. Using scissors cut the stems from the leaves.
3. Put around ¾ of the leaves into a large bowl.
4. Cube the feta and add to the bowl with the spinach leaves.
5. Cut the sundried tomatoes into thin strips and put on top of the feta.
6. Add the *boczek*.
7. Slice the avocado in half.
8. Twist the halves to open the avocado.
9. Take the stone out of one of the halves. *(Note 3)*
10. Cube the avocado and add to the bowl. *(Note 4)*
11. Pour the sundried tomato oil over the salad.
12. Cut the cherry tomatoes in half and add to the salad.
13. Put the remaining spinach on top. *(Note 5)*
14. Pour the dressing over the salad.
15. Add the roasted sunflower seeds.
16. Peel the onion and chop finely.
17. Add to the salad.
18. Add pepper to taste.
19. Put into the fridge for around 1 hour.

Preparing the croutons
1. Toast the slices of bread until golden brown on both sides. *(Note 6)*
2. Cut into 1cm cubes.
3. Put into a separate bowl.

To serve
1. Put a portion of the salad on a plate.
2. Sprinkle with croutons. *(Note 7)*

NOTES

1. You can swap the avocado for a handful of olives.
2. The paper towel will absorb excess fat.
3. To take the stone out of the avocado, put the half with the stone in one hand. Take a knife with your other hand and hit the stone so the blade of the knife sticks into the stone. Mind your fingers. Pick up the knife along with the stone. Alternatively run a spoon around the stone and scoop it out.
4. To cube the avocado, take one half in one hand. Take a knife into the other hand. Score the inside of the avocado in a 0.5 cm grid pattern, deep enough so that the knife is touching the avocado skin, then run a spoon around the edge of the skin to remove the cubed avocado.
5. If the leaves are too big, you can tear them.
6. If you don't have a toaster, you can toast the bread in the oven.
7. Don't add the croutons too early because they will soak up the dressing and become soggy.

KITCHEN ACCESSORIES

- ☐ frying pan
- ☐ large bowl
- ☐ bowl
- ☐ small bowl
- ☐ knife
- ☐ chopping board
- ☐ large plate
- ☐ 3 tablespoons
- ☐ toaster
- ☐ wooden spoon
- ☐ garlic crusher (press)
- ☐ scissors
- ☐ paper towel

GOOD TO KNOW

vegetarian option
- use a vegetarian bacon alternative

gluten-free option
- use gluten-free bread to prepare croutons

contains dairy
- contains feta cheese
- contains natural yoghurt

contains pork
- contains *boczek*

pork-free option
- use turkey ham as an alternative

fridge
- until the next day

kcal
- 773 per serving, 4638 total

Party Food

"GREEK" FISH (RYBA PO GRECKU)

*Delicious Greek style dish made with fish and vegetables: carrot, parsley root, celeriac and onion.
It can be served both warm and cold, for dinner or just with a slice of bread.*

Difficulty	Serves	Preparation	Defrosting	Resting	Frying	Cooking	Total
INTERMEDIATE	8	1 H	4 H	2 H	~20 MIN	~25 MIN	~8 H

INGREDIENTS

For the fish
- ☐ 500g white fish fillets *(Note 1)*
- ☐ 1 onion (~150g)
- ☐ 3 tbsp plain flour
- ☐ 1 tsp salt
- ☐ 1 litre milk

For the vegetables
- ☐ 150g tomato paste
- ☐ 5-6 carrots (~500g)
- ☐ 5 onions (~450g)
- ☐ 2 parsnips (~300g)
- ☐ 1 celeriac (~400g)
- ☐ 5 allspice berries
- ☐ 4 bay leaves
- ☐ 150ml water
- ☐ 100ml cooking oil
- ☐ 1 tsp salt
- ☐ pepper to taste

For frying
- ☐ 6 tbsp cooking oil

To serve
- ☐ a slice of your favourite bread

 Polish products differ from the ones available locally. You will find more information about allspice in the chapter "About the products" on page 328.

DIRECTIONS

Preparing the fish (frozen)
1. Take the fish out of the freezer and rinse the ice.
2. Place on a large plate to defrost. This can take around 4 hours. *(Note 2)*
3. Cover the plate with aluminium foil, leaving some free space on the sides.
4. Pour the water out from time to time.

Preparing the fish (fresh/defrosted)
1. Check for and remove any bones in the fillets.
2. Chop the fillets into smaller pieces.

Soaking the fish
1. Pour the milk into a medium saucepan.
2. Add salt to the milk and stir until dissolved.
3. Set the saucepan aside.
4. Peel the onion, cut in half and then into thin slices.
5. Beginning with the onion, construct layers of onion and fish in a bowl finishing with onion on top.
6. Pour milk into the bowl to cover the fish.
7. Put the bowl in the fridge for 2 hours.

Preparing the fillets
1. Take the fillets out of the fridge.
2. Carefully pour the contents into a sieve to remove the milk.
3. Remove the onion from the fillets, the onion can be discarded.
4. Set a sieve over a bowl and let the fillets drain. Discard the milk.
5. Set the bowl aside.

Preparing the vegetables
1. Peel the carrot, parsnip and celeriac.
2. Grate using a grater with large holes.
3. Transfer to a separate bowl.
4. Peel the onion and chop finely.
5. Put the hob on medium heat.
6. Heat the oil in a large pot.
7. Turn the hob down to low heat.
8. Add the chopped onion.
9. Occasionally stir with a wooden spoon.
10. Fry until translucent.
11. When the onion is translucent, add the water to the pot.
12. Add prepared vegetables.
13. Add the spices: bay leaves, allspice, salt and pepper.
14. Mix well.
15. Cover the pot and simmer on low heat for around 15-20 minutes. *(Note 3)*
16. Occasionally stir with a wooden spoon.
17. While waiting, start flouring and frying the fish.

Flouring the fish
1. Put the flour into a soup plate.
2. Lay a fillet on the flour.
3. Sprinkle flour on both sides.
4. Transfer to a separate large plate.
5. Repeat with all the fillets.
6. Set aside.

Frying
1. Put the hob on medium heat.
2. Heat the oil in a frying pan.
3. Turn the hob down to low heat.
4. Put the fillets in the pan.
5. Fry on both sides until golden. Each side can take around 2-3 minutes. *(Note 4)*
6. Put the fried fillets onto a plate lined with paper towel. *(Note 5)*

Preparing the salad
1. After the vegetables have been simmering for 15-20 minutes add the fried fillets to the vegetables.
2. Add the tomato paste.
3. Stir to gently break the fish fillets.
4. Cover and simmer for around 5 minutes.
5. Turn off the hob.
6. Take out the bay leaves and allspice berries.

To serve
- Serve warm or cold with bread.

NOTES

1. You can use cod, blue grenadier, pollock or hake fillets.
2. Put only one layer of fish on the plate. If you have more, put them on a second plate. Don't put the fillets on top of each other because they won't defrost and might freeze together. Water will leak from the fish which you need to pour out. Don't put the fillets on a paper towel because they might stick.
3. Don't boil the vegetables for too long – you don't want them to be soft. They should be crunchy, since they will keep cooking when mixed with the fish.
4. While frying, check if the edges of the fish have become golden. When it happens, that side should be ready.
5. The paper towel will absorb excess fat.

KITCHEN ACCESSORIES

- ☐ large pot with lid
- ☐ medium saucepan
- ☐ frying pan
- ☐ 2 bowls
- ☐ measuring jug
- ☐ knife
- ☐ peeling knife
- ☐ chopping board
- ☐ soup plate

- ☐ 2 large plates
- ☐ tablespoon
- ☐ teaspoon
- ☐ wooden spoon
- ☐ silicone spatula
- ☐ grater
- ☐ sieve
- ☐ aluminium foil
- ☐ paper towel

GOOD TO KNOW

gluten-free option
- swap flour for a gluten-free version
- use gluten-free bread to serve

contains dairy
- contains milk

contains fish
- contains fish fillets

fridge
- for up to 3 days
- can be eaten hot or cold – reheat the dish on a frying pan or microwave

kcal
- without bread
  320 per serving, 2560 total

CHICKEN JELLY

A delicate and delicious chicken jelly with a hard-boiled egg and vegetables: carrots, sweetcorn and peas. Perfect for parties and buffets.

Difficulty	Makes	Preparation	Cooking	Resting	Total
INTERMEDIATE	8	1 H	40 MIN	~4 H 20 MIN	~6 H

INGREDIENTS

For the broth
- ☐ 3 chicken thighs (~1.2kg)
- ☐ 2 carrots (~280g)
- ☐ 1 parsnip (~100g)
- ☐ 1 piece of celeriac (~200g)
- ☐ 10cm piece of leek (green part, ~50g)
- ☐ 1 onion (~100g)
- ☐ 2 garlic cloves (or 1½ tsp garlic powder)
- ☐ 4 allspice berries
- ☐ 3 bay leaves
- ☐ 1 tsp peppercorns
- ☐ salt to taste
- ☐ ~2 litres water

For the eggs
- ☐ 4 large eggs
- ☐ ~1 litre water *(Note 1)*

For the jelly
- ☐ 2 bunches of parsley (~60 g)
- ☐ ~40g gelatine *(Note 2)*
- ☐ 1 tinned sweetcorn (340g)
- ☐ 1 tinned peas (200g)

To serve
- ☐ a slice of your favourite bread

 Polish products differ from the ones available locally. You will find more information about allspice in the chapter "About the products" on page 328.

DIRECTIONS

Preparing the eggs – part 1
1. Put the hob on medium heat.
2. Pour the water into a medium saucepan and bring to a boil.

Preparing the broth – part 1
1. Put the meat into a large pot.
2. Cover the meat with water (around 2 litres).
3. Add the spices: peppercorns, allspice and bay leaves.
4. Put the hob on medium heat.
5. Bring the water to a boil.
6. Reduce the heat and simmer for around 1 hour.
7. Check the water level when simmering and refill if too much water has evaporated. There should be enough water to cover all the ingredients.
8. During the cooking process, foam can appear on the surface. Remove using a slotted spoon. *(Note 3)*

Preparing the vegetables
1. Peel the carrot and cut lengthwise.
2. Peel the parsnip and cut into large pieces; leave the end whole.
3. Peel the celeriac and cut into large pieces.
4. Take the outer leaves off the leek and cut off any withered parts.

Party Food

5. Cut 10cm off the top of the leek and rinse to remove the grit.
6. Slice the leek into 3 smaller pieces.
7. Peel the garlic.
8. Transfer the prepared vegetables to a plate.

Preparing the onion
1. Peel the onion and cut in half.
2. Put on the gas, cut side down and burn on the flame. This can take around 4-5 minutes. *(Note 4)*
3. Put the onion on the plate next to the other vegetables.

Preparing the eggs – part 2
1. The water should already be boiling.
2. Using a spoon, carefully lower the eggs into the water.
3. Boil for 8 minutes.
4. Turn off the heat.
5. Pour the hot water out and cover the eggs with cold water to cool.
6. Set the saucepan aside.

Preparing the broth – part 2
1. To the meat, add the vegetables prepared earlier: carrot, parsnip, celeriac, leek, garlic and burnt onion. *(Note 5)*
2. After around 1 hour of simmering, check if the meat is soft. Be careful: the meat will be very hot! *(Note 6)*
3. Check the water level when simmering and refill if too much water has evaporated. There should be enough water to cover all the ingredients.
4. At the end of cooking, add salt to taste.
5. Turn off the hob.

Preparing the gelatine
1. After cooking the broth, strain into a separate large pot.
2. Put the boiled meat and vegetables on a plate and wait until cool enough to handle. This can take around 20 minutes. *(Note 7)*
3. Put the gelatine in the broth and stir thoroughly to dissolve.
4. Set aside. *(Note 8)*
5. While waiting, prepare the eggs and all the other ingredients.

Preparing the eggs – part 3
1. Peel the eggs.
2. Rinse the eggs to get rid of any shell.
3. Put in a soup plate and cut in half.

Preparing the rest of the ingredients
1. Cube the cooked and cooled carrots, parsnips and celeriac.
2. Put into a bowl and set aside.
3. Using a fork, separate the meat from the bones and chop finely. *(Note 9)*
4. Put into a separate bowl and set aside.
5. Open the tin of sweetcorn, strain and set aside.
6. Open the tin of peas, strain and set aside.
7. Rinse the parsley and chop finely.
8. Leave on the chopping board and set aside.

Preparing the jelly
1. Put an egg half into a small bowl.
2. Then add layers of:
   - 1 tbsp parsley
   - a handful of carrot, parsnip and celeriac pieces
   - 1 tsp canned peas
   - a few meat pieces
   - 1 tbsp sweetcorn
3. Repeat with the remaining 7 small bowls. *(Note 10)*
4. Pour the broth with the gelatine over all the ingredients.
5. Set aside to cool completely and then put into the fridge so that the jelly sets completely. This can take around 4 hours.

To serve
1. Loosen the jelly from within a bowl using a knife.
2. Put the bowl upside down on a plate so the jelly falls out.
3. Serve with a slice of your bread of choice.

NOTES

1. The amount of water needed for cooking the eggs will depend on the size of the saucepan. There should be enough water to cover the eggs completely.
2. Use 20g of gelatine per litre of broth.
3. Removing the foam will make the jelly clearer.
4. You can also cut the onion into very thick slices and burn them in a frying pan (without any oil) which you put on low heat. This can take around 10 minutes.
5. Add the vegetables to the broth only after removing the foam with a slotted spoon.
6. When the meat is soft, you can turn off the heat. If not, cook it until it's tender.
7. You won't need the onions, leek and garlic, as well as the bay leaves and allspice berries.
8. Don't worry – gelatine doesn't set too quickly, so you have enough time to prepare other jelly ingredients.
9. Warm meat falls off the bone very easily. It's going to be much more difficult when the meat is cold.
10. If some of the ingredients remain, distribute them between bowls.

KITCHEN ACCESSORIES

- ☐ 2 large pots
- ☐ medium saucepan
- ☐ 8 small bowls
- ☐ 2 bowls
- ☐ knife
- ☐ peeling knife
- ☐ chopping board
- ☐ soup plate

- ☐ large plate
- ☐ 2 tablespoons
- ☐ teaspoon
- ☐ fork
- ☐ slotted spoon
- ☐ tin opener
- ☐ sieve

GOOD TO KNOW

gluten-free option
- use gluten-free bread to serve

contains pork
- contains gelatine – check the type of gelatine

pork-free option
- use agar instead of gelatine

contains beef
- contains gelatine – check the type of gelatine

beef-free option
- use agar instead of gelatine

fridge
- for up to 3 days

kcal
- without bread
  502 per serving, 4016 total

7. CAKES AND DESSERTS

Since I can remember, my mum baked a pie every Saturday. It was usually apple pie with apples straight from the orchard or dewdrop cheesecake. We usually snook a piece on Saturday, even though the pie was meant for Sunday afternoon. Our family usually visited us then, and mum could treat them to a freshly baked cake.

Cakes and other sweet baked goods are very common in Poland. When you visit someone, you can be almost certain you will be treated to a coffee or tea and something sweet – my grandmother Emilia, for example, baked amazing sweet *twaróg* biscuits and my mum for special occasions prepares more labour intensive cakes such as the Napoleon, *kremówka* or coconut cream pie with plum jam. A cake or other dessert is also a great gift for our host when we are visiting someone – I always bring the tiramisu that my friends often ask about. I brought back the recipe for this dessert from Italy; right after I returned to Poland, I prepared a couple of versions to recreate the flavour I remembered with ingredients I had on hand, so that the mascarpone cream was perfectly sweet and the sponge fingers as moist as they should be. I've never shared this recipe with anyone – but I am going to make an exception for you.

Taking into consideration the changing seasons and the availability of fruit, many seasonal cakes are baked in Poland – in the spring we bake rhubarb cake, cherry and custard pie is a great choice in the summer, while in the autumn we might choose the delicious plum or walnut pies. As you can see – we're never short on occasions to eat something sweet. We also make very special sweets for Fat Thursday, for Easter and Christmas – you will find the recipes in the following chapters!

I encourage you to bake something tasty and share it with your loved ones – I am sure that no one will be able to refuse at least a piece of delicious cake!

VICTORIA SPONGE

A delicious Polish take on an English recipe for a very soft sponge with jam and a delicious vanilla cream filling.
This classic Anglo-Polish Victoria Sponge is a cake perfect for every occasion.

Difficulty	Serves	Preparation	Baking	Resting	Total
INTERMEDIATE	12	1 H	30 MIN	30 MIN	2 H

INGREDIENTS

For the sponge
- ☐ 80g plain flour
- ☐ 80g potato starch
- ☐ 80g sugar
- ☐ 16g vanilla sugar
- ☐ 5 large eggs
- ☐ 1 tsp baking powder

For the cream filling
- ☐ 150g unsalted butter (+ more for buttering the tin)
- ☐ 16g vanilla sugar
- ☐ 2 tbsp sugar
- ☐ 1 tbsp potato starch
- ☐ 1 tbsp plain flour
- ☐ 250ml milk

For the filling
- ☐ ~150g strawberry jam *(Note 1)*

For soaking the sponge
- ☐ 1 tea bag (black tea)
- ☐ 1 tsp sugar
- ☐ 250ml hot water
- ☐ lemon juice

For the decoration
- ☐ 2 tbsp icing sugar

 Polish products differ from the ones available locally. You will find more information about potato starch and vanilla sugar in the chapter "About the products" on page 328.

DIRECTIONS

Preparing the cream filling – part 1
Preparing the butter
1. Take the butter out of the fridge.
2. Cube the butter.
3. Transfer to a large bowl.
4. Set the bowl aside. *(Note 2)*

Preparing the sponge
Preparing the cake tin
1. Using scissors, cut the baking paper as a single sheet, to cover the bottom and inner sides of the tin.
2. Brush the cake tin with butter so the paper sticks.
3. Line the cake tin with the baking paper.
4. Grease the baking paper with more butter.
5. Set the cake tin aside.

Cakes and Desserts

Preparing the flour and sugar
1. Sift the flour and starch into a separate bowl.
2. Add the baking powder.
3. Set the bowl aside.
4. Measure the sugar into another separate small bowl.

Preparing the egg whites
1. Separate the yolks from the whites. Put the yolks in a large bowl and the whites in the bowl of a food mixer. *(Note 3)*
2. Add 1 tbsp of the prepared sugar to the egg whites. *(Note 4)*
3. Whisk the egg whites to stiff peaks. This can take around 10 minutes.
4. While waiting, prepare the yolks.

Preparing the yolks
1. To the bowl with the yolks add the vanilla sugar and the remaining sugar.
2. Using a hand mixer combine all of the ingredients. This can take around 5 minutes.
3. Set the prepared yolks aside.

Preparing the oven
1. Preheat the oven to 180°C / 350°F or gas 4.

Preparing the cake batter
1. Add the egg whites to the bowl with the yolks spoon by spoon.
2. Fold in the egg white with a spatula.
3. Add the flour gradually.
4. Mix to combine the ingredients with the hand mixer turned off. *(Note 5)*
5. Whisk thoroughly to combine all the ingredients.
6. Pour the mixture into the prepared baking tin.
7. Spread evenly using a spatula.

Baking
1. Bake for around 30 minutes. *(Note 6)*
2. Don't open the oven while baking, so the sponge doesn't sink.
3. When the sponge is ready, remove from the tin and place on a cooling rack to cool completely. This can take around 30 minutes.
4. While waiting, prepare the cream filling.

Preparing the cream filling – part 2
Preparing the milk and flour
1. Pour around 100ml of milk into a bowl.
2. Add the plain flour and potato starch.
3. Using a hand mixer, combine all the ingredients. Whisk for around 1 minute.
4. Set the bowl aside.

Preparing the mixture
1. Put the hob on low heat.
2. Put the remaining milk in a medium saucepan (around 150ml).
3. Bring to a boil. *(Note 7)*
4. Add the milk with the flour to the boiling milk.
5. Keep stirring with a wooden spoon until uniform. *(Note 8)*
6. When the mixture starts bubbling, cook for 2 minutes.
7. Turn off the hob.
8. Add the sugar and vanilla sugar.
9. Mix well.
10. Set aside to cool completely. This can take around 30 minutes. *(Note 9)*
11. Stir from time to time.

Finishing the cream filling
1. The mixture needs to have cooled before continuing.
2. Using a hand mixer, whip the butter in the large bowl.
3. Add the mixture spoon by spoon.
4. Whisk until the ingredients are combined.

Preparing the cake
Preparing the tea (Notes 10 and 11)
1. Brew the tea in a cup.
2. Add sugar and lemon juice.
3. Stir for the sugar to dissolve.

Layering the sponge
1. Remove the baking paper from the cake.
2. Using a bread knife, cut the sponge in half lengthwise. The sponge may still be warm! *(Note 12)*
3. Add fresh baking paper to the baking tin and set aside. *(Note 13)*
4. Only start layering the sponge with cream filling when the cake has cooled completely.

5. Put the base of the sponge in the cake tin.
6. Sprinkle with tea. *(Note 14)*
7. Spread the jam evenly over the sponge using a spatula.
8. Put the cream filling on the jam layer. *(Note 15)*
9. Spread evenly.
10. Sprinkle the second sponge with tea on the inner side. *(Note 16)*
11. Put the second sponge on top of the cream filling, so that the wet side touches the filling.
12. Put the cake in the fridge for around 30 minutes so the cream filling can set.

To serve
- Sprinkle the cake with icing sugar.

NOTES

1. You can swap the strawberry jam with raspberry jam. You will find a recipe for raspberry jam in the "Pantry" chapter.
2. When the butter is at room temperature, it's easier to fold into the mixture.
3. If you don't have a food mixer, you can prepare the batter in a large bowl using a hand mixer.
4. The remaining sugar will be added to the bowl with the yolks.
5. This will prevent the mixer from blowing the flour everywhere.
6. After around 30 minutes, check if the sponge is cooked inside. Be careful: the sponge will be very hot! Insert a toothpick right to the bottom of the sponge. If some batter is stuck to the toothpick, bake the sponge for 5 more minutes. After this time check the sponge again and bake for 5 additional minutes if it's not ready.
7. When the milk is close to boiling, it starts to foam and bubble so watch it to ensure it does not boil over.
8. Lumps are going to form at first, but as you keep stirring, you'll get a uniform mixture.
9. You can cool the mixture quicker by pouring cold water into the sink and resting the saucepan in the cold water. The mixture should cool completely in around 10 minutes.
10. You don't have to use all the tea to soak the sponge.
11. You can prepare the tea earlier. It doesn't matter if you use hot or cold tea.
12. If you cut the sponge, it will cool down faster.
13. Baking paper will secure the sides of the sponge while you make more layers.
14. Wait for the sponge to soak up the tea before you add the jam.
15. Don't put the whole filling in one spot, because then it will be combined with the jam. Spoon the filling in several spots and only then start spreading it on the sponge.
16. Wait for the sponge to soak up the tea.

KITCHEN ACCESSORIES

- ☐ medium saucepan
- ☐ 2 large bowls
- ☐ 2 bowls
- ☐ cup
- ☐ measuring jug
- ☐ knife
- ☐ bread knife
- ☐ chopping board
- ☐ 2 tablespoons
- ☐ 2 teaspoons
- ☐ hand mixer
- ☐ food mixer
- ☐ wooden spoon
- ☐ spatula
- ☐ scissors
- ☐ toothpick
- ☐ sieve
- ☐ kitchen scale
- ☐ cooling rack
- ☐ cake tin (diameter 20cm, height 7cm)
- ☐ baking paper

GOOD TO KNOW

 vegetarian

 contains dairy
- contains butter
- contains milk

 fridge
- for up to 3 days

 kcal
- 265 per serving, 3180 total

GOES WELL WITH

 **Raspberry Jam**
11. Pantry, page 313

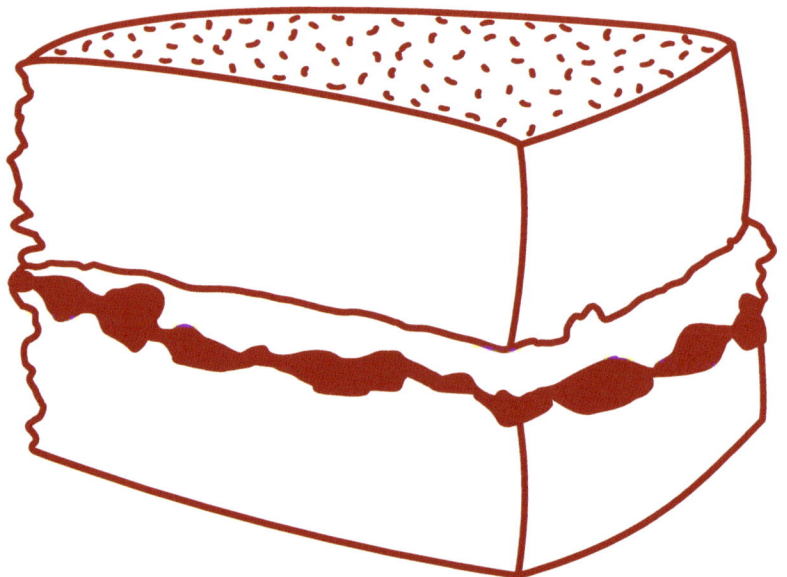

Cakes and Desserts

WALNUT SPONGE WITH ALMOND CREAM

A very delicate, soft sponge made with ground walnuts layered with a delicious almond cream.
Make yourself a cup of tea, cut yourself a slice of cake and enjoy the moment.

Difficulty	Serves	Preparation	Baking	Resting	Total
INTERMEDIATE	15	1 H 10 MIN	50 MIN	30 MIN	2 H 30 MIN

INGREDIENTS

For the sponge
- 320g coarsely milled wheat flour (krupczatka)
- 200g sugar
- 130g walnuts
- 32g vanilla sugar
- 10 large eggs

For the cream filling
- 180g unsalted butter (+ more for buttering the tin)
- 30g almond sugar *(Note 1)*
- 3 tbsp sugar
- 2 tbsp potato starch
- 2 tbsp plain flour
- 500ml milk

For soaking the sponge
- 1 tea bag (black tea)
- 1 tsp sugar
- 250ml hot water
- lemon juice

For the decoration
- 4 tbsp icing sugar

 Polish products differ from the ones available locally. You will find more information about almond sugar, mąka krupczatka, potato starch and vanilla sugar in the chapter "About the products" on page 328.

DIRECTIONS

Preparing the cream filling – part 1
Preparing the butter
1. Take the butter out of the fridge.
2. Cube the butter.
3. Transfer to a large bowl.
4. Set the bowl aside. *(Note 2)*

Cakes and Desserts

Preparing the sponge
Preparing the baking tin
1. Using scissors, cut the baking paper as a single sheet, to cover the bottom and inner sides of the tin.
2. Brush the baking tin with butter so the paper sticks.
3. Line the baking tin with the baking paper.
4. Grease the baking paper with more butter.
5. Set the baking tin aside.

Preparing the ingredients
1. Separate the yolks from the whites. Put the yolks in a small bowl and the whites in the bowl of a food mixer. *(Note 3)*
2. Sift the flour into a separate bowl.
3. Measure the sugar into another separate small bowl.
4. Finely chop 1 tbsp of walnuts.
5. Put into a separate bowl.
6. Grind the rest of the nuts. *(Note 4)*
7. Add to the bowl with the chopped nuts.

Preparing the cake batter – part 1
1. Add both sugars to the egg whites.
2. Whisk the egg whites to stiff peaks. This can take around 10 minutes.

Preparing the oven
1. Preheat the oven to 180°C / 350°F or gas 4.

Preparing the batter – part 2
1. Add the yolks to the whipped mixture.
2. Add the flour and prepared nuts.
3. Whisk until the ingredients are combined. This can take around 10 minutes.
4. Pour the mixture into the prepared baking tin.
5. Spread evenly using a spatula.

Baking
1. Bake for around 50 minutes, until golden. *(Note 5)*
2. When the sponge is ready, remove from the tin and place on a cooling rack to cool completely. This can take around 30 minutes.
3. While waiting, prepare the cream filling.

Preparing the cream filling – part 2
Preparing the milk and flour
1. Pour around 100ml of milk into a bowl.
2. Add the plain flour and potato starch.
3. Using a hand mixer, combine all the ingredients. Whisk for around 1 minute.
4. Set the bowl aside.

Preparing the mixture
1. Put the hob on low heat.
2. Put the remaining milk in a medium saucepan (around 400ml).
3. Bring to a boil. *(Note 6)*
4. Add the milk with the flour to the boiling milk.
5. Keep stirring with a wooden spoon until uniform. *(Note 7)*
6. When the mixture starts bubbling, cook for 3 more minutes.
7. Turn off the hob.
8. Add the sugar and almond sugar.
9. Mix well.
10. Set aside to cool completely. This can take around 30 minutes. *(Note 8)*
11. Stir from time to time.

Finishing the cream filling
1. The mixture needs to have cooled before continuing.
2. Using a hand mixer, whip the butter in the large bowl.
3. Add the mixture spoon by spoon.
4. Whisk until the ingredients are combined.

Preparing the cake
Preparing the tea (Notes 9 and 10)
1. Brew the tea in a cup.
2. Add sugar and lemon juice.
3. Stir for the sugar to dissolve.

Layering the sponge
1. Remove the baking paper from the cake.
2. Using a bread knife, cut the sponge in half lengthwise. The sponge may still be warm. *(Note 11)*
3. Add fresh baking paper to the baking tin and set aside. *(Note 12)*
4. Only start layering the sponge with cream filling when the cake has cooled completely.
5. Put the base of the sponge in the baking tin.
6. Sprinkle with tea. *(Note 13)*
7. Spread the cream filling evenly over the sponge using a spatula.
8. Sprinkle the second sponge with tea on the inner side. *(Note 14)*
9. Put the second sponge on top of the cream filling, so that the wet side touches the filling.
10. Put the cake in the fridge for around 30 minutes so the cream filling can set.

To serve
- Sprinkle the cake with icing sugar.

NOTES

1. You can swap the almond sugar with 30g of vanilla sugar.
2. When the butter is at room temperature, it's easier to fold into the mixture.
3. If you don't have a food mixer, you can prepare the batter in a large bowl using a hand mixer.
4. You can use a blender instead of the nut grinder.
5. After around 50 minutes, check if the sponge is cooked inside. Be careful: the sponge will be very hot! Insert a toothpick right to the bottom of the sponge. If some batter is stuck to the toothpick, bake the sponge for 5 more minutes. After this time check the sponge again and bake for 5 additional minutes if it's not ready.
6. When the milk is close to boiling, it starts to foam and bubble so watch it to ensure it does not boil over.
7. Lumps are going to form at first, but as you keep stirring, you'll get a uniform mixture.
8. You can cool the mixture quicker by pouring cold water into the sink and resting the saucepan in the cold water. The mixture should cool completely in around 10 minutes.
9. You don't have to use all the tea to soak the sponge.
10. You can prepare the tea earlier. It doesn't matter if you use hot or cold tea.
11. If you cut the sponge, it will cool down faster.
12. Baking paper will secure the sides of the sponge while you make more layers.
13. When the tea has soaked into the sponge add the cream filling straight away. If left too long, it will become difficult to spread the cream over the sponge.
14. Wait for the sponge to soak up the tea.

KITCHEN ACCESSORIES

- ☐ medium saucepan
- ☐ large bowl
- ☐ 4 bowls
- ☐ small bowl
- ☐ cup
- ☐ measuring jug
- ☐ knife
- ☐ bread knife
- ☐ chopping board
- ☐ 2 tablespoons
- ☐ teaspoon
- ☐ nut grinder (or hand blender)
- ☐ hand mixer
- ☐ food mixer
- ☐ wooden spoon
- ☐ spatula
- ☐ scissors
- ☐ toothpick
- ☐ sieve
- ☐ kitchen scale
- ☐ cooling rack
- ☐ baking tin (measured inside 35 x 20 x 7cm)
- ☐ baking paper

GOOD TO KNOW

vegetarian

contains dairy
- contains butter
- contains milk

contains nuts
- contains walnuts
- contains almond sugar

fridge
- for up to 3 days

kcal
- 392 per serving, 5880 total

Cakes and Desserts 57

TIRAMISU

Delicious Italian tiramisu is also very popular in Poland. Check out this amazing dessert with the rich flavour of coffee and amaretto liqueur and a delicate light cream.

Difficulty	Serves	Preparation	Resting	Total
SIMPLE	10	~1 H	2 H	3 H

INGREDIENTS

For the coffee
- 6 tsp instant espresso coffee
- 1 litre water
- 100ml amaretto

For the cream mixture
- 500g mascarpone
- 140g sugar
- 4 large eggs

For the tiramisu
- 2½ tbsp cocoa powder
- 300g sponge fingers

DIRECTIONS

Preparing the coffee
1. Put the hob on medium heat.
2. Pour 250 ml of water into a small saucepan or kettle and bring to a boil.
3. Put the coffee in a medium saucepan.
4. Cover with boiling water.
5. Mix well.
6. Add 750 ml of cold water.
7. Add the amaretto.
8. Mix well.
9. Set aside.

Preparing the cream mixture
Preparing the yolks
1. Separate the yolks from the whites into two separate small bowls.
2. Add the yolks to a food mixer bowl. *(Note 1)*
3. Add the sugar, leaving 2 tbsp aside. *(Note 2)*
4. Whisk the yolks with the sugar. This can take around 5 minutes.
5. Add the mascarpone.
6. Whisk so that all ingredients are combined together. This can take around 5 minutes.
7. Set the yolk mixture aside.

Preparing the egg whites
1. Add the egg whites to a separate bowl.
2. Add the remaining sugar.
3. Whisk the egg whites to stiff peaks. This can take around 10 minutes.
4. Set the egg whites aside.

Cakes and Desserts

Combining both mixtures
1. Add the egg whites to the bowl with the yolks spoon by spoon.
2. Fold in the egg white with a spatula. *(Note 3)*
3. Set the cream mixture aside.

Preparing the tiramisu
1. Pour the coffee into a soup plate. *(Note 4)*
2. Soak the sponge fingers in the coffee and lay in a single layer in a serving dish. *(Note 5)*
3. Put half the cream mixture on the sponge fingers.
4. Spread evenly.
5. Using a teaspoon, put the cocoa in a sieve and sprinkle the cream mixture, until fully covered.
6. Put another layer of coffee-soaked sponge fingers on the cream mixture.
7. Cover with the remaining cream mixture.
8. Spread evenly.
9. Sprinkle with cocoa powder.
10. Clean the edges of the serving dish. *(Note 6)*
11. Cover with aluminium foil.
12. Put into the fridge for around 2 hours.

To serve
- Serve a portion of tiramisu with a cup of espresso.

NOTES

1. If you don't have a food mixer, you can prepare the cream mixture in a large bowl using a hand mixer.
2. You will use the remaining sugar when whisking the egg whites.
3. Delicately, with circular movements, stir the whipped whites into the yolks and mascarpone, so that two mixtures combine. Don't mix too fast so as not to lose the air in the whisked egg whites. This will make for a more delicate mixture.
4. If the biscuits absorb all coffee from the plate, add some more. You don't need to use all of the coffee.
5. You will layer all the ingredients in a serving dish. When ready, you can cut the tiramisu into portions. Alternatively you can swap the serving dish for small bowls and you'll have your prepared portions ready to serve. Soak the sponge fingers long enough to soak up the coffee and become tender. Be careful they don't dissolve. Soaking time will depend on how dry and crumbly they are. Some sponge fingers are sprinkled with sugar – you might need to soak them longer.
6. You can wipe the edges of the serving dish with a wet paper towel.

KITCHEN ACCESSORIES

- ☐ medium saucepan
- ☐ small saucepan
- ☐ serving dish
  (measured inside 32 x 25 x 6cm)
- ☐ bowl
- ☐ 2 small bowls
- ☐ measuring jug
- ☐ soup plate
- ☐ small plate
- ☐ 2 tablespoons
- ☐ 2 teaspoons
- ☐ food mixer
- ☐ small sieve
- ☐ aluminium foil
- ☐ paper towel

GOOD TO KNOW

 vegetarian

 contains dairy
- contains mascarpone

 contains alcohol
- contains amaretto

 fridge
- until the next day

 kcal
- 324 per serving, 3240 total

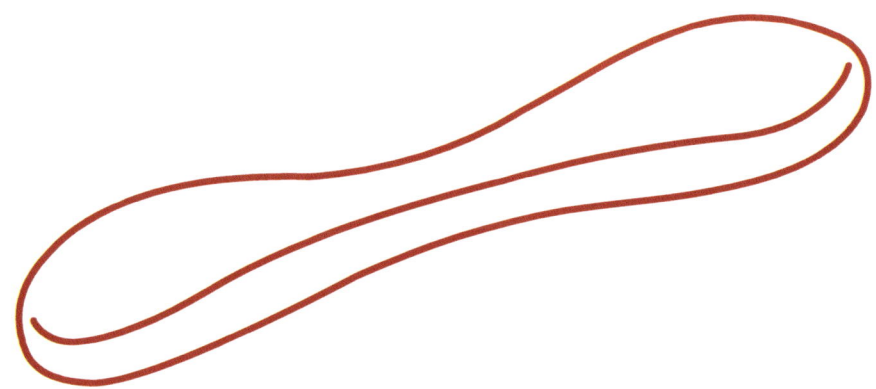

Cakes and Desserts

RHUBARB CAKE

A fantastic seasonal cake where the sweetness of the cake meets the tartness of the rhubarb.
Sprinkled with icing sugar, it's a real crowd pleaser at picnics and parties!

Difficulty	Serves	Preparation	Baking	Resting	Total
INTERMEDIATE	21	40 MIN	50 MIN	2 H	3 H 30 MIN

INGREDIENTS

For the cake batter
- ☐ 400g plain flour
- ☐ 200g sugar
- ☐ 32g vanilla sugar
- ☐ 7 large eggs
- ☐ 1 tsp baking powder
- ☐ 1 tsp bicarbonate of soda
- ☐ 180ml cooking oil

For the filling
- ☐ 500g fresh rhubarb *(Note 1)*

For the decoration
- ☐ 4 tbsp icing sugar

For the baking tin
- ☐ 1 tbsp butter

 Polish products differ from the ones available locally. You will find more information about vanilla sugar in the chapter "About the products" on page 328.

DIRECTIONS

Preparing the rhubarb
1. Cut off the thickened side and the leaf. *(Note 2)*
2. Wash and dry the remaining stem.
3. Cut into 1cm pieces.
4. Put the rhubarb in a bowl and set aside.

Preparing the baking tin
1. Using scissors, cut the baking paper as a single sheet, to cover the bottom and inner sides of the tin.
2. Brush the baking tin with butter so the paper sticks.
3. Line the baking tin with the baking paper.
4. Grease the baking paper with more butter.
5. Set the baking tin aside.

Preparing the oven
1. Preheat the oven to 180°C / 350°F or gas 4.

Preparing the cake batter
1. Crack the eggs into a large bowl, and add the sugar and vanilla sugar.
2. Whisk until the ingredients are combined.
3. Add the oil.
4. Whisk again.
5. Sift the flour into the bowl.
6. Add the baking powder and bicarbonate of soda.
7. Mix to combine the ingredients with the hand mixer turned off. *(Note 3)*
8. Whisk thoroughly to combine all the ingredients.

Preparing the cake
1. Pour the cake batter into the prepared baking tin.
2. Spread evenly using a spatula.
3. Put the rhubarb on top of the cake, pressing slightly into the batter. *(Note 4)*

Baking
1. Bake for around 50 minutes. *(Note 5)*
2. When the cake is ready, place on a cooling rack to cool completely.
3. Remove the baking paper from the cake.

To serve
- Sprinkle with icing sugar.

NOTES

1. You can swap fresh rhubarb for the same amount of frozen rhubarb. Take it out of the freezer 1 hour before you bake the cake and put it in a soup plate to partly defrost. If the rhubarb is still partly frozen it will retain juice and keep the cake moist while baking.
2. Rhubarb leaves are not edible, because they are rich in oxalic acid which is toxic and can be harmful.
3. This will prevent the mixer from blowing the dry ingredients everywhere.
4. If you're using frozen rhubarb, drain the water gathered on the plate.
5. After around 50 minutes, check if the sponge is cooked inside. Be careful: the sponge will be very hot! Insert a toothpick right to the bottom of the sponge. If some batter is stuck to the toothpick, bake the sponge for 5 more minutes. After this time check the sponge again and bake for 5 additional minutes if it's not ready.

KITCHEN ACCESSORIES

- ☐ large bowl
- ☐ bowl
- ☐ measuring jug
- ☐ knife
- ☐ chopping board
- ☐ tablespoon
- ☐ teaspoon
- ☐ hand mixer
- ☐ spatula

- ☐ scissors
- ☐ toothpick
- ☐ sieve
- ☐ kitchen scale
- ☐ cooling rack
- ☐ baking tin (measured inside 35 x 20 x 7cm)
- ☐ baking paper

GOOD TO KNOW

vegetarian

contains dairy
- contains butter

pantry
- store in a dry place up to 3 days

kcal
- 224 per serving, 4704 total

CHOCOLATE CAKE WITH APPLES, DRIED FRUIT AND NUTS

A soft, moist chocolate sponge enriched with fresh apples and dried fruits, and sprinkled with icing sugar. A perfect treat for a special day.

Difficulty	Serves	Preparation	Baking	Resting	Total
INTERMEDIATE	21	40 MIN	50 MIN	2 H	3 H 30 MIN

INGREDIENTS

For the cake batter
- ☐ 400g plain flour
- ☐ 200g sugar
- ☐ 32g vanilla sugar
- ☐ 7 large eggs
- ☐ 3 tbsp cocoa powder
- ☐ 1 tbsp ground cinnamon
- ☐ 1 tsp baking powder
- ☐ 1 tsp bicarbonate of soda
- ☐ 180ml cooking oil

For the filling
- ☐ 3 apples (~510g)
- ☐ 100g walnuts
- ☐ 100g dried cranberries
- ☐ 100g dried apricots
- ☐ 100g raisins
- ☐ 500ml water

For the decoration
- ☐ 4 tbsp icing sugar

For the baking tin
- ☐ 1 tbsp butter

 Polish products differ from the ones available locally. You will find more information about vanilla sugar in the chapter "About the products" on page 328.

DIRECTIONS

Preparing the dried fruits and nuts
1. Put the hob on medium heat.
2. Pour the water into a medium saucepan or kettle and bring to a boil.
3. Put the cranberries, apricots and raisins in a bowl.
4. Cover with boiling water (around 250ml). *(Note 1)*
5. Set aside for around 5 minutes. *(Note 2)*
6. Peel the apples and cut into quarters.
7. Remove the pips and stems.
8. Cut the apples into 1cm cubes.
9. Put into a separate bowl.
10. Finely chop the walnuts and put into the bowl with the apples.
11. Drain the water from the fruit.
12. Once again cover with boiling water (around 250ml).
13. Set aside for around 5 minutes.
14. Pour the water out.

15. Put the cranberries and raisins into the bowl with the apples and nuts.
16. Finely chop the apricots and add to the bowl with the fruit and nuts.
17. Set the bowl aside.

Preparing the baking tin
1. Using scissors, cut the baking paper as a single sheet, to cover the bottom and inner sides of the tin.
2. Brush the baking tin with butter so the paper sticks.
3. Line the baking tin with the baking paper.
4. Grease the baking paper with more butter.
5. Set the baking tin aside.

Preparing the oven
1. Preheat the oven to 180°C / 350°F or gas 4.

Preparing the cake batter
1. Crack the eggs into a large bowl, and add the sugar and vanilla sugar.
2. Whisk until the ingredients are combined.
3. Add the oil.
4. Whisk again.
5. Sift the flour into the bowl.
6. Add the baking powder, bicarbonate of soda, cocoa powder and cinnamon.
7. Mix to combine the ingredients with the hand mixer turned off. *(Note 3)*
8. Whisk thoroughly to combine all the ingredients.
9. Add the fruit and nuts.
10. Mix thoroughly with a spatula so that the fruit and nuts are covered with batter.

Preparing the cake
1. Pour the cake batter into the prepared baking tin.
2. Spread evenly using a spatula.
3. Form a well in the middle and push some of the batter to the edges. *(Note 4)*

Baking
1. Bake for around 50 minutes. *(Note 5)*
2. When the cake is ready, place on a cooling rack to cool completely.
3. Remove the baking paper from the cake.

To serve
- Sprinkle the cake with icing sugar.

NOTES

1. Some dried fruit has sulphur dioxide (E220) added to it to conserve and protect the product from moisture and mould, this step helps to remove the sulphur dioxide.
2. Dried fruits will soften and slightly swell in hot water.
3. This will prevent the mixer from blowing the dry ingredients everywhere.
4. While baking the cake rises more in the middle and less on the edges. Therefore you should leave a well in the middle of the batter.
5. After around 50 minutes, check if the sponge is cooked inside. Be careful: the sponge will be very hot! Insert a toothpick right to the bottom of the sponge. If some batter is stuck to the toothpick, bake the sponge for 5 more minutes. After this time check the sponge again and bake for 5 additional minutes if it's not ready.

KITCHEN ACCESSORIES

- ☐ medium saucepan
- ☐ large bowl
- ☐ 2 bowls
- ☐ measuring jug
- ☐ knife
- ☐ peeling knife
- ☐ chopping board
- ☐ 2 tablespoons
- ☐ 2 teaspoons
- ☐ hand mixer
- ☐ spatula
- ☐ scissors
- ☐ toothpick
- ☐ sieve
- ☐ kitchen scale
- ☐ cooling rack
- ☐ baking tin (measured inside 35 x 20 x 7cm)
- ☐ baking paper

GOOD TO KNOW

 vegetarian

 contains dairy
- contains butter

 contains nuts
- contains walnuts

 pantry
- store in a dry place up to 3 days

 kcal
- 288 per serving, 6048 total

Cakes and Desserts

APPLE PIE

Iconic Polish apple pie with freshly sliced apples and cinnamon is a delicious treat for sharing – it tastes amazing not only in the autumn!

Difficulty	Serves	Preparation	Baking	Resting	Total
SIMPLE	36	1 H 40 MIN	~1 H	2 H	~4 H 40 MIN

INGREDIENTS

For the dough
- ☐ 430g plain flour (+ more for dusting)
- ☐ 200g unsalted butter (+ more for buttering the tin)
- ☐ 135g sugar
- ☐ 32g vanilla sugar
- ☐ 2 large eggs
- ☐ 3 tbsp sour cream
- ☐ 2 tsp baking powder

For the filling
- ☐ 1.5kg apples *(Notes 1 and 2)*
- ☐ 6-10 tbsp sugar *(Note 3)*
- ☐ 6-8 tbsp breadcrumbs
- ☐ 4-6 tsp ground cinnamon *(Note 4)*
- ☐ ½ lemon

For the decoration
- ☐ 4 tbsp icing sugar

 Polish products differ from the ones available locally. You will find more information about sour cream and vanilla sugar in the chapter "About the products" on page 328.

DIRECTIONS

Preparing the butter
1. Take the butter out of the fridge.
2. Cube the butter.
3. Transfer to a small bowl.
4. Set the bowl aside. *(Note 5)*

Preparing the apples
1. Peel the apples and cut into quarters.
2. Remove the pips and stems.
3. Finely slice the apples into 2mm slices.
4. Put into a large bowl.
5. Roll the lemon on the kitchen counter. *(Note 6)*
6. Cut in half.
7. Juice one half into the bowl. *(Note 7)*
8. Mix well.
9. Set the bowl aside.

Preparing the dough
1. Sift the flour into the bowl of a food mixer. *(Note 8)*
2. Add the sugar, vanilla sugar and baking powder.
3. Crack one egg into the bowl, separate the other egg and add the yolk, then add the sour cream. Discard the egg white.
4. Mix until the ingredients are combined.
5. Add the butter.
6. Knead the dough until smooth and elastic. This can take around 10 mins in the food mixer and a little bit longer if kneading the dough by hand. *(Note 9)*

Cakes and Desserts

Preparing the baking tin
1. Using scissors, cut the baking paper to fit the bottom of the baking tin.
2. Brush the baking tin with butter so the paper sticks.
3. Line the baking tin with the baking paper.
4. Set the baking tin aside.

Preparing the apple pie – part 1
1. Sprinkle a work surface with flour. Transfer the dough onto the work surface.
2. Roll out the dough into a thick sausage shape and with a knife mark 3 equal parts.
3. Cut off ⅓ of the dough and set aside. *(Note 10)*
4. Sprinkle the remaining ⅔ with plain flour.
5. Roll out to the size of the baking tin, enough to fit to the bottom and sides.
6. Put into the prepared baking tin. *(Note 11)*
7. Carefully press the dough into the baking tin, in particular into the edges and corners.
8. Set the baking tin with the dough aside.

Preparing the filling
1. Cover the dough with breadcrumbs. *(Note 12)*
2. Layer the prepared apples. *(Note 13)*
3. Sprinkle the apples with sugar and cinnamon. *(Note 14)*

Preparing the oven
1. Preheat the oven to 180°C / 350°F or gas 4.

Preparing the apple pie – part 2
1. Sprinkle the work surface with more flour. Transfer the remaining dough onto the work surface.
2. Sprinkle the dough with flour.
3. Roll out to the size of the baking tin.
4. Cover the apples in the baking tin with the dough. *(Note 15)*
5. Using your fingers, carefully press the edges of the top part of the dough with the dough spread on the sides.
6. Prick the dough with a fork. *(Note 16)*

Baking
1. Bake for around 50 minutes to 1 hour, until golden.
2. After baking the pie, leave in the baking tin to cool completely. *(Note 17)*

To serve
- Sprinkle the pie with icing sugar.

NOTES

1. The apples for the pie should be hard, so they don't break down completely while baking. Varieties I would choose for this are; *Malinówka Oberlandzka*, Rubin, Kosztela, McIntosh, Reinette, Antonovka, Champion.
2. You can swap fresh apples for sliced preserved apples. You will need ten 280ml jars for the pie. You will find the recipe for <u>preserved apple alices</u> in the "Pantry" chapter. If you decide to use apples from the jar, you can omit the sugar and lemon.
3. The amount of sugar depends on the sweetness of the apples – you can add more sugar to tart apples and less – to sweet ones.
4. The amount of cinnamon depends on your taste.
5. When the butter is at room temperature, the dough will be easier to knead.
6. Before cutting the lemon, roll it for a while on the kitchen counter, pressing slightly with your hand. This will help you extract all the juice from the lemon.
7. Adding lemon juice will keep the apples from getting dark.

8. If you don't have a food mixer, you can knead the dough by hand on the work surface. Sift the flour onto the work surface. Add the dry ingredients and make a well in the middle. Add the wet ingredients. Start combining the ingredients with a knife. Then knead the dough by hand.
9. After kneading, the dough should be smooth, slightly sticky but not enough to stick to your hands.
10. You will use one third of the dough to cover the apples.
11. The dough is very crumbly and might be difficult to transfer to the baking tin in one piece. To transfer it more easily, carefully wrap the dough around the rolling pin and transfer onto and into the baking tin.
12. Breadcrumbs will absorb excess apple juice. They will help to bake the dough and prevent it from getting too wet.
13. If there's excess juice in the bowl with the sliced apples, drain it off, so as not to add to the pie along with the apples. You can make a drink with the apple juice. Just dilute it with water.
14. If you're using preserved apple slices, don't sprinkle them with sugar. If there is liquid in the jar do not add to the pie.
15. Carefully wrap the dough around the rolling pin and transfer onto the baking tin. Roll it on top, covering the apples.
16. Any juice should evaporate while the pie is baking. The holes in the top allow this to happen.
17. Freshly baked pie can break when you try to cut and remove a portion from the tin. When it's cold, the inside will have set, which prevents it from breaking and the apples from spilling out of the pie.

KITCHEN ACCESSORIES

- ☐ large bowl
- ☐ small bowl
- ☐ knife
- ☐ peeling knife
- ☐ chopping board
- ☐ 2 tablespoons
- ☐ 2 teaspoons
- ☐ fork
- ☐ food mixer
- ☐ scissors
- ☐ sieve
- ☐ rolling pin
- ☐ pastry board
- ☐ kitchen scale
- ☐ baking tin (measured inside 35 x 20 x 7cm)
- ☐ baking paper

GOOD TO KNOW

vegetarian

contains dairy
- contains butter
- contains sour cream

pantry
- store in a dry place up to 4 days

kcal
- 154 per serving, 5544 total

GOES WELL WITH

Preserved Apple Slices
11. Pantry, page 307

PLUM PIE

*A warm, sunny autumn captured in a delicious plum pie.
Full of the flavour of plums with cinnamon and sweet icing sugar.*

Difficulty	Serves	Preparation	Baking	Resting	Total
SIMPLE	21	50 MIN	~1 H	2 H	~3 H 50 MIN

INGREDIENTS

For the dough
- ☐ 430g plain flour (+ more for dusting)
- ☐ 200g unsalted butter (+ more for buttering the tin)
- ☐ 135g sugar
- ☐ 32g vanilla sugar
- ☐ 2 large eggs
- ☐ 3 tbsp sour cream
- ☐ 2 tsp baking powder

For the filling
- ☐ ~1.5kg purple (common) plums
- ☐ 6-8 tbsp breadcrumbs
- ☐ 4-6 tsp ground cinnamon *(Note 1)*

For the decoration
- ☐ 4 tbsp icing sugar

 Polish products differ from the ones available locally. You will find more information about purple plums, sour cream and vanilla sugar in the chapter "About the products" on page 328.

DIRECTIONS

Preparing the butter
1. Take the butter out of the fridge.
2. Cube the butter.
3. Transfer to a small bowl.
4. Set the bowl aside. *(Note 2)*

Preparing the plums
1. Rinse the plums and transfer to a paper towel. *(Note 3)*
2. Remove the stones and keep the plums whole by cutting the plums lengthwise, without cutting all the way around.
3. Transfer the fruit to a large bowl and set aside.

Preparing the dough – part 1
1. Sift the flour into the bowl of a food mixer. *(Note 4)*
2. Add the sugar, vanilla sugar and baking powder.
3. Crack one egg into the bowl, separate the other egg and add the yolk, then add the sour cream. Discard the egg white.
4. Mix until the ingredients are combined.
5. Add the butter.
6. Knead the dough until smooth and elastic. This can take around 10 mins in the food mixer and a little bit longer if kneading the dough by hand. *(Note 5)*

Cakes and Desserts

Preparing the baking tin
1. Using scissors, cut the baking paper to fit the bottom of the baking tin.
2. Brush the baking tin with butter so the paper sticks.
3. Line the baking tin with the baking paper.
4. Set the baking tin aside.

Preparing the dough – part 2
1. Sprinkle a work surface with flour. Transfer the dough onto the work surface.
2. Roll out the dough into a thick sausage shape and with a knife mark 3 equal parts.
3. Cut off ⅓ of the dough and set aside. *(Note 6)*
4. Sprinkle the remaining ⅔ with plain flour.
5. Roll out to the size of the baking tin, enough to fit to the bottom and sides.
6. Put into the prepared baking tin. *(Note 7)*
7. Carefully press the dough into the baking tin, in particular into the edges and corners. *(Note 8)*
8. Set the baking tin with the dough aside.

Preparing the filling
1. Cover the dough with breadcrumbs. *(Note 9)*
2. Lay the plums on the dough, cut side up.
3. Sprinkle the plums with cinnamon.

Preparing the oven
1. Preheat the oven to 180°C / 350°F or gas 4.

Preparing the pie
1. Sprinkle the work surface with more flour. Transfer the remaining dough onto the work surface.
2. Sprinkle the dough with flour.
3. Roll to the size of the baking tin.
4. Using a pastry wheel, cut into 2cm wide strips. *(Note 10)*
5. Lay the strips on the plums to create a lattice crust. *(Note 11)*
6. Using your fingers, carefully press the edges of the dough with the ends of the strips to stick them together.

Baking
1. Bake for around 50 minutes to 1 hour, until golden.
2. After baking the pie, leave in the baking tin to cool completely. *(Note 12)*

To serve
- Sprinkle with icing sugar.

NOTES

1. The amount of cinnamon depends on your taste.
2. When the butter is at room temperature, the dough will be easier to knead.
3. The paper towel will absorb excess water.
4. If you don't have a food mixer, you can knead the dough by hand on the work surface. Sift the flour onto the work surface. Add the dry ingredients and make a well in the middle. Add the wet ingredients. Start combining the ingredients with a knife. Then knead the dough by hand.
5. After kneading, the dough should be smooth, slightly sticky but not enough to stick to your hands.
6. You will use one third of the dough to cover the plums.

7. The dough is very crumbly and might be difficult to transfer to the baking tin in one piece. To transfer it more easily, carefully wrap the dough around the rolling pin and transfer onto and into the baking tin.
8. You might feel like there's not enough dough after you spread it out. It will rise slightly while baking and fill the gaps between the plums.
9. Breadcrumbs will absorb excess plum juice. They will help to bake the dough and prevent it from getting too wet.
10. You can use a pizza knife instead of the pastry wheel.
11. The plum juice will evaporate while the pie is baking. It might even rise to the top of the pie. The gaps between the lattice stripes allow it to evaporate.
12. Freshly baked pie can break when you try to cut and remove a portion from the tin. When it's cold, the inside will have set, which prevents it from breaking and the plum juice from spilling out of the pie.

KITCHEN ACCESSORIES

- ☐ large bowl
- ☐ small bowl
- ☐ knife
- ☐ pastry wheel (or pizza knife)
- ☐ chopping board
- ☐ 2 tablespoons
- ☐ 2 teaspoons
- ☐ food mixer
- ☐ scissors
- ☐ sieve
- ☐ rolling pin
- ☐ pastry board
- ☐ kitchen scale
- ☐ baking tin (measured inside 35 x 20 x 7cm)
- ☐ baking paper
- ☐ paper towel

GOOD TO KNOW

 vegetarian

 contains dairy
- contains butter
- contains sour cream

 pantry
- store in a dry place up to 4 days

 kcal
- 236 per serving, 4956 total

CHERRY AND CUSTARD PIE

This pie is an amazing mix of sour cherries and sweet budyń (Polish style custard). So perfectly balanced, it will become a real crowd pleaser.

Difficulty
INTERMEDIATE

Serves
36

Preparation
1 H 10 MIN

Baking
~50 MIN

Resting
12 H

Total
~14 H

INGREDIENTS

For the dough
- 430g plain flour (+ more for dusting)
- 200g unsalted butter (+ more for buttering the tin)
- 135g sugar
- 32g vanilla sugar
- 2 large eggs
- 3 tbsp sour cream
- 2 tsp baking powder

For the filling
For the cherries
- 2.5kg cherries
- 400g sugar
- 6-8 tbsp breadcrumbs

For the budyń
- 2 packets vanilla *budyń* for 0.5 litre of milk (80g) *(Note 1)*
- 700ml milk *(Note 2)*
- 1½ tbsp sugar (optional) *(Note 3)*

For the decoration
- 4 tbsp icing sugar

 Polish products differ from the ones available locally. You will find more information about budyń, sour cream and vanilla sugar in the chapter "About the products" on page 328.

DIRECTIONS

Day before baking: evening
Preparing the cherries – part 1
1. Rinse the cherries and remove any stems.
2. Remove the pits.
3. Transfer the fruit to a large bowl.
4. Cover with sugar.
5. Put the bowl in the fridge for around 12 hours.

Baking day
Preparing the butter
1. Take the butter out of the fridge.
2. Cube the butter.
3. Transfer to a small bowl.
4. Set the bowl aside. *(Note 4)*

Cakes and Desserts

Preparing the cherries – part 2
1. Put the cherries in a large pot.
2. Put the hob on low heat.
3. Heat the cherries with the sugar until the sugar dissolves.
4. Stir from time to time.
5. Set the sieve over a large bowl.
6. Put the cherries in the sieve and press lightly with a spoon to drain excess juice.
7. Set the bowl aside.

Preparing the baking tin
1. Using scissors, cut the baking paper to fit the bottom of the baking tin.
2. Brush the baking tin with butter so the paper sticks.
3. Line the baking tin with the baking paper.
4. Set the baking tin aside.

Preparing the dough
1. Sift the flour into the bowl of a food mixer. *(Note 5)*
2. Add the sugar, vanilla sugar and baking powder.
3. Crack one egg into the bowl, separate the other egg and add the yolk, then add the sour cream. Discard the egg white.
4. Mix until the ingredients are combined.
5. Add the butter.
6. Knead the dough until smooth and elastic. This can take around 10 mins in the food mixer and a little bit longer if kneading the dough by hand. *(Note 6)*
7. Sprinkle a work surface with flour. Transfer the dough onto the work surface.
8. Roll out the dough into a thick sausage shape and with a knife mark 3 equal parts.
9. Cut off ⅓ of the dough, divide into 4 parts and put on a plate. *(Notes 7 and 8)*
10. Put the plate in the freezer.
11. Sprinkle the remaining ⅔ with plain flour.
12. Roll out to the size of the baking tin, enough to fit to the bottom and sides.
13. Put into the prepared baking tin. *(Note 9)*
14. Carefully press the dough into the baking tin, in particular into the edges and corners.
15. Set the baking tin with the dough aside.

Preparing the filling
1. Cover the dough with breadcrumbs. *(Note 10)*
2. Put the cherries on the breadcrumbs. *(Note 11)*
3. Set the baking tin with the dough aside.

Preparing the *budyń*
Preparing the milk
1. Pour 400ml of milk into a measuring jug.
2. Pour the milk into a medium saucepan.
3. Add the sugar to the saucepan.
4. Add 300ml more milk to the measuring jug.
5. Add the *budyń* powder to the measuring jug.
6. Whisk to get rid of all the lumps.
7. Set aside.

Preparing the budyń mixture
1. Put the hob on low heat.
2. Heat the milk to dissolve the sugar. *(Note 12)*
3. Add the milk with the *budyń* to the boiling milk.
4. Keep stirring with a wooden spoon until uniform.
5. When the mixture starts bubbling, cook for 2 more minutes, stirring constantly.
6. Turn off the hob.
7. Pour hot *budyń* over the cherries.
8. Spread evenly using a spatula.

Preparing the oven
1. Preheat the oven to 180°C / 350°F or gas 4.

Preparing the pie
1. Take the dough out of the freezer.
2. With a knife mark 4 equal parts on the spread *budyń*.
3. Using one piece of frozen dough per quarter of the marked *budyń*. Grate the frozen dough using a large grater over the top. *(Note 13)*

Baking

1. Bake for around 40-50 minutes, until golden.
2. After baking the pie, leave in the baking tin to cool completely. *(Note 14)*

To serve

- Sprinkle with icing sugar.

NOTES

1. You can swap vanilla *budyń* for the same amount of sweet cream *(śmietankowy) budyń*.
2. The amount of milk is purposefully reduced in this recipe, so that the *budyń* is thicker.
3. Check on the packet if the *budyń* is already sweetened. If that's the case, don't add any more sugar. If it's unsweetened, add 1½ tbsp of sugar, so that the pie is not too sweet.
4. When the butter is at room temperature, the dough will be easier to knead.
5. If you don't have a food mixer, you can knead the dough by hand on the work surface. Sift the flour onto the work surface. Add the dry ingredients and make a well in the middle. Add the wet ingredients. Start combining the ingredients with a knife. Then knead the dough by hand.
6. After kneading, the dough should be smooth, slightly sticky but not enough to stick to your hands.
7. You will use one third of the dough to cover the *budyń*.
8. If you divide the dough into smaller parts, it will freeze quicker.
9. The dough is very crumbly and might be difficult to transfer to the baking tin in one piece. To transfer it more easily, carefully wrap the dough around the rolling pin and transfer onto and into the baking tin.
10. Breadcrumbs will absorb excess cherry juice. They will help to bake the dough and prevent it from getting too wet.
11. If there's excess juice in the bowl with the cherries, drain it off, so as not to add to the pie along with the cherries. You can make a drink with the cherry juice. Just dilute it with water.
12. When the milk is close to boiling, it starts to foam and bubble so watch it to ensure it does not boil over.
13. Dividing the dough into quarters and grating each part on one quarter of the *budyń* allows for a uniform coverage of the whole pie.
14. Freshly baked pie can break when you try to cut and remove a portion from the tin. When it's cold, the inside will have set, which prevents it from breaking and the *budyń* from spilling out of the pie.

KITCHEN ACCESSORIES

- ☐ large pot
- ☐ medium saucepan
- ☐ large bowl
- ☐ small bowl
- ☐ measuring jug
- ☐ knife
- ☐ chopping board
- ☐ plate
- ☐ 2 tablespoons
- ☐ 2 teaspoons
- ☐ food mixer
- ☐ stoner
- ☐ wooden spoon
- ☐ spatula
- ☐ whisk
- ☐ grater
- ☐ scissors
- ☐ sieve
- ☐ rolling pin
- ☐ pastry board
- ☐ kitchen scale
- ☐ baking tin (measured inside 35 x 20 x 7cm)
- ☐ baking paper

GOOD TO KNOW

 vegetarian

 contains dairy
- contains butter
- contains milk
- contains sour cream

 pantry
- store in a dry place up to 4 days

 kcal
- 226 per serving, 8136 total

82 **Cakes and Desserts**

COCONUT CREAM PIE WITH PLUM JAM

A delightful shortcrust pastry with a tart plum jam and a thick layer of sweet coconut cream. Absolutely delicious!

Difficulty	Serves	Preparation	Baking	Resting	Total
INTERMEDIATE	36	40 MIN	~1 H	2 H	3 H 40 MIN

INGREDIENTS

For the dough
- ☐ 570g plain flour (+ more for dusting)
- ☐ 250g unsalted butter (+ more for buttering the tin)
- ☐ 200g sugar
- ☐ 4 large eggs
- ☐ 3 tbsp sour cream
- ☐ 1 tbsp baking powder
- ☐ 1 tbsp cocoa powder

For the filling
- ☐ 300g desiccated coconut
- ☐ ~300g plum jam *(Note 1)*
- ☐ 250g sour cream
- ☐ 3 tbsp sugar
- ☐ 2 tbsp potato starch

 Polish products differ from the ones available locally. You will find more information about potato starch and sour cream in the chapter "About the products" on page 328.

DIRECTIONS

Preparing the butter
1. Take the butter out of the fridge.
2. Cube the butter.
3. Transfer to a small bowl.
4. Set the bowl aside. *(Note 2)*

Preparing the baking tin
1. Using scissors, cut the baking paper to fit the bottom of the baking tin.
2. Brush the baking tin with butter so the paper sticks.
3. Line the baking tin with the baking paper.
4. Set the baking tin aside.

Preparing the dough
1. Separate the yolks from the whites into two separate small bowls.
2. Sift the flour into the bowl of a food mixer. *(Note 3)*
3. Add the sugar and baking powder.
4. Add the yolks and sour cream.
5. Mix until the ingredients are combined.
6. Add the butter.
7. Knead the dough until smooth and elastic. This can take around 10 mins in the food mixer and a little bit longer if kneading the dough by hand. *(Note 4)*

8. Sprinkle a work surface with flour. Transfer the dough onto the work surface.
9. Roll out the dough into a thick sausage shape and with a knife mark 3 equal parts.
10. Cut off ⅔ of the dough and set aside.
11. Add the cocoa to the remaining one third of the dough.
12. Knead the dough to combine the ingredients and until uniform in colour.
13. Divide the dough with the cocoa into 4 parts and put on a plate. *(Notes 5 and 6)*
14. Put the plate in the freezer for around 1 hour.
15. Divide the remaining two thirds in half.
16. Take the first half and use your fingers to spread the dough across the bottom of the baking.
17. Divide the second half into four parts and spread each evenly on the sides of the baking tin; be careful to stick the sides together and with the dough on the bottom. *(Note 7)*
18. While waiting, prepare the coconut mixture.

Preparing the coconut mixture
1. Add the egg whites to a clean food mixer bowl. *(Note 8)*
2. Add the sugar.
3. Whisk the egg whites to stiff peaks. This can take around 10 minutes.
4. To the egg mixture add the desiccated coconut, potato starch and sour cream.
5. Whisk until the ingredients are combined. This can take around 5 minutes.

Preparing the oven
1. Preheat the oven to 180°C / 350°F or gas 4.

Preparing the pie
1. Using a spoon, smooth the dough in the baking tin.
2. Spread the *powidła śliwkowe* evenly over the dough using a spatula.
3. Put the coconut mixture on the *powidła śliwkowe*.
4. Spread evenly.
5. Take the cocoa dough out of the freezer.
6. Mark with a knife 4 equal parts on the coconut mixture.
7. Using one piece of frozen dough per quarter of the marked coconut mixture. Grate the frozen dough using a large grater over the top. *(Note 9)*

Baking
1. Bake for 1 hour.
2. After baking the pie, leave in the baking tin to cool completely. *(Note 10)*

NOTES

1. You can buy plum jam *(powidła śliwkowe)* or make it yourself. You will find a recipe for powidła śliwkowe in the "Pantry" chapter.
2. When the butter is at room temperature, the dough will be easier to knead.
3. If you don't have a food mixer, you can knead the dough by hand on the work surface. Sift the flour onto the work surface. Add the dry ingredients and make a well in the middle. Add the wet ingredients. Start combining the ingredients with a knife. Then knead the dough by hand.
4. After kneading, the dough should be smooth, slightly sticky but not enough to stick to your hands.
5. The cocoa dough will cover the coconut custard.
6. If you divide the dough into smaller parts, it will freeze quicker.

7. If you're using a square tin, cut the dough into quarters. Spread each one on one of the sides. If you're using a rectangular tin, cut the dough into 2 smaller and 2 bigger parts. Spread the bigger parts on the longer sides and the smaller parts on the shorter sides. If you're using a round tin, cut the dough into quarters. Make four cuts on the bottom (at 12, 6, 3 and 9 o'clock). Spread each part of the dough between the cuts.
8. If you don't have a food mixer, you can prepare the coconut mixture in a large bowl using a hand mixer.
9. Dividing the dough into quarters and grating each part on one quarter of the coconut mixture allows for a uniform coverage of the whole pie.
10. Fresh baked pie can break when you try to cut and remove a portion from the tin. When it's cold, the inside will have set, which prevents it from breaking and the coconut mixture from spilling out of the pie.

KITCHEN ACCESSORIES

- ☐ bowl
- ☐ 3 small bowls
- ☐ knife
- ☐ chopping board
- ☐ plate
- ☐ 2 tablespoons
- ☐ teaspoon
- ☐ food mixer

- ☐ spatula
- ☐ grater
- ☐ scissors
- ☐ sieve
- ☐ pastry board
- ☐ kitchen scale
- ☐ baking tin (measured inside 35 x 20 x 7cm)
- ☐ baking paper

GOOD TO KNOW

 vegetarian

 contains dairy
- contains butter
- contains sour cream

 pantry
- store in a dry place up to 4 days

 kcal
- 154 per serving, 5544 total

GOES WELL WITH

 *Powidła Śliwkowe* **(Plum Jam)**
11. Pantry, page 317

DEWDROP CHEESECAKE

A delightful, delicate cheesecake with a beautiful layer of foam decorated with caramel dewdrops. Perfect for sharing on every occasion.

   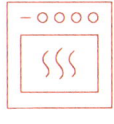  

Difficulty	Serves	Preparation	Baking	Resting	Total
INTERMEDIATE	36	1 H	~1 H 10 MIN	~2 H	4 H 10 MIN

INGREDIENTS

For the dough
- ☐ 270g plain flour (+ more for dusting)
- ☐ 90g sugar
- ☐ 80g unsalted butter (+ more for buttering the tin)
- ☐ 16g vanilla sugar
- ☐ 1 large egg
- ☐ 1 tbsp sour cream
- ☐ 1½ tsp baking powder

 Polish products differ from the ones available locally. You will find more information about budyń, sour cream, twaróg and vanilla sugar in the chapter "About the products" on page 328.

For the cheese mixture
- ☐ 1.2kg low-fat *twaróg*
- ☐ 180g sugar
- ☐ 16g vanilla sugar
- ☐ 3 packets of vanilla *budyń* for 0.5 litre of milk (120g) *(Note 1)*
- ☐ 2 large eggs
- ☐ 4 egg yolks
- ☐ 500ml milk *(Note 2)*
- ☐ 250ml cold water
- ☐ 120ml cooking oil

For the egg whites foam
- ☐ 4 egg whites *(Note 3)*
- ☐ 4 tbsp sugar

DIRECTIONS

Preparing the butter
1. Take the butter out of the fridge.
2. Cube the butter.
3. Transfer to a small bowl.
4. Set the bowl aside. *(Note 4)*

Preparing the baking tin
1. Using scissors, cut the baking paper to fit the bottom of the baking tin.
2. Brush the baking tin with butter so the paper sticks.
3. Line the baking tin with the baking paper.
4. Set the baking tin aside.

Preparing the dough
1. Sift the flour onto a pastry board.
2. Add the sugar, vanilla sugar and baking powder.
3. Make a well in the dry ingredients.
4. Add the sour cream, butter and egg.
5. Chop the dough with a knife until the ingredients are combined. This can take around 5 minutes. *(Note 5)*
6. When larger pieces of dough start to form, begin kneading by hand.
7. Sprinkle the dough with flour, to prevent the dough sticking. *(Note 6)*

Cakes and Desserts

8. Roll out the dough to a thickness of about 3mm.
9. Put into the prepared baking tin. *(Note 7)*
10. The dough should be spread on the bottom of the baking tin and up the sides to a height of 5-6cm.
11. Carefully press the dough into the baking tin, in particular into the edges and corners.
12. Set the baking tin with the dough aside.

Preparing the oven
1. Preheat the oven to 180°C / 350°F or gas 4.

Preparing the cheese mixture
1. Separate 4 yolks from the whites. Put the yolks in a large pot and the whites in a large bowl. Set the whites aside. *(Note 3)*
2. Crack two eggs into the large pot with the yolks.
3. Add the *twaróg*, *budyń*, sugar, vanilla sugar and milk.
4. Using a hand blender, blend until a uniform mixture.
5. Add the water and oil.
6. Blend again.
7. Pour the mixture into the baking tin up to the level of the dough.

Baking – part 1
1. Bake for around 1 hour 10 minutes.
2. Check if the cheese mixture has been baked. *(Note 8)*
3. When the cheesecake is almost baked, prepare the egg white foam.

Preparing the egg white foam
1. Add 4 tbsp of sugar to the egg whites.
2. Using a hand mixer, whisk until stiff.
3. Remove the cheesecake from the oven and place on a cooling rack.
4. Put the foam on top.
5. Spread evenly using a spatula.

Baking – part 2
1. Put the cheesecake back in the oven.
2. Bake until the foam starts to become golden. This can take 6-8 minutes. *(Note 9)*
3. After baking the cheesecake, leave in the baking tin to cool completely and allow the dewdrops to form. *(Note 10)*

NOTES

1. You can swap vanilla *budyń* for the same amount of sweet cream *(śmietankowy) budyń*.
2. The amount of milk is purposefully reduced in this recipe, so that the *budyń* is thicker.
3. For the foam use the egg whites left over after making the cheese mixture.
4. When the butter is at room temperature, the dough will be easier to knead.
5. It's best to chop the dough using two knives. Use one knife to chop the butter with the flour and the second knife to collect the butter from the first one. After you chop the butter, it will form little lumps with the flour.
6. If the dough is too tough, add 1 tsp sour cream and knead again. If that doesn't help add a little more sour cream.
7. The dough is very crumbly and might be difficult to transfer to the baking tin in one piece. To transfer it more easily, carefully wrap the dough around the rolling pin and transfer onto and into the baking tin.
8. Take the baking tin out of the oven and shake it slightly. Be careful: the baking tin will be very hot! If the cheese mixture in the middle is still wobbly, bake for 10 more minutes.

9. If the foam bakes for too long and the colour becomes a golden brown, the drops won't appear on the top after it cools.
10. Freshly baked cheesecake can break when you try to cut and remove a portion from the tin. When it's cold, the inside will have set, which prevents it from breaking and the cheese mixture from spilling out of the cheesecake.

KITCHEN ACCESSORIES

- ☐ large pot
- ☐ large bowl
- ☐ small bowl
- ☐ measuring jug
- ☐ 2 knives
- ☐ chopping board
- ☐ 2 tablespoons
- ☐ 2 teaspoons
- ☐ hand blender

- ☐ hand mixer
- ☐ spatula
- ☐ scissors
- ☐ sieve
- ☐ rolling pin
- ☐ pastry board
- ☐ kitchen scale
- ☐ baking tin (measured inside 35 x 20 x 7cm)
- ☐ baking paper

GOOD TO KNOW

 vegetarian

 contains dairy
- contains butter
- contains milk
- contains sour cream
- contains *twaróg*

 fridge
- for up to 4 days

 kcal
- 193 per serving, 6948 total

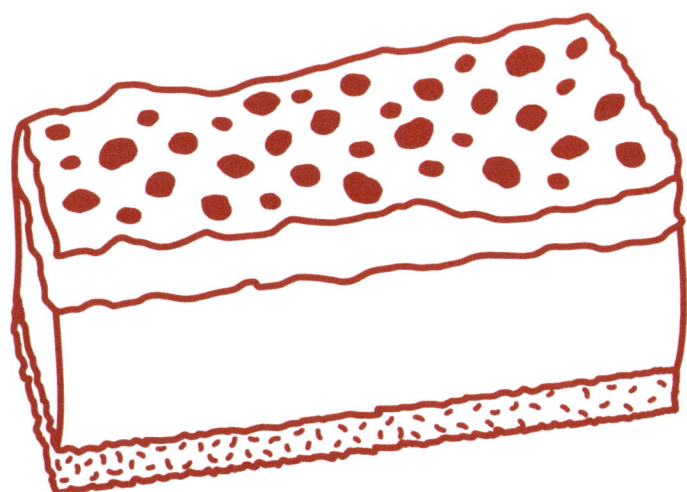

VIENNESE CHEESECAKE

*A deliciously sweet and slightly tart cheesecake.
An easy cake that will delight your guests.
Decorate it with icing sugar or melted chocolate.*

Difficulty INTERMEDIATE	**Serves** 12	**Preparation** ~1 H	**Baking** 1 H 20 MIN	**Resting** 1 H	**Total** ~3 H 20 MIN

INGREDIENTS

For the cheese mixture
- ☐ 500g semi-skimmed *twaróg*
- ☐ 100g unsalted butter (+ more for buttering the tin)
- ☐ 100g sugar
- ☐ 16g vanilla sugar *(Note 1)*
- ☐ 4 large eggs
- ☐ 1 tbsp plain flour
- ☐ 1 tbsp potato starch
- ☐ ½ tsp salt

For the dried fruit
- ☐ 50g raisins
- ☐ 50g candied orange peel *(Note 2)*
- ☐ 1 tsp plain flour
- ☐ 500ml water

For the decoration
- ☐ 2 tbsp icing sugar

For the glaze (optional) *(Note 3)*
- ☐ 50g milk chocolate
- ☐ 25g unsalted butter
- ☐ 25ml milk

 Polish products differ from the ones available locally. You will find more information about candied orange peel, potato starch, twaróg and vanilla sugar in the chapter "About the products" on page 328.

DIRECTIONS

Preparing the dried fruits
1. Put the hob on medium heat.
2. Pour the water into a small saucepan or kettle and bring to a boil.
3. Put the raisins in a bowl.
4. Cover with boiling water (around 250ml). *(Note 4)*
5. Set aside for around 5 minutes. *(Note 5)*
6. Chop the orange peel and put into a separate bowl.
7. Drain the water from the raisins.
8. Once again cover with boiling water (around 250ml).
9. Set aside for around 5 minutes.
10. Pour the water out.
11. Lay the raisins on a paper towel. *(Note 6)*
12. Put the raisins in the bowl with the candied orange peel.
13. Add 1 tsp plain flour to the bowl.
14. Stir, so that all the fruit are covered with flour.
15. Set the bowl aside.

Cakes and Desserts

Preparing the cake tin
1. Using scissors, cut the baking paper as a single sheet, to cover the bottom and inner sides of the tin. *(Note 7)*
2. Brush the cake tin with butter so the paper sticks.
3. Line the cake tin with the baking paper.
4. Grease the baking paper with more butter.
5. Set the cake tin aside.

Preparing the butter
1. Cube the butter.
2. Put the hob on low heat.
3. Add the butter to a small saucepan.
4. Melt on a low heat to prevent burning.
5. When the butter is liquid, set aside.

Preparing the *twaróg* mixture
1. Separate the yolks from the whites, into two separate large bowls. Set the whites aside.
2. Add the *twaróg* to the yolks.
3. Add the plain flour, potato starch, half of sugar, vanilla sugar and melted butter.
4. Add the vanilla extract. (optional)
5. Blend until smooth.
6. Set the bowl aside.

Preparing the egg whites
1. Add the salt and the remaining sugar to the bowl with the egg whites.
2. Using a hand mixer, whisk until stiff. This can take around 10-15 minutes.

Preparing the oven
1. Preheat the oven to 150°C / 300°F or gas 2.

Preparing the cheese mixture
1. Gradually add the *twaróg* mixture to the whisked egg whites.
2. Mix until combined.
3. Add the fruit.
4. Thoroughly combine all the ingredients.
5. Pour the mixture into the prepared cake tin.
6. Spread evenly using a spatula.

Baking
1. Bake for around 1 hour.
2. After 1 hour raise the temperature to 180°C / 350°F or gas 4 and bake for 20 minutes.
3. Don't open the oven while baking.
4. Turn off the oven and leave the cake inside to cool. This can take around 30 minutes.
5. Take the cheesecake out of the oven and leave in the cake tin to cool completely. *(Note 8)*
6. Place the cold cheesecake onto a cooling rack.
7. Remove the baking paper.

To serve
- Sprinkle the cheesecake with icing sugar.
- Alternatively, cover with a chocolate glaze. Make the glaze using the recipe below.

Preparing the glaze (optional)
1. Pour the milk into a small saucepan.
2. Put the hob on low heat.
3. Add the butter.
4. Break the chocolate into smaller pieces and add to the saucepan.
5. Keep stirring, so that all ingredients melt and a uniform mixture forms.
6. Pour the glaze on the cheesecake.
7. Spread evenly.
8. Put the cheesecake in the fridge for around 30 minutes.

NOTES

1. You can swap the vanilla sugar with 2 tsp vanilla extract.
2. Instead of candied orange peel, you can use candied lemon or lime peel. In the "Pantry" chapter you will find a recipe for the perfect candied orange peel.
3. You can make the glaze yourself or use a store-bought chocolate glaze. You will need 100g of glaze.
4. Some dried fruit has sulphur dioxide (E220) added to it to conserve and protect the product from moisture and mould, this step helps to remove the sulphur dioxide.
5. Raisins will soften and slightly swell in hot water.
6. The paper towel will absorb excess water. Squeeze the raisins so they release as much liquid as possible.
7. Have the baking paper be about 2-3cm above the edge of your cake tin. The cheesecake will rise while baking – and this will prevent it from spilling over.
8. During this time, the cheesecake will fall and set, and also form a ripple on the sides.

KITCHEN ACCESSORIES

- ☐ small saucepan
- ☐ 2 large bowls
- ☐ 2 bowls
- ☐ measuring jug
- ☐ knife
- ☐ chopping board
- ☐ 2 tablespoons
- ☐ 2 teaspoons
- ☐ hand blender

- ☐ hand mixer
- ☐ spatula
- ☐ scissors
- ☐ kitchen scale
- ☐ cooling rack
- ☐ cake tin (diameter 20cm, height 7cm)
- ☐ baking paper
- ☐ paper towel

GOOD TO KNOW

vegetarian

contains dairy
- contains butter
- contains milk
- contains *twaróg*

fridge
- for up to 4 days

kcal
- without icing sugar and chocolate glaze
  187 per serving, 2244 total
- with icing sugar
  192 per serving, 2304 total
- with chocolate glaze
  268 per serving, 3216 total

GOES WELL WITH

Candied Orange Peel
11. Pantry, page 321

Cakes and Desserts

APPLE AND TWARÓG CAKE

A delightful pastry with a sweet cheese filling and a tangy apple and orange mixture. Covered with delicious chocolate.

Difficulty	Serves	Preparation	Baking	Resting	Total
INTERMEDIATE	36	~1 H	1 H	3 H	~5 H

INGREDIENTS

For the dough
- 430g plain flour (+ more for dusting)
- 200g unsalted butter (+ more for buttering the tin)
- 135g sugar
- 32g vanilla sugar
- 2 large eggs
- 3 tbsp sour cream
- 2 tsp baking powder

For the cheese mixture
- 500g low-fat *twaróg*
- 100g unsalted butter
- 1 large egg
- 1 packet sweet cream *budyń* for 0.5 litre of milk (40g) *(Note 1)*
- 4 tbsp sugar
- 130ml milk

For the apple mixture *(Note 2)*
- 1kg apples
- 1 packet orange jelly (70g) *(Note 3)*
- 2 tbsp sugar
- 100ml water

For the glaze
- 100g unsalted butter
- 1 large egg
- 3 tbsp milk
- 2½ tbsp icing sugar *(Note 4)*
- 6 tsp cocoa powder

> *Polish products differ from the ones available locally. You will find more information about budyń, jelly, sour cream, twaróg and vanilla sugar in the chapter "About the products" on page 328.*

DIRECTIONS

Preparing the pastry
Preparing the butter
1. Take the butter out of the fridge.
2. Cube the butter.
3. Transfer to a small bowl.
4. Set the bowl aside. *(Note 5)*

Preparing the baking tin
1. Using scissors, cut the baking paper to fit the bottom of the baking tin.
2. Brush the baking tin with butter so the paper sticks.
3. Line the baking tin with the baking paper.
4. Set the baking tin aside.

Preparing the dough – part 1
1. Sift the flour into the bowl of a food mixer. *(Note 6)*
2. Add the sugar, vanilla sugar and baking powder.
3. Crack one egg into the bowl, separate the other egg and add the yolk, then add the sour cream. Discard the egg white.
4. Mix until the ingredients are combined.
5. Add the butter.
6. Knead the dough until smooth and elastic. This can take around 10 mins in the food mixer and a little bit longer if kneading the dough by hand. *(Note 7)*

Preparing the oven
1. Preheat the oven to 180°C / 350°F or gas 4.

Preparing the dough – part 2
1. Sprinkle a work surface with flour. Transfer the dough onto the work surface.
2. Roll out the dough into a thick sausage shape and cut into 3 equal parts.
3. Set two parts of the dough aside.
4. Sprinkle one part with flour.
5. Roll out to the size of the baking tin base.
6. Put into the prepared baking tin. *(Note 8)*
7. Carefully press the dough into the baking tin, in particular into the edges.

Baking
1. Bake for around 20 minutes, until golden.

Preparing the dough – part 3
1. While baking one batch of the dough, roll out the next.
2. After baking, put the pastry on a cooling rack.
3. Remove the baking paper from the pastry. *(Note 9)*
4. Line the baking tin with fresh baking paper.
5. Put another rolled out batch of the dough into the baking tin and bake.
6. Repeat for the remaining dough, remembering to change the baking paper.
7. After baking all the pastry layers, layer the baking tin with fresh baking paper, to cover the bottom and inner sides of the tin. *(Note 10)*
8. Put the first pastry layer, that has already cooled, into the baking tin. *(Note 11)*
9. Set the baking tin aside.

Preparing the cheese mixture
1. When all the pastry layers are ready, start preparing the cheese mixture.
2. To a large pot add the *twaróg*, *budyń*, egg, milk and sugar.
3. Using a hand blender, blend until a uniform mixture.
4. Put the hob on medium heat.
5. Heat the mixture to thicken.
6. Occasionally stir with a wooden spoon.
7. When air bubbles begin to appear on the surface of the mixture, heat for 5 minutes, stirring constantly.
8. Turn off and remove from the heat and set the pot aside.

Preparing the cake – part 1
1. Pour the hot cheese mixture onto the first pastry layer in the baking tin.
2. Spread evenly using a spatula.
3. Layer the second pastry layer on top.
4. Press slightly to stick.
5. Set the baking tin with the cake aside.

Preparing the apple mixture
Apple mixture made with fresh apples
1. Peel the apples and cut into quarters.
2. Remove the pips and stems.
3. Cut the apples into 0.5cm cubes. *(Note 12)*
4. Add to a large saucepan.
5. Pour the water into the saucepan. *(Note 13)*
6. Put the hob on low heat.
7. Bring the water to a simmer.
8. Simmer, semi-covered for around 20-30 minutes. *(Note 14)*
9. Occasionally stir with a wooden spoon.
10. After the water evaporates, keep stirring the apples, so they don't burn. *(Note 15)*
11. The apples should be soft and mushy. *(Note 16)*
12. Using a hand blender, blend to get a uniform consistency.
13. Add the orange jelly and sugar.
14. Mix thoroughly, to combine the jelly with the apples.
15. Turn off and remove from the heat and set the saucepan aside.
16. Pour cold water into the sink and place the saucepan with the apples inside. Allow to cool. This can take around 10 minutes.
17. Stir from time to time so the mixture thickens.

Apple mixture made apple sauce (optional)
1. Put the hob on medium heat.
2. To a large pot add around 1 litre of water and start boiling. *(Note 17)*
3. Put a medium saucepan into the pot with the water.
4. Add the apple sauce and jelly into the saucepan. *(Note 18)*
5. Mix thoroughly, to combine the jelly with the apples. *(Note 19)*
6. Turn off and remove from the heat and set the pot aside.
7. Pour cold water into the sink and place the pot with the apples inside. Allow to cool. This can take around 10 minutes.
8. Stir from time to time so the mixture thickens.

Preparing the cake – part 2
1. Pour the apple mixture onto the second pastry layer in the baking tin.
2. Spread evenly using a spatula.
3. Cover the apple mixture with the third pastry layer.
4. Press lightly to stick.
5. Set the baking tin with the cake aside to cool completely. *(Note 20)*

Preparing the chocolate glaze
1. Ensure the cake is cooled completely before adding the chocolate glaze.
2. Crack the egg into a bowl.
3. Add the icing sugar and cocoa powder.
4. Whisk thoroughly to combine all the ingredients.
5. Put the hob on medium heat.
6. Pour the milk into a medium saucepan.
7. Cube the butter.
8. Add the butter to the saucepan and let it melt.
9. Heat until sizzling.
10. Add the hot butter to the bowl with cocoa powder.
11. Thoroughly combine all the ingredients. *(Notes 21 and 22)*

Preparing the cake – part 3
1. Pour the glaze onto the cake.
2. Spread evenly.
3. Set the cake aside in a cool place for around 3 hours.

NOTES

1. You can swap sweet cream *budyń* for the same amount of vanilla *budyń*.
2. You can use apple sauce to make the apple mixture. You will find the recipe for <u>apple sauce</u> in the "Pantry" chapter. Instead of apples and sugar you will need two 280ml jars. You still need the orange jelly for the mixture.
3. You can swap orange jelly for lemon or peach jelly.
4. Icing sugar will dissolve quicker and is then easier to distribute. If you don't have any icing sugar, you can use regular sugar – just stir the glaze until dissolved.
5. When the butter is at room temperature, the dough will be easier to knead.
6. If you don't have a food mixer, you can knead the dough by hand on the work surface. Sift the flour onto the work surface. Add the dry ingredients and make a well in the middle. Add the wet ingredients. Start combining the ingredients with a knife. Then knead the dough by hand.
7. After kneading, the dough should be smooth, slightly sticky but not enough to stick to your hands.
8. The dough is very crumbly and might be difficult to transfer to the baking tin in one piece. To transfer it more easily, carefully wrap the dough around the rolling pin and transfer into the baking tin.
9. It is easier to remove the baking paper while the pastry is warm. Removing the paper when the pastry is cold might damage it, since the pastry might stick to the paper.
10. Baking paper will secure the sides of the cake while you make more layers.
11. You will put the cheese mixture on the pastry in the baking tin, and then add more layers on top.
12. Cubed apples cook faster.
13. Adding water will prevent the apples from burning before they start releasing their juice.
14. The time you need to soften the apples depends on the variety you use.
15. If they start sticking to the bottom and burning, transfer to another saucepan and keep simmering and stirring.
16. Check if they are soft. Be careful: they will be very hot!
17. The amount of water needed will depend on the size of your pots. There should be enough water so you can put another saucepan in the pot without spilling.
18. If you're cooking the water in a large pot, be careful not to burn yourself when it starts boiling.
19. Heat the apples until they are hot and the jelly dissolves.
20. After you cover the apple mixture with the pastry layer, it can heat up. This will make the chocolate glaze cool slower. Wait for the cake to cool completely.
21. If the glaze is too thin, add 1-2 tsp cocoa powder and stir again to combine.
22. Check if the glaze is sweet enough. Be careful: it will be very hot! If it's not sweet enough, add more icing sugar. Stir for the sugar to dissolve.

KITCHEN ACCESSORIES

- ☐ large pot
- ☐ large saucepan with lid
- ☐ medium saucepan
- ☐ bowl
- ☐ measuring jug
- ☐ knife
- ☐ peeling knife
- ☐ chopping board
- ☐ 2 tablespoons
- ☐ 2 teaspoons
- ☐ hand blender
- ☐ food mixer
- ☐ wooden spoon
- ☐ spatula
- ☐ whisk
- ☐ scissors
- ☐ sieve
- ☐ rolling pin
- ☐ pastry board
- ☐ kitchen scale
- ☐ cooling rack
- ☐ baking tin (measured inside 35 x 20 x 7cm)
- ☐ baking paper

GOOD TO KNOW

vegetarian

contains dairy
- contains butter
- contains milk
- contains sour cream
- contains *twaróg*

contains pork
- contains jelly – check if it's made with pork gelatine

fridge
- for up to 4 days

kcal
- 205 per serving, 7380 total

GOES WELL WITH

Apple Sauce
11. Pantry, page 309

Cakes and Desserts

NAPOLEON

*Delicious layers of cake and custard, finished with a crumble.
A perfect cake for parties and celebrations.*

Difficulty	Serves	Preparation	Baking	Resting	Total
INTERMEDIATE	36	~1 H	1 H	3 H	5 H

INGREDIENTS

For the dough
- ☐ 430g plain flour (+ more for dusting)
- ☐ 200g unsalted butter (+ more for buttering the tin)
- ☐ 135g sugar
- ☐ 32g vanilla sugar
- ☐ 2 large eggs
- ☐ 3 tbsp sour cream
- ☐ 2 tsp baking powder

For the custard
- ☐ 220g sugar
- ☐ 32g vanilla sugar
- ☐ 6 large eggs
- ☐ 4 tbsp potato starch
- ☐ 3 tbsp plain flour
- ☐ 1 litre milk

 Polish products differ from the ones available locally. You will find more information about potato starch, sour cream and vanilla sugar in the chapter "About the products" on page 328.

DIRECTIONS

Preparing pastry
Preparing the butter
1. Take the butter out of the fridge.
2. Cube the butter.
3. Transfer to a small bowl.
4. Set the bowl aside. *(Note 1)*

Preparing the baking tin
1. Using scissors, cut the baking paper to fit the bottom of the baking tin.
2. Brush the baking tin with butter so the paper sticks.
3. Line the baking tin with the baking paper.
4. Set the baking tin aside.

Preparing the dough – part 1
1. Sift the flour into the bowl of a food mixer. *(Note 2)*
2. Add the sugar, vanilla sugar and baking powder.
3. Crack one egg into the bowl, separate the other egg and add the yolk, then add the sour cream. Discard the egg white.
4. Mix until the ingredients are combined.
5. Add the butter.
6. Knead the dough until smooth and elastic. This can take around 10 mins in the food mixer and a little bit longer if kneading the dough by hand. *(Note 3)*

Preparing the oven
1. Preheat the oven to 180°C / 350°F or gas 4.

Preparing the dough – part 2
1. Sprinkle a work surface with flour. Transfer the dough onto the work surface.
2. Roll out the dough into a thick sausage shape and cut into 3 equal parts.
3. Set two parts of the dough aside.
4. Sprinkle one part with flour.
5. Roll out to the size of the baking tin base.
6. Put into the prepared baking tin. *(Note 4)*
7. Carefully press the dough into the baking tin, in particular into the edges.

Baking
1. Bake for around 20 minutes, until golden.

Preparing the dough – part 3
1. While baking one batch of the dough, roll out the next.
2. After baking, put the pastry on a chopping board.
3. Remove the baking paper from the pastry. *(Note 5)*
4. Cut off about 0.5cm from each edge of the pastry, creating neat edges. *(Note 6)*
5. Put the pastry on a rack to cool.
6. Put the cut edges into a bowl. *(Note 7)*
7. Line the baking tin with fresh baking paper.
8. Put another rolled out batch of the dough into the baking tin and bake.
9. Repeat for the remaining dough, remembering to; change the baking paper and cutting off the edges of the pastry when baked.
10. After baking all the pastry layers, layer the baking tin with fresh baking paper, to cover the bottom and inner sides of the tin. *(Note 8)*
11. Set the baking tin aside.

Preparing the crumble
1. Put the collected edges of the pastry into a resealable plastic food bag.
2. Close tightly.
3. Roll to crush into small pieces.
4. Put the crushed pastry back into the bowl.

Preparing the custard
Preparing the mixture
1. When the pastry layers have cooled completely, start preparing the custard.
2. Crack 4 eggs into a large bowl, separate 2 eggs and add the yolks. Discard the egg whites.
3. Add the sugar.
4. Whisk for around 5 minutes.
5. Gradually add the potato starch and plain flour.
6. Whisk the mixture thoroughly while adding flour.
7. After adding all the flour, pour in 200ml of milk. *(Note 9)*
8. Whisk until the ingredients are combined.

Cooking the custard
1. Put the hob on low heat.
2. Put the remaining milk in a medium saucepan (800ml).
3. Bring to a boil. *(Note 10)*
4. Add the prepared mixture to the milk.
5. Keep stirring with a wooden spoon until uniform. *(Note 11)*
6. When the custard starts bobbling, cook for 3 minutes. *(Note 12)*
7. Turn off the hob.
8. Add the vanilla sugar.
9. Mix well. *(Note 13)*

Preparing the cake
1. Put one pastry layer in the baking tin.
2. Pour ⅓ of the hot custard on top.
3. Spread evenly using a spatula.
4. Cover with the second pastry layer.
5. Pour the second ⅓ of the hot custard on top.
6. Spread evenly.
7. Cover with the third pastry layer.
8. Pour the last ⅓ of the hot custard on top.
9. Spread evenly.
10. Sprinkle the crumble evenly on the custard. *(Note 14)*
11. Set the cake aside in a cool place for around 3 hours.

NOTES

1. When the butter is at room temperature, the dough will be easier to knead.
2. If you don't have a food mixer, you can knead the dough by hand on the work surface. Sift the flour onto the work surface. Add the dry ingredients and make a well in the middle. Add the wet ingredients. Start combining the ingredients with a knife. Then knead the dough by hand.
3. After kneading, the dough should be smooth, slightly sticky but not enough to stick to your hands.
4. The dough is very crumbly and might be difficult to transfer to the baking tin in one piece. To transfer it more easily, carefully wrap the dough around the rolling pin and transfer into the baking tin.
5. It is easier to remove the baking paper while the pastry is warm. Removing the paper when the pastry is cold might damage it, since the pastry might stick to the paper.
6. You need to cut the edges off when the pastry layers are still warm, so it doesn't break when you cut it.
7. You will use the edges of the pastry layers to make the crumble.
8. Baking paper will secure the sides of the cake while you make more layers.
9. Adding milk will loosen the consistency, which will make it easier to pour the mixture into the boiling milk.
10. When the milk is close to boiling, it starts to foam and bubble so watch it to ensure it does not boil over.
11. Lumps are going to form at first, but as you keep stirring, you'll get a uniform mixture.
12. Check that the custard does not taste like flour. If it does, cook a little bit longer. If it no longer tastes of flour, turn off the hob. Be careful: the custard will be very hot!
13. Check it for sweetness. If it's not sweet enough, you can add more vanilla sugar.
14. You can carefully press the crumble to the custard using a spatula. Remember to wash it after spreading the last layer of the custard on the cake.

KITCHEN ACCESSORIES

- ☐ large pot
- ☐ large bowl
- ☐ bowl
- ☐ measuring jug
- ☐ knife
- ☐ chopping board
- ☐ 2 tablespoons
- ☐ 2 teaspoons
- ☐ hand mixer
- ☐ food mixer
- ☐ wooden spoon
- ☐ spatula
- ☐ scissors
- ☐ sieve
- ☐ rolling pin
- ☐ pastry board
- ☐ kitchen scale
- ☐ cooling rack
- ☐ baking tin (measured inside 35 x 20 x 7cm)
- ☐ baking paper
- ☐ resealable plastic food bag

GOOD TO KNOW

 vegetarian

 contains dairy
- contains butter
- contains milk
- contains sour cream

 fridge
- for up to 3 days

 kcal
- 168 per serving, 6048 total

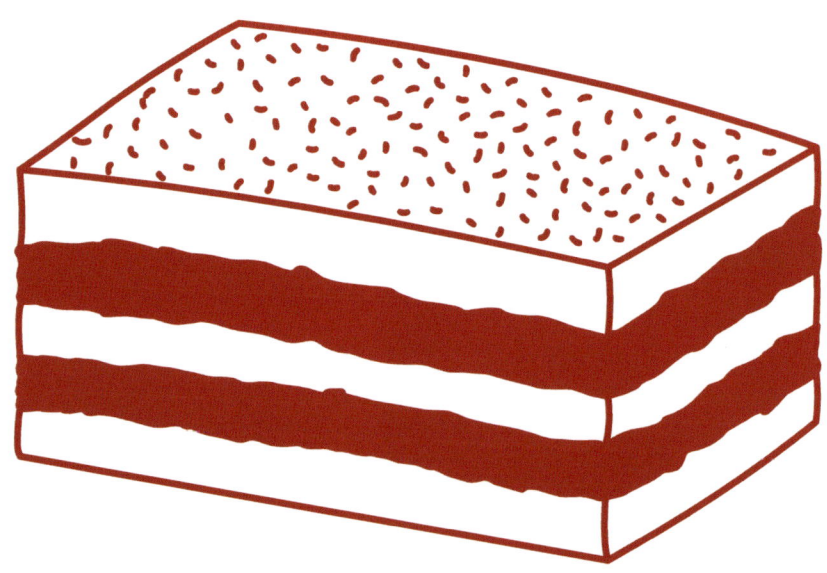

106   **Cakes and Desserts**

KOCIE OCZKA

"Cat's Eyes" – delightful shortbread biscuits with a plum jam, sprinkled with icing sugar. A perfect sweet treat for when you travel, or to share with your family and friends.

Difficulty	Makes	Preparation	Baking	Resting	Total
INTERMEDIATE	~50	~1 H 10 MIN	1 H	20 MIN	~2 H 30 MIN

INGREDIENTS

For the dough
- ☐ 400g plain flour (+ more for dusting)
- ☐ 250g unsalted butter
- ☐ 32g vanilla sugar
- ☐ 2 large eggs
- ☐ 2-3 tbsp sour cream *(Note 1)*
- ☐ 1 tsp baking powder

For the filling
- ☐ ~300g plum jam *(Notes 2 and 3)*

For the decoration
- ☐ ~4 tbsp icing sugar

 Polish products differ from the ones available locally. You will find more information about sour cream and vanilla sugar in the chapter "About the products" on page 328.

DIRECTIONS

Preparing the butter
1. Take the butter out of the fridge.
2. Cube the butter.
3. Transfer to a small bowl.
4. Set the bowl aside. *(Note 4)*

Preparing the baking tray
1. Using scissors, cut the baking paper to fit the baking tray.
2. Line the baking tray with the baking paper.
3. Set aside.

Preparing the dough
1. Separate the yolks from the whites into two separate small bowls. Discard the egg whites.
2. Sift the flour onto a pastry board.
3. Add the vanilla sugar and baking powder.
4. Make a well in the dry ingredients.
5. Add the butter and yolks.
6. Using a knife cut through the butter and dough mixture until resembles breadcrumbs. This can take around 10 minutes. *(Note 5)*
7. Collect the dough with a knife to form a pile.
8. Add 2 tbsp sour cream.
9. Chop the dough with a knife until the ingredients are combined. This can take around 3 minutes. *(Note 6)*
10. When larger pieces of dough start to form, begin kneading by hand. *(Note 7)*
11. Sprinkle the dough with flour, to prevent the dough sticking.

Cakes and Desserts

Preparing the oven
1. Preheat the oven to 180°C / 350°F or gas 4.

Cutting the biscuits – part 1
1. Roll out the dough into a thick sausage shape and cut into 3 equal parts.
2. Set two parts of the dough aside.
3. Sprinkle the pastry board and the dough with flour.
4. Roll out the dough to a thickness of about 2mm.
5. Using a large 5-cm cutter cut out circles in the dough.
6. Add the edges that are left to the remaining dough.
7. Using a small 1.5cm cutter cut out holes in half of the prepared circles.
8. Gather the cut out inner circles and add to the remaining dough.
9. Put the prepared circles on the baking tray 1cm apart. *(Note 8)*
10. Prick the circles without a hole with a fork in a couple of places. *(Note 9)*

Baking
1. Bake for around 15-20 minutes, until golden.

Cutting the biscuits – part 2
1. While the first batch is baking, roll the dough and prepare the next batch.
2. When the biscuits are baked, place on a cooling rack to cool completely.

Preparing the biscuits
1. Spread the jam on the circles without holes. *(Note 10)*
2. Place the biscuits with holes on top. *(Note 11)*
3. Sprinkle with icing sugar.

NOTES

1. You need 2 tbsp sour cream to make the dough. You may add the additional tablespoon if the dough doesn't stick together.
2. You can buy plum jam (*powidła śliwkowe*) or make it yourself. You will find a recipe for *powidła śliwkowe* in the "Pantry" chapter.
3. You can swap the plum jam (*powidła śliwkowe*) for any type of marmalade or jam. You will find a recipe for raspberry jam in the "Pantry" chapter.
4. When the butter is at room temperature, the dough will be easier to knead.
5. It's best to chop the dough using two knives. Use one knife to chop the butter with the flour and the second knife to collect the butter from the first one. After you chop the butter, it will form little lumps with the flour.
6. If the dough keeps falling apart and doesn't hold together, add 1 tbsp of sour cream and continue chopping.
7. After kneading, the dough should be smooth, slightly sticky but not enough to stick to your hands.
8. You can lay the cookies on the baking tray close to each other since they will only rise a little bit.
9. The fork pricks will allow the biscuits to rise evenly.
10. Spread the jam on the top of the biscuits – not on the side that touched the baking tray.
11. Position the biscuits with a hole upside-down, so that the side that was resting on the baking tray is now the top.

KITCHEN ACCESSORIES

- ☐ bowl
- ☐ small bowl
- ☐ 2 knives
- ☐ chopping board
- ☐ 2 tablespoons
- ☐ 2 teaspoons
- ☐ fork
- ☐ scissors
- ☐ sieve
- ☐ rolling pin
- ☐ pastry board
- ☐ kitchen scale
- ☐ cooling rack
- ☐ baking tray (measured inside 30x26cm)
- ☐ cookie cutter (round, diameter 5cm)
- ☐ cookie cutter (round, diameter 1.5cm)
- ☐ baking paper

GOOD TO KNOW

 vegetarian

 contains dairy
- contains butter
- contains sour cream

 pantry
- store in a dry place up to 4 days

 kcal
- 87 per cookie, 437 total

GOES WELL WITH

 **Raspberry Jam**
11. Pantry, page 313

 **Powidła Śliwkowe (Plum Jam)**
11. Pantry, page 317

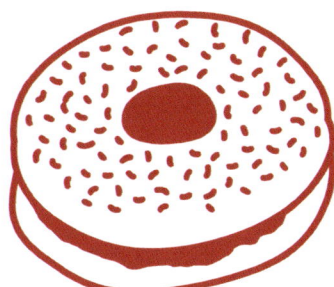

Cakes and Desserts

WALNUT PIE

A delicate, moist, and buttery walnut cake with a layer of slightly tart plum jam. Perfect with a cup of tea.

Difficulty	Serves	Preparation	Baking	Resting	Total
INTERMEDIATE	36	~1 H 20 MIN	~40 H	2 H	~4 H

INGREDIENTS

For the dough
- ☐ 250g plain flour (+ more for dusting)
- ☐ 200g unsalted butter (+ more for buttering the tin)
- ☐ 2 large eggs
- ☐ 6 tbsp cold water

For the decoration
- ☐ 4 tbsp icing sugar

For the mixture
- ☐ 300g walnuts
- ☐ 120g icing sugar
- ☐ 45g almond sugar *(Note 1)*
- ☐ 9 large eggs
- ☐ ~450g plum jam *(Note 2)*

 Polish products differ from the ones available locally. You will find more information about almond sugar in the chapter "About the products" on page 328.

DIRECTIONS

Preparing the butter
1. Take the butter out of the fridge.
2. Cube the butter.
3. Transfer to a small bowl.
4. Set the bowl aside. *(Note 3)*

Preparing the baking tin
1. Using scissors, cut the baking paper as a single sheet, to cover the bottom and inner sides of the tin.
2. Brush the baking tin with butter so the paper sticks.
3. Line the baking tin with the baking paper.
4. Set the baking tin aside.

Preparing the dough
1. Separate the yolks from the whites of two eggs. Put the yolks in a small bowl and the whites in the bowl of a food mixer. Set the whites aside. *(Notes 4 and 5)*
2. Sift the flour onto a pastry board.
3. Make a well in the flour.
4. Add the butter and yolks.
5. Using a knife cut through the butter and dough mixture until resembles breadcrumbs. This can take around 10 minutes. *(Note 6)*
6. Collect the dough with a knife to form a pile.
7. Add 6 tbsp of water.
8. Chop the dough with a knife until the ingredients are combined. This can take around 3 minutes. *(Note 7)*

9. When larger pieces of dough start to form, begin kneading by hand.
10. Sprinkle the dough with flour, to prevent the dough sticking.
11. Roll out the dough into a thick sausage shape and with a knife mark 3 equal parts.
12. Cut off ⅓ of the dough and set aside. *(Note 8)*
13. Sprinkle the remaining ⅔ with plain flour.
14. Roll out to the size of the baking tin, enough to fit to the bottom and sides.
15. Put into the prepared baking tin. *(Note 9)*
16. Carefully press the dough into the baking tin, in particular into the edges and corners.
17. Set the baking tin with the dough aside.

Preparing the mixture
Preparing the ingredients
1. Grind the walnuts in a nut grinder. *(Note 10)*
2. Transfer to a small bowl.
3. Measure the icing sugar into a separate small bowl.

Preparing the egg whites
1. Separate the yolks from the whites of the nine remaining eggs. Put the yolks in a large bowl and add the whites to the remaining egg whites from earlier, into the bowl of the food mixer. *(Note 11)*
2. Add the almond sugar to the egg whites.
3. Whisk the egg whites to stiff peaks. This can take around 10 minutes.
4. While waiting, prepare the yolks.

Preparing the yolks
1. Add the icing sugar into the bowl with the yolks.
2. Using a hand mixer combine all of the ingredients. This can take around 5 minutes.
3. Set the prepared yolks aside.

Preparing the filling
1. When the egg whites are at the stiff peaks stage, begin to combine all the ingredients.
2. Slowly add the yolks, whisking continuously.
3. Add the ground walnuts.
4. Whisk until the ingredients are combined.
5. Set the filling aside.

Preparing the oven
1. Preheat the oven to 180°C / 350°F or gas 4.

Preparing the pie
1. Put a layer of plum jam on the dough in the baking tin.
2. Spread evenly with a spatula.
3. Cover with the filling.
4. Spread evenly using a spatula. *(Note 12)*
5. Sprinkle the work surface with more flour. Transfer the remaining dough onto the work surface.
6. Sprinkle the dough with flour.
7. Roll out to the size of the baking tin.
8. Transfer the dough onto the prepared pie. *(Note 13)*
9. Using your fingers, carefully press the edges of the dough to seal the top.
10. Prick the dough with a fork. *(Note 14)*

Baking
1. Bake for around 40 minutes, until golden.
2. After baking the pie, leave in the baking tin to cool down completely. *(Note 15)*

To serve
- Sprinkle with icing sugar.

NOTES

1. You can swap the almond sugar with 45g of vanilla sugar.
2. You can buy plum jam (*powidła śliwkowe*) or make it yourself. You will find a recipe for <u>*powidła śliwkowe*</u> in the "Pantry" chapter.
3. When the butter is at room temperature, the dough will be easier to knead.

4. You will use the egg whites to make the filling.
5. If you don't have a food mixer, you can prepare the mixture in a large bowl using a hand mixer.
6. It's best to chop the dough using two knives. Use one knife to chop the butter with the flour and the second knife to collect the butter from the first one. After you chop the butter, it will form little lumps with the flour.
7. If the dough keeps falling apart and doesn't hold together, add 1 tbsp of water and continue chopping.
8. You will use one third of the dough to cover the filling.
9. The dough is very crumbly and might be difficult to transfer to the baking tin in one piece. To transfer it more easily, carefully wrap the dough around the rolling pin and transfer onto and into the baking tin.
10. You can use a blender instead of the nut grinder.
11. If you don't have a food mixer, add the egg whites to the remaining whites in the large bowl.
12. Remember to wash the spatula after you spread the plum jam.
13. Carefully wrap the dough around the rolling pin and transfer onto the baking tin. Roll it on top, covering the filling.
14. The holes will prevent the dough from rising.
15. Freshly baked pie can break when you try to cut and remove a portion from the tin. When it's cold, the inside will have set, which prevents it from breaking and the filling from spilling out of the pie.

KITCHEN ACCESSORIES

- ☐ large bowl
- ☐ 4 small bowls
- ☐ 2 knives
- ☐ chopping board
- ☐ tablespoon
- ☐ fork
- ☐ nut grinder (or hand blender)
- ☐ hand mixer
- ☐ food mixer
- ☐ spatula
- ☐ scissors
- ☐ sieve
- ☐ rolling pin
- ☐ pastry board
- ☐ kitchen scale
- ☐ baking tin (measured inside 35 x 20 x 7cm)
- ☐ baking paper

GOOD TO KNOW

 vegetarian

 contains dairy
- contains butter

 contains nuts
- contains walnuts
- contains almond sugar

 pantry
- store in a dry place up to 4 days

 kcal
- 194 per serving, 6984 total

GOES WELL WITH

 *Powidła Śliwkowe* **(Plum Jam)**
11. Pantry, page 317

EASY KREMÓWKA

A delicious take on a traditional Polish cake made with delicate sheets of pastry filled with sweet vanilla custard and sprinkled with icing sugar. Perfect for every special occasion.

Difficulty	Serves	Preparation	Baking	Resting	Total
INTERMEDIATE	15	1 H 20 MIN	40 MIN	1 H	3 H

INGREDIENTS

For the dough
- ☐ 150g plain flour (+ more for dusting)
- ☐ 150g unsalted butter (+ more for buttering the tin)
- ☐ 1 egg yolk
- ☐ 3 tbsp cold water

For the custard
- ☐ 110g sugar
- ☐ 16g vanilla sugar
- ☐ 3 large eggs
- ☐ 2 tbsp potato starch
- ☐ 1½ tbsp plain flour
- ☐ 500ml milk

For the decoration
- ☐ 4 tbsp icing sugar

 Polish products differ from the ones available locally. You will find more information about potato starch and vanilla sugar in the chapter "About the products" on page 328.

DIRECTIONS

Preparing the pastry
Preparing the butter
1. Take the butter out of the fridge.
2. Cube the butter.
3. Transfer to a small bowl.
4. Set the bowl aside. *(Note 1)*

Preparing the dough – part 1
1. Sift the flour onto a pastry board.
2. Make a well in the flour.
3. Add the butter and the yolk.
4. Chop the dough with a knife until the ingredients are combined. This can take around 10 minutes. *(Note 2)*
5. Collect the dough with a knife to form a pile.
6. Add 3 tbsp of water.
7. Chop the dough with a knife until the ingredients are combined. This can take around 3 minutes. *(Note 3)*
8. When larger pieces of dough start to form, begin kneading by hand.
9. Sprinkle the dough with flour, to prevent the dough sticking.
10. Roll out the dough into a thick sausage shape and cut in half.
11. Transfer to a small plate.
12. Put the plate in the fridge for around 15 minutes.

Preparing the baking tin
1. Using scissors, cut the baking paper as a single sheet, to cover the bottom and inner sides of the tin.
2. Brush the baking tin with butter so the paper sticks.
3. Line the baking tin with the baking paper.
4. Set the baking tin aside.

Preparing the oven
1. Preheat the oven to 180°C / 350°F or gas 4.

Preparing the dough – part 2
1. Put one part of the dough on the pastry board. Keep the rest in the fridge.
2. Sprinkle the pastry board and the dough with flour.
3. Roll out to the size of the baking tin base.
4. Put into the prepared baking tin. *(Note 4)*
5. Carefully press the dough into the baking tin, in particular into the edges.

Baking
1. Bake for around 15-20 minutes, until golden.

Preparing the dough – part 3
1. While baking one batch of the dough, roll out the next.
2. After baking, place the pastry with baking paper on a cooling rack to cool. *(Note 5)*
3. Line the baking tin with fresh baking paper.
4. Put another rolled out batch of the dough into the baking tin and bake.
5. Leave the pastry in the baking tin to cool completely.

Preparing the custard
Preparing the mixture
1. When the pastry layers have cooled completely, start preparing the custard.
2. Crack 2 eggs into a large bowl and add a single yolk. Discard the egg white.
3. Add the sugar.
4. Whisk for around 5 minutes.
5. Gradually add the potato starch and plain flour.
6. Whisk the mixture thoroughly while adding the flour.
7. After adding all the flour, pour in 100ml of milk. *(Note 6)*
8. Whisk until the ingredients are combined.

Cooking the custard
1. Put the hob on low heat.
2. Put the remaining milk in a large saucepan (400ml).
3. Bring to a boil. *(Note 7)*
4. Add the prepared mixture to the milk.
5. Keep stirring with a wooden spoon until uniform. *(Note 8)*
6. When the custard starts bobbling, cook for 3 minutes. *(Note 9)*
7. Turn off the hob.
8. Add the vanilla sugar.
9. Mix well. *(Note 10)*

Preparing the cake
1. Pour the hot custard on the pastry layer in the baking tin.
2. Spread evenly using a spatula.
3. Cover with the second pastry layer.
4. Set the cake aside in a cool place for around 1 hour.

To serve
- Sprinkle the cake with icing sugar.

NOTES

1. When the butter is at room temperature, the dough will be easier to knead.
2. It's best to chop the dough using two knives. Use one knife to chop the butter with the flour and the second knife to collect the butter from the first one. After you chop the butter, it will form little lumps with the flour.
3. If the dough keeps falling apart and doesn't hold together, add 1 tbsp of water and continue chopping.
4. The dough is very crumbly and might be difficult to transfer to the baking tin in one piece. To transfer it more easily, carefully wrap the dough around the rolling pin and transfer into the baking tin.
5. Don't move the pastry layer without paper, because it's very crumbly and could break.
6. Adding milk will loosen the consistency, which will make it easier to pour the mixture into the boiling milk.
7. When the milk is close to boiling, it starts to foam and bubble so watch it to ensure it does not boil over.
8. Lumps are going to form at first, but as you keep stirring, you'll get a uniform mixture.
9. Check that the custard does not taste like flour. If it does, cook a little bit longer. If it no longer tastes of flour, turn off the hob. Be careful: the custard will be very hot!
10. Check it for sweetness. If it's not sweet enough, you can add more vanilla sugar.

KITCHEN ACCESSORIES

- ☐ large saucepan
- ☐ large bowl
- ☐ 3 small bowls
- ☐ measuring jug
- ☐ 2 knives
- ☐ chopping board
- ☐ small plate
- ☐ 2 tablespoons
- ☐ 2 teaspoons
- ☐ hand mixer

- ☐ wooden spoon
- ☐ spatula
- ☐ scissors
- ☐ sieve
- ☐ rolling pin
- ☐ pastry board
- ☐ kitchen scale
- ☐ cooling rack
- ☐ baking tin (measured inside 35 x 20 x 7cm)
- ☐ baking paper

GOOD TO KNOW

 vegetarian

 contains dairy
- contains butter
- contains milk

 fridge
- for up to 3 days

 kcal
- 204 per serving, 3060 total

CREAM HORNS

Horns made of dough filled with a sweet custard and sprinkled with vanilla sugar are for many a defining taste of their childhood! Make them now and allow yourself a little sweet treat!

Difficulty
INTERMEDIATE

Makes
35

Preparation
1 H 30 MIN

Baking
1 H

Resting
30 MIN

Total
3 H

INGREDIENTS

For the dough
- 500g plain flour
- 250g unsalted butter
- 250g sour cream
- ½ tsp salt

For baking the horns
- 64g vanilla sugar *(Note 1)*
- 2 egg whites
- 100ml cooking oil

For the custard
- 300g unsalted butter
- 48g vanilla sugar
- 2 egg yolks *(Note 2)*
- 4 tbsp sugar
- 4 tbsp potato starch
- 4 tbsp plain flour
- 1 litre milk

 Polish products differ from the ones available locally. You will find more information about potato starch, sour cream and vanilla sugar in the chapter "About the products" on page 328.

DIRECTIONS

Preparing the custard – part 1
Preparing the butter
1. Take the butter out of the fridge.
2. Cube the butter.
3. Transfer to a large bowl.
4. Set the bowl aside. *(Note 3)*

Preparing the horns
Preparing the butter
1. Take the butter out of the fridge.
2. Cube the butter.
3. Transfer to a small bowl.
4. Set the bowl aside. *(Note 4)*

Preparing the dough
1. Sift the flour onto a pastry board.
2. Make a well in the flour.
3. Add the salt, butter and sour cream.
4. Chop the dough with a knife until the ingredients are combined. This can take around 10 minutes. *(Note 5)*
5. When larger pieces of dough start to form, begin kneading by hand.
6. Knead for around 20 minutes. Don't add any more flour. *(Note 6)*
7. Roll out the dough into a thick sausage shape and cut in half.
8. Wrap each portion with cling film.
9. Put the dough in the fridge for around 30 minutes.

Preparing the baking tray
1. Using scissors, cut the baking paper to fit the baking tray.
2. Line the baking tray with the baking paper.
3. Set aside.

Before baking
1. Pour the oil into a small bowl.
2. Brush the pastry horn moulds with the oil using a brush.
3. Set aside.
4. Separate the yolks from the whites. Put the yolks in a large bowl and the whites in a small one. Set the yolks aside.
5. Whisk the egg whites with a fork and set aside.
6. Pour the vanilla sugar into a soup plate and set aside.

Preparing the oven
1. Preheat the oven to 200°C / 400°F or gas 6.

Preparing the horns
1. Put one part of the dough on the pastry board. Don't throw away the cling film.
2. Sprinkle the pastry board and the dough with flour.
3. Prepare the horns following the instructions in the panel.
4. Repeat for the rest of the horns.

Baking
1. Bake for around 15-20 minutes, until golden.
2. When ready, carefully remove the pastry horn moulds using a tea towel. Be careful: the horns and mould will be very hot!
3. When the horns are baked, place on a cooling rack to cool completely.

INSTRUCTIONS

To prepare the horns, follow these instructions:

Roll the dough into a rectangle.

Using a pastry wheel align the sides of the dough to create a rectangle with a longer side of 35cm. (Note 7)

Roll the leftover pieces of dough into a ball, wrap in cling film and put into the fridge.

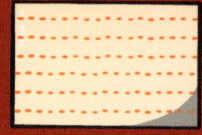
Using a pastry wheel, cut the dough into 2.5 x 35 cm strips.

Roll the dough strips onto the pastry horn mould from the top, leaving about 1cm of free space at the top. (Note 8)

Wrap the strips of the dough, so that they slightly overlap.

Leave 2-3mm at the bottom of the pastry horn mould so it's easier to remove after baking.

Brush the horns with whisked egg white.

Roll in the vanilla sugar.

Lay on the prepared baking tray, leaving around 2cm between them. (Note 9)

Preparing the custard – part 2
Preparing the mixture
1. When the horns have cooled completely, start preparing the custard.
2. Add the sugar into the bowl with the yolks.
3. Whisk for around 5 minutes.
4. Gradually add the potato starch and plain flour.
5. Whisk the mixture thoroughly while adding the flour.
6. After adding all the flour, pour in 200ml of milk. *(Note 10)*
7. Whisk until the ingredients are combined.

Cooking the custard
1. Put the hob on low heat.
2. Put the remaining milk in a medium saucepan (800ml).
3. Bring to a boil. *(Note 11)*
4. Add the prepared mixture to the milk.
5. Keep stirring with a wooden spoon until uniform. *(Note 12)*
6. When the custard starts bobbling, cook for 3 minutes. *(Note 13)*
7. Turn off the hob.
8. Add the vanilla sugar.
9. Mix well. *(Note 14)*
10. Set aside to cool completely. This can take around 30 minutes. *(Note 15)*
11. Stir from time to time.

Finishing the custard
1. The mixture needs to have cooled before continuing.
2. Using a hand mixer, whip the butter prepared earlier.
3. Add the mixture spoon by spoon.
4. Whisk until the ingredients are combined.

Filling the horns
1. Put the custard in a pastry bag. *(Note 16)*
2. Fill the horns on both sides.

Cakes and Desserts

NOTES

1. You can swap the vanilla sugar with the same amount of regular sugar – around 5 tbsp.
2. For the custard you should use the remaining yolks.
3. When the butter is at room temperature, it's easier to fold into the custard.
4. When the butter is at room temperature, the dough will be easier to knead.
5. It's best to chop the dough using two knives. Use one knife to chop the butter with the flour and the second knife to collect the butter from the first one. After you chop the butter, it will form little lumps with the flour.
6. At first the dough will stick to your hands, keep kneading and it will eventually stop sticking.
7. 35cm is the right amount of dough to create a strip you can wrap around a horn mould that is 12cm high. If the strips are too short, they might not be enough to wrap around the mould. If that is the case, stick another strip at the end of the first one and keep wrapping. If the strip of dough is too long remove any excess dough ensuring there is 2-3mm of space at the bottom of the pastry horn mould.
8. When you leave enough free space, you can easily fill the horn with cream from that side.
9. You can lay the horns on the baking tray close to each other since they will only rise a little bit.
10. Adding milk will loosen the consistency, which will make it easier to pour the mixture into the boiling milk.
11. When the milk is close to boiling, it starts to foam and bubble so watch it to ensure it does not boil over.
12. Lumps are going to form at first, but as you keep stirring, you'll get a uniform mixture.
13. Check that the custard does not taste like flour. If it does, cook a little bit longer. If it no longer tastes of flour, turn off the hob. Be careful: the custard will be very hot!
14. Check it for sweetness. If it's not sweet enough, you can add more vanilla sugar.
15. You can cool the custard quicker by pouring cold water into the sink and resting the saucepan in the cold water. The custard should cool completely after around 15 minutes.
16. If you don't have a piping bag, you can use a resealable plastic food bag. Put one corner of the bag in a glass. Wrap the rest of the edges around the glass. Using a spoon, put the custard in the bag. Take the bag out of the glass and close it. Press all of the custard into one corner. Cut that corner (around 0.5cm) with scissors.

KITCHEN ACCESSORIES

- ☐ large pot
- ☐ 2 large bowls
- ☐ 3 small bowls
- ☐ measuring jug
- ☐ 2 knives
- ☐ pastry wheel (or pizza knife)
- ☐ chopping board
- ☐ soup plate
- ☐ 2 tablespoons
- ☐ teaspoon
- ☐ fork
- ☐ hand mixer
- ☐ wooden spoon
- ☐ brush
- ☐ scissors
- ☐ sieve
- ☐ rolling pin
- ☐ pastry board
- ☐ kitchen scale
- ☐ cooling rack
- ☐ baking tray (measured inside 30x26cm)
- ☐ 12 pastry horn moulds (12cm long)
- ☐ piping bag (or resealable plastic food bag)
- ☐ tea towel
- ☐ cling film / plastic wrap
- ☐ baking paper

GOOD TO KNOW

 vegetarian

 contains dairy
- contains butter
- contains milk
- contains sour cream

 fridge
- for up to 3 days

 kcal
- 258 per roll, 9030 total

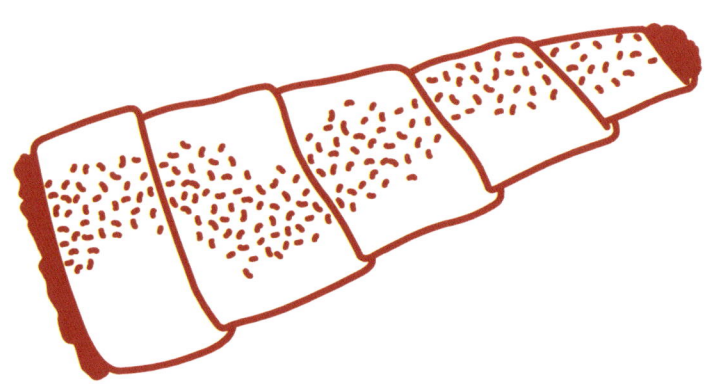

Cakes and Desserts

MARMALADE BISCUITS

Biscuits filled with delicious Polish marmalade, sprinkled with icing sugar. A perfect sweet snack you can take to school or work or to share with your friends. Ideal with tea or coffee.

Difficulty	Makes	Preparation	Baking	Resting	Total
SIMPLE	100	40 MIN	1 H 20 MIN	20 MIN	2 H 20 MIN

INGREDIENTS

For the dough
- ☐ 500g plain flour (+ more for dusting)
- ☐ 250g unsalted butter
- ☐ 250g sour cream
- ☐ 50g fresh yeast (or 14g instant yeast)

For the filling
- ☐ ~550g marmalade *(Notes 1 and 2)*

For the decoration
- ☐ ~4 tbsp icing sugar

 Polish products differ from the ones available locally. You will find more information about marmalade, sour cream and yeast in the chapter "About the products" on page 328.

DIRECTIONS

Preparing the butter
1. Take the butter out of the fridge.
2. Cube the butter.
3. Transfer to a small bowl.
4. Set the bowl aside. *(Note 3)*

Preparing the baking tray
1. Using scissors, cut the baking paper to fit the baking tray.
2. Line the baking tray with the baking paper.
3. Set aside.

Preparing the dough
1. Sift the flour into the bowl of a food mixer. *(Note 4)*
2. Add the sour cream.
3. Crumble the yeast onto the sour cream.
4. Using the tip of the knife, mix the yeast with the sour cream, but not with the flour. *(Note 5)*
5. Set aside for around 10 minutes.
6. Mix until the ingredients are combined.
7. Add the butter.
8. Knead the dough until smooth and elastic. This can take around 10 mins in the food mixer and a little bit longer if kneading the dough by hand. *(Note 6)*

Preparing the oven
1. Preheat the oven to 180°C / 350°F or gas 4.

Preparing the biscuits – part 1
1. Sprinkle a work surface with flour. Transfer the dough onto the work surface.
2. Roll out the dough into a thick sausage shape and cut into 4 equal parts.
3. Leave one part of the dough on the work surface. Transfer the rest to a bowl and cover with a tea towel.
4. Prepare the biscuits following the instructions in the panel.

Baking
1. Bake for around 20 minutes, until golden.

INSTRUCTIONS

To prepare the biscuits, follow the instructions:

 Roll out the dough to a thickness of about 2mm.

 Put ½ tsp of marmalade in the middle of every square. (Note 8)

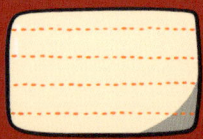 Using a pastry wheel, cut the dough into 5cm wide strips.

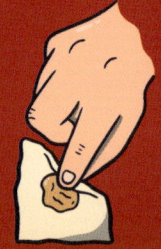 Connect the opposite corners of the square to form a triangle.

 Then cut crosswise at 5cm intervals.

 Gently press the corner of the triangle with your finger. (Note 9)

 After cutting, you should get 5 x 5cm squares. (Note 7)

 Lay the biscuits on the prepared baking tray, leaving around 1.5cm between them. (Note 10)

Preparing the biscuits – part 2

1. While the first batch is baking, roll the dough and prepare the next batch.
2. When the biscuits are baked, place on a cooling rack to cool completely.

To serve

- Sprinkle with icing sugar.

NOTES

1. It's best to use thick marmalade which won't spill during baking.
2. You can use plum jam (*powidła śliwkowe*) instead of marmalade, but it has to be very thick. You can buy plum jam (*powidła śliwkowe*) or make it yourself. You will find a recipe for *powidła śliwkowe* in the "Pantry" chapter.
3. When the butter is at room temperature, the dough will be easier to knead.
4. If you don't have a food mixer, you can knead the dough by hand in a large bowl. Sift the flour into the bowl and follow the remaining instructions.
5. You need to dissolve the yeast in the sour cream before you start kneading the dough.
6. If you are kneading the dough by hand, at first it will stick to your hands a lot. Keep stretching the dough while kneading. After kneading, the dough should be smooth and only slightly sticky. It might feel slightly oily. It shouldn't stick to your hands. If it continues to stick to your hands after 10 minutes of kneading, add 1 tbsp flour and knead for 5 minutes. If it's still too sticky, add another tbsp flour and knead for 5 more minutes. I wouldn't add more than 2 tbsp flour.
7. Add the edges that are left to the remaining dough. Remember to always cover the dough you are not using with a tea towel, so it doesn't dry out.
8. It's easiest to use 2 teaspoons. Spoon the marmalade on to the first teaspoon. Use the second teaspoon to slide the marmalade on the dough.
9. Pressing the dough will prevent the biscuit from opening while it bakes.
10. Place the biscuits with their shorter sides facing each other, maintaining spaces to visually create a square. This way you can bake more biscuits in one batch.

KITCHEN ACCESSORIES

- ☐ bowl
- ☐ knife
- ☐ pastry wheel (or pizza knife)
- ☐ chopping board
- ☐ 2 tablespoons
- ☐ 2 teaspoons
- ☐ food mixer
- ☐ scissors
- ☐ sieve
- ☐ rolling pin
- ☐ pastry board
- ☐ kitchen scale
- ☐ cooling rack
- ☐ baking tray (measured inside 3C
- ☐ tea towel
- ☐ baking paper

GOOD TO KNOW

 vegetarian

 contains dairy
- contains butter
- contains sour cream

 pantry
- store in an airtight container up to 5 days

 kcal
- 58 per biscuit, 5800 total

GOES WELL WITH

 *Powidła Śliwkowe* (Plum Jam)
11. Pantry, page 317

SWEET TWARÓG BISCUITS

*Delicious little moreish biscuits made with twaróg and sprinkled with sugar
These wonderful bites are crumbly and flavourful... It's very hard to only have one!*

Difficulty	Makes	Preparation	Baking	Resting	Total
SIMPLE	~80 *	1 H 20 MIN	1 H 20 MIN	20 MIN	3 H

INGREDIENTS

- ☐ 250g plain flour (+ more for dusting)
- ☐ 250g unsalted butter
- ☐ 250g low-fat *twaróg*
- ☐ 200g sugar
- ☐ 2 large eggs

 Polish products differ from the ones available locally. You will find more information about twaróg in the chapter "About the products" on page 328.

DIRECTIONS

Preparing the butter
1. Take the butter out of the fridge.
2. Cube the butter.
3. Transfer to a small bowl.
4. Set the bowl aside. *(Note 1)*

Preparing the baking tray
1. Using scissors, cut the baking paper to fit the baking tray.
2. Line the baking tray with the baking paper.
3. Set aside.

Preparing the eggs and *twaróg*
1. Separate the yolks from the whites. Put the yolks in a small bowl and the whites in a large bowl.
2. Pass the *twaróg* through a potato ricer into a separate bowl. *(Note 2)*

Preparing the dough
1. Sift the flour onto a pastry board.
2. Make a well in the flour.
3. Add the yolks, butter and *twaróg*.
4. Chop the dough with a knife until the ingredients are combined. This can take around 10 minutes. *(Note 3)*
5. When larger pieces of dough start to form, begin kneading by hand.
6. Sprinkle the dough with flour to prevent the dough sticking.

Cutting the biscuits
1. Roll out the dough into a thick sausage shape and cut into 3 equal parts.
2. Set two parts of the dough aside.
3. Sprinkle the pastry board and the dough with flour.
4. Roll out the dough to a thickness of about 3-4mm.
5. Use a cookie cutter to cut out circles in the dough.
6. Add the edges that are left to the remaining dough.

* depends on the size of the cookie cutters

Preparing the oven
1. Preheat the oven to 180°C / 350°F or gas 4.

Preparing the egg white foam
1. Add 1 tsp of sugar to the bowl with the egg whites.
2. Using a hand mixer, whisk until stiff.
3. Put the remaining sugar into a soup plate.

Preparing the biscuits – part 1
1. Take a circle in one hand.
2. Using a brush, brush the top of the circle with the egg whites foam.
3. Put the circle onto the plate with the sugar, whites side down, so that the sugar sticks to the biscuit.
4. Put the biscuits on the baking tray, sugar side up 1.5cm apart. *(Note 4)*
5. Repeat with all the biscuits.

Baking
1. Bake for around 20 minutes, until golden.

Cutting the biscuits – part 2
1. While the first batch is baking, roll the dough and prepare the next batch.
2. When the biscuits are baked, place on a cooling rack to cool completely.

NOTES
1. When the butter is at room temperature, the dough will be easier to knead.
2. You can use a meat mincer with large holes instead of a potato ricer.
3. It's best to chop the dough using two knives. Use one knife to chop the butter with the flour and the second knife to collect the butter from the first one. After you chop the butter, it will form little lumps with the flour.
4. You can lay the biscuits on the baking tray close to each other since they will only rise a little bit.

KITCHEN ACCESSORIES
- ☐ large bowl
- ☐ 2 bowls
- ☐ small bowl
- ☐ 2 knives
- ☐ chopping board
- ☐ soup plate
- ☐ 2 tablespoons
- ☐ teaspoon
- ☐ hand mixer
- ☐ potato ricer (or meat mincer)
- ☐ brush
- ☐ scissors
- ☐ sieve
- ☐ rolling pin
- ☐ pastry board
- ☐ kitchen scale
- ☐ cooling rack
- ☐ baking tray (measured inside 30x26cm)
- ☐ cookie cutters of various shapes
- ☐ baking paper

GOOD TO KNOW

 vegetarian

 contains dairy
- contains butter
- contains *twaróg*

 pantry
- store in a dry place up to 4 days

 kcal
- 49 per biscuits, 3920 total

KARPATKA

A snow-capped mountainous cake with a delicious sweet vanilla cream filling. Perfect for an afternoon celebration amongst friends.

Difficulty	Serves	Preparation	Baking	Resting	Total
INTERMEDIATE	15	2 H	~50 MIN	40 MIN	3 H 30 MIN

INGREDIENTS

For the dough
- 220g plain flour
- 100g unsalted butter
- 5 large eggs
- 2 tsp baking powder
- ½ tsp salt
- 300ml water

For the cream filling
- 200g unsalted butter
- 80g sugar
- 3 packets of vanilla *budyń* for 0.5 litre of milk (120g)
- 1 litre milk

To serve
- 2 tbsp icing sugar

 Polish products differ from the ones available locally. You will find more information about budyń in the chapter "About the products" on page 328.

DIRECTIONS

Preparing the cake layers
Preparing the cake batter – part 1
1. Put the hob on medium heat.
2. Pour the water into a medium saucepan and bring to a boil.
3. Add the butter and salt.
4. Occasionally stir with a wooden spoon to melt the butter and dissolve the salt.
5. Bring the water to a boil.
6. Turn the hob down to low heat.
7. Add the flour.
8. Keep stirring until a uniform consistency. This can take around 5 minutes. *(Note 1)*
9. Turn off the hob.
10. Set aside to cool; the mixture should remain slightly warm. This can take around 20 minutes. *(Note 2)*
11. Stir from time to time.

Preparing the baking tray
1. Using scissors, cut the baking paper to fit the baking tray.
2. Line the baking tray with the baking paper.
3. Set aside.

Preparing the oven
1. Preheat the oven to 200°C / 400°F or gas 6.

Cakes and Desserts

Preparing the cake batter – part 2
1. When the mixture has cooled a little, take the following steps.
2. Crack the eggs into a small bowl.
3. Add the eggs one by one to the batter and keep mixing, so that they combine with the rest of the batter.
4. After adding the last egg keep mixing until a uniform consistency.
5. Add the baking powder.
6. Whisk until the ingredients are combined.
7. Pour half of the cake batter on the baking tray. *(Note 3)*
8. Spread with a spatula. *(Note 4)*

Baking
1. Bake on the middle rack for around 20 minutes, until golden.
2. Tilt the oven door and leave the cake layer to rest for 5 minutes. *(Note 5)*
3. After that place the cake layer on a cooling rack to cool completely.
4. Leave the baking paper in the baking tray.

Preparing the oven
1. Once again preheat the oven to 200°C / 400°F or gas 6.

Preparing the mixture – part 3
1. Put the second half of the cake batter on a baking tray.
2. Spread with a spatula.
3. Bake according to the instructions above and set aside to cool completely.

Preparing the cream filling
Preparing the milk
1. Pour 750ml of milk into a measuring jug.
2. Pour the milk into a large pot.
3. Add the sugar to the pot.
4. Add 250ml more milk to the measuring jug.
5. Add the *budyń* powder to the measuring jug.
6. Whisk to get rid of all the lumps.
7. Set aside.

Preparing the budyń mixture
1. Put the hob on low heat.
2. Heat the milk to dissolve the sugar. *(Note 6)*
3. Add the milk with the *budyń* to the boiling milk.
4. Keep stirring with a wooden spoon until uniform.
5. When the mixture starts bubbling, cook for 2 more minutes, stirring constantly.
6. Turn off the hob.
7. Set aside to cool completely. This can take around 40 minutes. *(Note 7)*
8. Stir from time to time.

Combining the ingredients
1. Cube the butter and put in a large bowl.
2. Whisk the butter.
3. Add the mixture spoon by spoon.
4. Whisk until the ingredients are combined. *(Note 8)*
5. Set the prepared cream filling aside.

Preparing the karpatka
1. When the cake layers are cold, take the following steps.
2. Put one cake layer in a baking tray. *(Note 9)*
3. Spread the cream filling evenly using a spatula.
4. Cover with the second cake layer, risen (uneven) side up.
5. Put into the fridge for around 40 minutes.

To serve
- Sprinkle with icing sugar.

NOTES

1. Lumps are going to form at first, but as you keep stirring, you'll get a uniform mixture.
2. You can cool the mixture quicker by pouring cold water into the sink and resting the saucepan in the cold water. The mixture should cool completely in around 10 minutes.
3. Bake one cake layer (half of the portion) at a time. Baking both cakes at a time on two trays will prevent the bottom cake from rising.
4. You don't have to spread the cake batter evenly. There can be more in one spot and less in the next. This is how "mountains" and "valleys" will be created. What's important is that the cake butter covers the baking paper.
5. While waiting, excess moisture will evaporate, and the pastry will dry out.
6. When the milk is close to boiling, it starts to foam and bubble so watch it to ensure it does not boil over.
7. You can cool the *budyń* quicker by pouring cold water into the sink and resting the pot in the cold water. The *budyń* should cool completely in around 20 minutes.
8. Don't mix butter and *budyń* for too long so that the mixture doesn't split.
9. Choose the cake layer that's less "wavy" as the bottom of the *karpatka*.

KITCHEN ACCESSORIES

- ☐ large pot
- ☐ medium saucepan
- ☐ large bowl
- ☐ small bowl
- ☐ measuring jug
- ☐ knife
- ☐ chopping board
- ☐ 2 tablespoons
- ☐ teaspoon
- ☐ hand mixer
- ☐ wooden spoon
- ☐ spatula
- ☐ whisk
- ☐ scissors
- ☐ cooling rack
- ☐ baking tray (measured inside 30x26cm)
- ☐ baking paper

GOOD TO KNOW

 vegetarian

 contains dairy
- contains butter
- contains milk

 fridge
- for up to 3 days

 kcal
- 310 per serving, 4652 total

KAJMAK PISCHINGER

*A simple and delicious vanilla cream called kajmak layered between wafers.
A delicacy which is super easy to make
and even easier to accidentally eat all by yourself.*

Difficulty
SIMPLE

Serves
25

Preparation
30 MIN

Cooking
~25 MIN

Resting
30 MIN

Total
~1 H 25 MIN

INGREDIENTS

For the Pischinger
- 1 packet of wafers
  (5 pieces, 160g, 27 x 27cm)

For the *kajmak* (Note 1)
- 300g cane sugar
- 150g unsalted butter
- 1 vanilla pod *(Note 2)*
- 1 litre full-fat milk
- 200ml double cream

 Polish products differ from the ones available locally. You will find more information about sour cream and wafers in the chapter "About the products" on page 328.

DIRECTIONS

Preparing the *kajmak*
1. Put the hob on medium heat.
2. Add the butter and sugar to a large pot.
3. Melt and dissolve, stirring constantly with a wooden spoon. This can take around 5 minutes.
4. Add the milk and cream.
5. Mix well.
6. Cut the vanilla pod in half lengthwise.
7. Scrape out the seeds using the blade of the knife.
8. Add the seeds and pod to the pot.
9. Turn the hob to high and bring to a boil.
10. Reduce the heat and simmer for around 20 minutes.
11. Stir from time to time at first, and then constantly. *(Note 3)*
12. Take the pot off the heat and set the pot aside.
13. Keep stirring and check the consistency. *(Note 4)*
14. When the *kajmak* stops bobbling, return the pot to the heat.
15. Again, bring to a boil, stirring constantly.
16. Take the pot off the heat and keep stirring until the *kajmak* stops bubbling. Repeat for around 5 minutes. *(Note 5)*
17. When the right consistency is achieved, turn off and remove from the heat and set the pot aside.
18. After around 30 minutes the mixture should be lukewarm.
19. Stir from time to time.

Preparing the Pischinger
1. Divide the *kajmak* into 4 parts within the pot.
2. Place the first wafer on a chopping board.
3. Put the first portion of the *kajmak* on the wafer.
4. Spread evenly with a spatula ensuring the cavities in the wafer are coated.
5. Place another wafer on top.
6. Layer with another portion of the *kajmak*.
7. Repeat until all the wafers and *kajmak* have been used. There needs to be a wafer at the top and bottom with *kajmak* between each layer.
8. Wrap the layered wafers with aluminium foil and leave on the chopping board.
9. Place something heavy on the wafers, e.g. a few books.
10. Leave for around 30 minutes.

To serve
- Cut into small pieces.

NOTES

1. You can use a store-bought caramel sauce (*kajmak*) in a tin (460g) and 200g of unsalted butter. Cut the butter (at room temperature) into small cubes and add to a large bowl. Mix to combine with a hand mixer. Add the caramel sauce and mix thoroughly until you get a uniform consistency. Spread the mixture on the wafers.
2. You can swap the vanilla pod for 1 tbsp vanilla extract.
3. While stirring, use a spoon to remove any milk that has settled on the walls of the pot and at the bottom to prevent burning.
4. The *kajmak* will stop bobbling and you can check the consistency. It should be thinner than yoghurt.
5. Repeat the heating process until you obtain a consistency thinner than yoghurt. Heating it longer will cause the milk to evaporate even more and thicken the mixture, so that there might not be enough to spread on the wafers.

KITCHEN ACCESSORIES

- ☐ large pot
- ☐ knife
- ☐ chopping board
- ☐ tablespoon
- ☐ wooden spoon
- ☐ spatula
- ☐ kitchen scale
- ☐ aluminium foil
- ☐ a couple of books or something heavy (to press the wafers)

GOOD TO KNOW

 vegetarian

 contains dairy
- contains butter
- contains milk
- contains double cream

 pantry
- store in a dry place up to 2 days

kcal
- 136 per serving, 3400 total

8. FAT THURSDAY

There is one day a year when lovers of sweets and baked goods have a day to celebrate and eating a *pączki* (doughnut) is obligatory! Fat Thursday is the beginning of the last week of carnival or Shrovetide. It's the last Thursday before Lent, when – according to the Catholic tradition – one should fast and abstain from rich foods.

The tradition is not to count calories on this day, so you can really go for it! Poles eat 100 million *pączki* on Fat Thursday – 2.5 per person! To prepare this amount of *pączki*, you need to use 2.5 thousand tons of flour, around 500 tons of sugar, 1.3 million litres of milk and 25 million eggs! *

From my childhood I remember that my grandmother Emilia prepared the *pączki* already on Wednesday, so they were ready for Fat Thursday. I fondly remember chopping boards and tabletops covered with tea towels, with *pączki* placed at equal intervals, set aside to rise. I remember that my grandmother kept boards on the kitchen cabinets because it was warmest high up and she was very nervous when someone came into the kitchen and let the warm air escape. The kitchen had to be hot for the yeast dough to rise. Grandma prepared *pączki* with rose petal jam, and especially for me, with plum jam (*powidła śliwkowe*). When they were ready, she sprinkled them with icing sugar. Amazing!

Fat Thursday is one of the sweetest days of the year. *Pączki* are available everywhere in huge quantities and various flavour combinations, so that nobody misses out. Buying them in a store saves time but preparing them at home gives great satisfaction – this chapter will show you how to prepare your own homemade *pączki*, *oponki* (sweetened *twaróg* doughnuts) and *faworki*, which can be an alternative for people who aren't fans of fluffy pastries filled with jam.

Are these delicacies enough to encourage you to celebrate Fat Thursday this year? There's only one answer, so I wish you happy baking.

---

* https://media.bnpparibas.pl/pr/727351/bank-bnp-paribas-tegoroczny-tlusty-czwartek-ze-wzrostem-cen-paczkow-od-kilkunastu-do-kilkudziesieciu-procent

PĄCZKI

*Traditional deep fried doughnuts called pączki, made with yeast dough.
Filled with jam and sprinkled with icing sugar
or covered with icing and candied orange peel.*

Difficulty	Makes	Preparation	Proving	Kneading	Frying	Total
CHALLENGING	25	40 MIN	1 H 50 MIN	~1 H	~20 MIN	~4 H

INGREDIENTS

For the dough
- 600g plain flour (+ more for dusting)
- 50g unsalted butter
- 50g sugar
- 50g fresh yeast (or 14g instant yeast)
- 16g vanilla sugar
- 8 large eggs
- 2 tbsp vodka (optional) *(Note 1)*
- ½ tsp salt
- 300ml milk

For frying
- ~3 litres rapeseed oil *(Note 2)*

For the doughnut filling
- 900g jam *(Note 3)*

To serve
- icing sugar
- candied orange peel (optional) *(Note 4)*

For the icing (optional)
- 100g icing sugar
- 3 tbsp lemon juice (or water)

 Polish products differ from the ones available locally. You will find more information about candied orange peel, vanilla sugar and yeast in the chapter "About the products" on page 328.

DIRECTIONS

Preparing the yeast
1. Put the hob on low heat.
2. Pour the milk into a medium saucepan.
3. Warm the milk until slightly warm but not hot.
4. While waiting, crumble the yeast into a large bowl.
5. Add 3 tbsp of sugar. Set the rest of the sugar aside.
6. Add 3 tbsp of flour. Set the rest of the flour aside.
7. Mix everything together to combine the yeast with sugar and remove any lumps of flour.
8. Add around 100ml warm milk to the bowl. Set the rest of the milk aside.
9. Mix until the consistency is thinner than yoghurt. If needed, add some more milk.
10. Cover the bowl with a tea towel.
11. Set aside in a warm place for around 30 minutes, so that the yeast triples in volume. *(Note 5)*

Preparing the butter
1. Put the hob on low heat.
2. Add the butter to a small saucepan.
3. Melt on a low heat to prevent burning.
4. When the butter is liquid, set aside.

Preparing the rest of the ingredients
1. Sift the flour into the bowl of a food mixer. *(Note 6)*
2. Set aside.
3. Separate the yolks from the whites, into two separate bowls. Discard the egg whites.
4. Set the prepared yolks aside.

Preparing the dough
1. When the yeast triples in size, start preparing the dough.
2. Check the temperature of the milk. If cold, put on the hob again, until lukewarm (not hot).
3. Add the salt to the milk.
4. Stir, so the salt dissolves.
5. Add the remaining sugar, vanilla sugar, yeast and egg yolks to the bowl with the flour.
6. Mix to combine the ingredients. This can take around 5 minutes in the food mixer and a little bit longer if kneading the dough by hand.
7. Gradually add the milk while kneading the dough.
8. When all the ingredients are combined, add the alcohol.
9. Gradually add the butter while kneading the dough.
10. Take the dough from the food processor and start kneading by hand. This can take around 20 minutes. *(Note 7)*
11. When the dough is ready, cover the bowl with a tea towel.
12. Set the bowl aside in a warm place for around 1 hour for the dough to rise, doubling in volume. *(Note 8)*

Preparing the *pączki*
1. After the dough has risen, put two tea towels on the counter or on two chopping boards and sprinkle with flour. *(Note 9)*
2. Sprinkle a work surface with flour. Transfer the dough onto the work surface.
3. Roll the dough into a 5cm thick, 1 m long cylinder. *(Note 10)*
4. Cut into equal parts and form each into a ball. *(Note 11)*
5. Place on prepared tea towels. *(Notes 12 and 13)*
6. Cover the balls with two separate tea towels and set aside in a warm place for around 20 minutes.

Frying
1. Before frying, have all the *pączki* made ready and prepare a slotted spoon and four large plates lined with paper towels.
2. Put the hob on medium heat.
3. Pour the oil in a large pot.
4. Heat the oil to 180°C / 350°F. *(Note 14)*
5. Gently drop each doughnut into the pot so that the side of the dough that was touching the tea towel is now on top. The side that has risen should be submerged in oil. *(Note 15)*
6. Cover the pot. *(Note 16)*
7. Fry the *pączki* for 1.5 minutes on one side.
8. Uncover the pot.
9. Turn the *pączki* using two wooden skewers. *(Note 17)*
10. Fry the other side of the *pączki* for 30-45 seconds, uncovered. *(Notes 18 and 19)*
11. Use a slotted spoon to take the fried *pączki* out of the oil.
12. Transfer the *pączki* onto the plates lined with paper towel. *(Note 20)*
13. Keep checking the temperature of the oil when frying the subsequent batches. *(Note 21)*
14. Repeat for the rest of the *pączki*.

Filling the *pączki*
1. Wait until the *pączki* have cooled before filling.
2. Put the jam in a piping bag. *(Note 22)*
3. Insert into the edge of the doughnut (on the side of the light stripe). *(Note 23)*
4. Fill the *pączki* with jam. *(Note 24)*
5. Repeat for the rest of the *pączki*.

To serve
- Put a portion of *pączki* on a plate and sprinkle with icing sugar.
- The *pączki* can also be decorated with icing and candied orange peel. Prepare the icing using the recipe below and cut the orange peel with scissors and then place on the *pączki* covered with fresh icing. Wait for the icing to set and the peel to stick.

Preparing the icing (optional)
1. Put the icing sugar into a small bowl.
2. Add lemon juice spoon by spoon, stirring until a yoghurt-like consistency. *(Note 25)*
3. Using a brush, spread the icing on the *pączki*.
4. Cut the candied orange peel and sprinkle on top. (optional)
5. Set the *pączki* aside for the icing to set.

NOTES

1. The vodka helps the *pączki* remain soft on the inside and crisper on the outside after cooling. Vodka is more volatile than water and evaporates quicker resulting in a dryer crust. Using an acidic spirit, like gin may also make the *pączki* fluffier. To make these without alcohol you can substitute the vodka for lemon juice or 10% spirit vinegar.
2. The amount of oil needed to fry the *pączki* depends on the size of the pot you're using. After you put the *pączki* in the pot, there should be enough oil to easily turn them over while frying.
3. You can swap the jam for the same amount of *powidła śliwkowe*. You can buy jam or make it yourself. You will find a recipe for jams and *powidła śliwkowe* in the "Pantry" chapter.
4. If using candied orange peel you will also need to prepare icing. In the "Pantry" chapter you will find a recipe for the perfect candied orange peel.
5. If the yeast doesn't triple in volume, it's possible the milk was too hot. If this happens, you need to prepare the yeast once again. If you can set your oven to 30°C / 90°F, you can put the bowl with the yeast inside covered with a tea towel. These are perfect conditions for yeast to rise.
6. If you don't have a food mixer, you can knead the dough by hand in a separate large bowl. Sift the flour into the bowl and follow the remaining instructions.
7. When kneading the dough, pull it up and stretch it. This will help aerate it. At first the dough will stick to your hands a lot. Don't add any flour at this stage, just keep kneading the dough. If the dough sticks to your hands after you have kneaded it, you can add a little bit of flour.
8. You can put the bowl of dough in the oven preheated to 30°C / 90°F. Remember to cover the bowl with a tea towel.

9. You will put the prepared *pączki* on the tea towels.
10. If the dough is still sticking, add a little bit of flour to peel it away from your hands and the board.
11. The dough will keep rising while you work with it, so quickly cut it into equal parts the size of a tennis ball or an apple. You are going to see a difference in size between the first and the last ball.
12. Keep the balls around 10cm apart.
13. If there's not enough space on the tea towels, sprinkle the board with flour and place the balls of dough there.
14. The easiest way to check the oil temperature will be to use a thermometer. If you don't have a food thermometer, you can check the temperature by dropping a tiny piece of dough in the oil. If the dough immediately floats to the top and turns brown, it means that the oil is already heated to a temperature of about 170-180°C / 340-350°F and is ready for frying the *pączki*.
15. One batch should consist of 3-4 *pączki*. Don't add too many *pączki* at once. There needs to be enough space in the pot to fry and turn the *pączki*.
16. Putting the *pączki* in the oil will lower its temperature. When you cover the pot, the temperature will rise quicker and the dough will rise a little on the top of the *pączki*.
17. Wooden skewers don't transfer the heat. They are also long enough to help you safely turn the *pączki*.
18. When the second half of the *pączki* is frying and the first half is on top, you can check if the *pączki* is golden brown on top. If not, turn it once again and fry the first side for 10 more seconds.
19. A bright strip should form around the *pączki*. It's a sign of the dough being light and well kneaded.
20. The paper towel will absorb excess oil.
21. The oil temperature may have increased during frying – this will make the *pączki* darker. If the oil is too hot you need to turn the heat down and wait for the temperature to drop. If the temperature is too low though, the *pączki* will not fry fully. Turn up the heat. The temperature of the oil should be around 170-180°C / 340-350°F.
22. If you don't have a piping bag, you can use a resealable plastic food bag. Put one corner of the bag in a glass. Wrap the rest of the edges around the glass. Using a spoon, put the jam in the bag. Take the bag out of the glass and close it. Press all of the jam into one corner. Cut that corner (around 0.5cm) with scissors.
23. If you find it difficult to insert the tip of the piping bag into the *pączki*, you can use a thin knife. Gently push it halfway into the *pączki*. Then insert the tip of the piping bag.
24. When you fill the *pączki*, move the tip of the piping bag around to spread the jam inside.
25. Be careful when adding the juice because it will dilute the icing. Thickening it will require adding a lot of icing sugar.

KITCHEN ACCESSORIES

- ☐ large pot with lid
- ☐ medium saucepan
- ☐ small saucepan
- ☐ large bowl
- ☐ 2 bowls
- ☐ small bowl (optional)
- ☐ measuring jug
- ☐ knife
- ☐ 4 large plates
- ☐ 2 tablespoons
- ☐ 2 teaspoons
- ☐ food mixer
- ☐ thermometer
- ☐ slotted spoon
- ☐ brush
- ☐ scissors (optional)
- ☐ 2 wooden skewers
- ☐ sieve
- ☐ pastry board
- ☐ kitchen scale
- ☐ piping bag (or resealable plastic food bag)
- ☐ 4 tea towels
- ☐ paper towel

GOOD TO KNOW

 vegetarian

 contains dairy
- contains butter
- contains milk

 contains alcohol
- contains vodka

 alcohol-free option
- you can skip the vodka
- you can swap the vodka for the same amount of lemon juice or 10% spirit vinegar

 pantry
- store in a cool place up to 3 days

 kcal
- without filling and garnishes
  195 per *pączki*, 4875 total
- with the filling, without garnishes
  231 per *pączki*, 5775 total
- with the filling and icing sugar
  241 per *pączki*, 6025 total
- with the filling and icing
  245 per *pączki*, 6125 total
- with the filling, icing and candied orange peel
  272 per *pączki*, 6800 total

GOES WELL WITH

 **Raspberry Jam**
11. Pantry, page 313

 ***Powidła Śliwkowe* (Plum Jam)**
11. Pantry, page 317

 **Candied Orange Peel**
11. Pantry, page 321

OPONKI

Traditional Polish doughnuts made with twaróg, fried on Fat Thursday. Sprinkle them with icing sugar right before serving and enjoy their delicious flavour.

Difficulty	Makes	Preparation	Frying	Total
INTERMEDIATE	55	45 MIN	~15 MIN	~1 H

INGREDIENTS

For the *oponki*
- ☐ 500g plain flour (+ more for dusting)
- ☐ 500g low-fat *twaróg*
- ☐ 135g sugar
- ☐ 16g vanilla sugar
- ☐ 3 large eggs
- ☐ 1 tbsp vodka (optional) *(Note 1)*
- ☐ 1½ tsp bicarbonate of soda

For frying
- ☐ ~3 litres rapeseed oil *(Note 2)*

To serve
- ☐ icing sugar

 Polish products differ from the ones available locally. You will find more information about twaróg and vanilla sugar in the chapter "About the products" on page 328.

DIRECTIONS

Preparing the dough
1. Pass the *twaróg* through a potato ricer.
2. Transfer into the bowl of a food mixer. *(Note 3)*
3. Sift the flour into the bowl.
4. Crack the eggs into the bowl.
5. Add the sugar, vanilla sugar and bicarbonate of soda.
6. Mix to combine the ingredients and add the alcohol.
7. Knead the dough. The dough should be slightly sticky. This can take around 5 minutes in the food mixer and a little bit longer if kneading the dough by hand.

Preparing the *oponki*
1. Put a tea towel on the kitchen counter or a chopping board and sprinkle with flour. *(Note 4)*
2. Sprinkle a work surface with flour. Transfer the dough onto the work surface.
3. Roll out the dough into a thick sausage shape and cut in half.
4. Transfer one part back to the bowl and cover with a separate tea towel. *(Note 5)*
5. Roll out the dough about 0.5cm thick.
6. Using a 9cm glass or cookie cutter, cut out circles in the dough.
7. Add the edges that are left to the remaining dough. *(Note 5)*
8. Using a 5cm shot glass or cookie cutter, cut out holes in the prepared circles.

9. Gather the cut out inner circles and add to the remaining dough under the tea towel. *(Note 5)*
10. Repeat for the rest of the *oponki*.
11. Place each on the prepared tea towel.

Frying
1. Before frying, prepare all the *oponki* and prepare a large plate lined with paper towels. *(Note 6)*
2. Put the hob on medium heat.
3. Pour the oil into a large pot. *(Note 7)*
4. Heat the oil to 180°C / 350°F. *(Note 8)*
5. Gently put a batch of *oponki* into the oil. *(Note 9)*
6. Turn the hob down to low heat.
7. When the *oponki* starts rising to the top, turn over using two wooden skewers and fry until golden. Each side can take around 30 seconds. *(Note 10)*
8. Put the fried *oponki* onto the plate lined with paper towel. *(Note 11)*

To serve
- Put a portion of *oponki* on a plate and sprinkle with icing sugar.
- The *oponki* can also be served with raspberry sorbet which can be made from the leftovers from making raspberry juice.

NOTES

1. The vodka helps the *oponki* remain soft on the inside and crisper on the outside after cooling. Vodka is more volatile than water and evaporates quicker resulting in a dryer crust. Using an acidic spirit, like gin may also make the *oponki* fluffier. To make these without alcohol you can substitute the vodka for lemon juice or 10% spirit vinegar.
2. The amount of oil needed to fry the *oponki* depends on the size of the pot you're using. After you put the *oponki* in the pot, there should be enough oil to easily turn them over while frying.
3. If you don't have a food mixer, you can knead the dough by hand in a large bowl. Transfer the *twaróg* into the bowl and follow the remaining instructions.
4. Place your prepared *oponki* on a tea towel, where they can wait to be fried.
5. Remember to always keep the dough you are not using in a bowl covered with a tea towel, so it doesn't dry out.
6. *Oponki* fry really fast; it's best to prepare all of them before you start frying.
7. I recommend using a wide, low pot, so that you can fry a bigger batch of *oponki* at once.
8. The easiest way to check the oil temperature will be to use a thermometer. If you don't have a food thermometer, you can check the temperature by dropping a tiny piece of dough in the oil. If the dough immediately floats to the top and turns brown, it means that the oil is already heated to a temperature of about 170-180°C / 340-350°F and is ready for frying the *oponki*.
9. Don't add too many *oponki* at once. There needs to be enough space in the pot to fry and turn the *oponki*.
10. Wooden skewers don't transfer the heat. They are also long enough to help you safely turn the *oponki* and take them out of the oil.
11. The paper towel will absorb excess oil.

KITCHEN ACCESSORIES

- ☐ large pot *(Note 8)*
- ☐ bowl
- ☐ glass (9cm diameter) or cookie cutter
- ☐ shot glass (5cm diameter) or cookie cutter
- ☐ knife
- ☐ large plate
- ☐ tablespoon
- ☐ teaspoon
- ☐ meat mincer
- ☐ food mixer
- ☐ thermometer
- ☐ 2 wooden skewers
- ☐ sieve
- ☐ rolling pin
- ☐ pastry board
- ☐ kitchen scale
- ☐ 2 tea towels
- ☐ paper towel

GOOD TO KNOW

vegetarian

contains dairy
- contains *twaróg*

contains alcohol
- contains vodka

alcohol-free option
- you can skip the vodka
- you can swap the vodka for the same amount of lemon juice or 10% spirit vinegar

pantry
- store in a cool place up to 3 days

kcal
- without icing sugar
  94 per *oponki*, 5170 total
- with icing sugar
  98 per *oponki*, 5390 total

GOES WELL WITH

Raspberry Juice
11. Pantry, page 295

Fat Thursday

FAWORKI

*Made with a dough and fried until golden,
they are served sprinkled with icing sugar.
Savour them with a cup of good tea or hot chocolate.*

Also known as: *Chrust, Chruściki, Jaworki*

Difficulty	Makes	Preparation	Frying	Total
INTERMEDIATE	40	1 H	~15 MIN	~1 H 15 MIN

INGREDIENTS

For the *faworki*
- 250g plain flour
- 4 large eggs
- 3 tbsp sour cream
- ½ tsp salt

For frying
- ~2 litres rapeseed oil *(Note 1)*

To serve
- icing sugar

 Polish products differ from the ones available locally. You will find more information about sour cream in the chapter "About the products" on page 328.

DIRECTIONS

Preparing the dough

1. Sift the flour into the bowl of a food mixer. *(Note 2)*
2. Add the egg yolks, sour cream and salt. Discard the egg white.
3. Mix until the ingredients are combined. *(Note 3)*
4. The dough should be firm and elastic. This can take around 5 minutes in the food mixer and a little bit longer if kneading the dough by hand. *(Note 4)*
5. Put a thick towel on the work surface. *(Note 5)*
6. Put a pastry board on the thick towel.
7. Put the dough on the pastry board.
8. Beat the dough either by throwing the dough against the pastry board or beating with a rolling pin for around 5 minutes. *(Note 6)*
9. Put a tea towel on the kitchen counter or a chopping board. *(Note 7)*
10. Roll out the dough into a thick sausage shape and cut in half.
11. Transfer one part back to the bowl and cover with a separate tea towel. *(Note 8)*
12. Roll out the dough into a rectangle about 2mm thick. *(Note 9)*

Preparing the *faworki*

- There are two methods for folding the *faworki* - the techniques can be found on page 158.
- Place the ready-to-fry *faworki* on a prepared tea towel.

Fat Thursday

Frying

1. Before frying, prepare all the *faworki* and prepare a large plate lined with paper towels. *(Note 10)*
2. Put the hob on medium heat.
3. Pour the oil into a large pot. *(Note 11)*
4. Heat the oil to 180°C / 350°F. *(Note 12)*
5. Gently put a batch of *faworki* into the oil. *(Note 13)*
6. Turn the hob down to low heat.
7. When the *faworki* starts rising to the top, turn over using two wooden skewers and fry until golden. Each side can take around 30 seconds. *(Note 14)*
8. Put the fried *faworki* onto the plate lined with paper towel. *(Note 15)*

To serve

- Put a portion of *faworki* on a plate and sprinkle with icing sugar.
- The *faworki* can also be served with raspberry sorbet which can be made from the leftovers from making raspberry juice.

NOTES

1. The amount of oil needed to fry the *faworki* depends on the size of the pot you're using. After you put the *faworki* in the pot, there should be enough oil to easily turn them over while frying.
2. If you don't have a food mixer, you can knead the dough by hand in a large bowl. Sift the flour into the bowl and follow the remaining instructions.
3. If you're kneading the dough by hand, knead the dough until it doesn't stick to your hands anymore.
4. If the dough is still too dry after kneading, add 1 tsp of sour cream at a time and keep kneading.
5. The towel will muffle the sound when you beat the dough.
6. Beating the dough will help to make it very soft and elastic.
7. Place your prepared *faworki* on a tea towel, where they can wait to be fried.
8. Remember to always keep the dough you are not using in a bowl covered with a tea towel, so it doesn't dry out.
9. Try to roll the dough out to a rectangle or a square shape. This will make it easier to cut the dough later on and reduce the amount of dough that will need to be rolled out again.
10. *Faworki* fry really fast; it's best to prepare all of them before you start frying.
11. I recommend using a wide, low pot, so that you can fry a bigger batch of *faworki* at once.

12. The easiest way to check the oil temperature will be to use a thermometer. If you don't have a food thermometer, you can check the temperature by dropping a tiny piece of dough in the oil. If the dough immediately floats to the top and turns brown, it means that the oil is already heated to a temperature of about 170-180°C / 340-350°F and is ready for frying the *faworki*.
13. Don't add too many *faworki* at once. There needs to be enough space in the pot to fry and turn the *faworki*.
14. Wooden skewers don't transfer the heat. They are also long enough to help you safely turn the *faworki* and take them out of the oil.
15. The paper towel will absorb excess oil.

KITCHEN ACCESSORIES

- ☐ large pot *(Note 11)*
- ☐ bowl
- ☐ knife
- ☐ pastry wheel (or pizza knife)
- ☐ large plate
- ☐ tablespoon
- ☐ teaspoon
- ☐ food mixer
- ☐ thermometer

- ☐ 2 wooden skewers
- ☐ sieve
- ☐ rolling pin
- ☐ pastry board
- ☐ kitchen scale
- ☐ 2 tea towels
- ☐ paper towel
- ☐ bathroom towel

GOOD TO KNOW

 vegetarian

 contains dairy
- contains sour cream

 pantry
- store in a cool place up to 4 days

 kcal
- without icing sugar
  84 per *faworki*, 3360 total
- with icing sugar
  88 per *faworki*, 3520 total

GOES WELL WITH

 **Raspberry Juice**
11. Pantry, page 295

Fat Thursday

FAWORKI FOLDING TECHNIQUES

You can wrap the *faworki* into a diamond or rectangle shape. Learn both techniques so that your *faworki* always looks perfect.

METHOD 1 – DIAMOND

 Using a pastry wheel, cut the dough into 3cm wide strips. (Note 1)

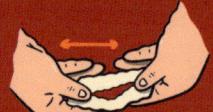 Spread the sides of the diamond to open the slit.

 Then cut crosswise at an angle, at 10-12cm intervals.

 Pass one end of the dough through the prepared slit.

 You should get diamond shapes. Add the edges that are left from cutting the diamonds to the remaining dough. (Note 2)

 Be careful not to tear the dough.

 Make a cut along the middle of each diamond without cutting the diamonds in half.

 Repeat for the rest of the faworki.

METHOD 2 – RECTANGLE

 Using a pastry wheel, cut the dough into 3cm wide strips. (Note 1)

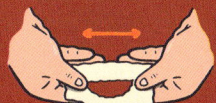 Spread the sides of the rectangle to open the slit.

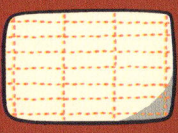 Then cut crosswise at 10-12cm intervals.

 Pass one end of the dough through the prepared slit.

 You should get rectangle shapes. Add the edges that are left from cutting the rectangles to the remaining dough. (Note 2)

 Be careful not to tear the dough.

 Make a cut along the middle of each rectangle without cutting the diamonds in half.

 Repeat for the rest of the faworki.

NOTES

1. You can use a pizza knife instead of the pastry wheel.
2. Remember to always keep the dough you are not using in a bowl covered with a tea towel, so it doesn't dry out.

Fat Thursday

9. EASTER

Easter is filled with symbolic food and delicious dishes. Easter traditions and meals can vary depending on the region of Poland, so I will talk about what I learned in my family home.

On Holy Saturday, my mum prepares an easter basket (*święconka*), which is brought to the church for the food to be blessed. The blessing represents life, resurrection, and salvation. The easter basket is made using willow to symbolise perseverance. My mum always includes: boiled eggs, which signify new life and the victory of life over death; bread and butter, to signify abundance; cold meats, to symbolise prosperity and affluence; salt, to signify durability and immortality; pepper and horseradish, to symbolise the passion of Jesus which according to tradition, are supposed to provide strength. The *święconka* is finished off with a small Easter *babka* signifying craftsmanship and perfection; a small lamb made of sugar, which symbolises the victory of life over death and the resurrection of Christ; and a chocolate rabbit which symbolises new life.

The *święconka* is then covered with white tea towel decorated by my mum at the edges with crochet patterns, and decorated with a few sprigs of boxwood which symbolise eternal life and rebirth. After the basket is blessed, it awaits Holy Sunday, when the foods can be eaten for a celebratory breakfast.

At breakfast the sugared lamb and rabbit stays in the centre of the Easter table. All the blessed foods are put on one platter – and at breakfast one should eat a bit of each of them. It's supposed to guarantee abundance and prosperity for another year. In my home the sausage, egg, and horseradish from the *święconka* basket are added to *żurek* which is served with a slice of buttered bread. While talking to my friend Madzia, I found out that *żurek* is not served for breakfast in her house. So as you can see, the tradition is different depending on the household and region of Poland. Nevertheless, her *żurek* is so delicious it will be the first recipe to open this chapter!

After breakfast it's time for something sweet – *babka* or *keks*, and when guests arrive in the afternoon, my mum serves her amazing vegetable salad (*sałatka jarzynowa*) and a delightful poppy seed roll (*makowiec*).

I believe that the recipes from this chapter will give you a taste of traditional Polish Easter cuisine – even if you do not celebrate this holiday!

EASTER ŻUREK

Traditional żurek with smoked boczek, kiełbasa and spices, finished with sour cream – an essential soup on the Polish Easter table.

One of the ingredients is bottled store-bought rye *zakwas*. If you want to make your own *zakwas*, you will find the recipe in the "Soups" chapter in volume 1.

Difficulty	Serves	Preparation	Frying	Cooking	Total
INTERMEDIATE	6	20 MIN	5 MIN	35 MIN	1 H

INGREDIENTS

For the żurek
- 220g *kiełbasa śląska* (Silesian *kiełbasa*)
- 220g *biała kiełbasa* (white *kiełbasa*)
- 150g smoked *boczek* (or smoked back bacon)
- 10 allspice berries
- 4 bay leaves
- 4 garlic cloves
- 1 chicken or vegetable bouillon cube
- ½ tsp sugar
- ½ tsp marjoram
- ½ tsp salt (+ more to taste)
- pepper to taste
- 2 litres water
- 1 bottle rye *zakwas* (500ml)

To thicken the soup
- 200ml sour cream

To serve (per portion)
- 1 large egg
- 700ml water
- a slice of rye bread

 Polish products differ from the ones available locally. You will find more information about allspice, kiełbasa, pork, sour cream, white sausage and zakwas in the chapter "About the products" on page 328.

DIRECTIONS

Preparing the żurek – part 1
1. Pour the water into a large pot.
2. Add the bouillon cube.
3. Peel the garlic.
4. Add to the pot.
5. Add the spices: allspice, bay leaves and ½ tsp salt.
6. Add the *kiełbasa śląska* cut into large pieces.
7. Put the hob on medium heat.
8. Bring the water to a boil.
9. Reduce the heat and simmer semi-covered for around 30 minutes.
10. While waiting, start preparing the *boczek* and *biała kiełbasa*.

Preparing the *boczek* and *biała kiełbasa*
1. Chop the *boczek* into 1cm cubes.
2. Finely slice the *biała kiełbasa*.
3. Put the hob on medium heat.
4. Put the *boczek* and *biała kiełbasa* in a frying pan.

5. Fry until golden and the fat has been released.
6. Occasionally stir with a wooden spoon.
7. Add the fried *boczek* and *biała kiełbasa* to the pot with the boiling soup along with the melted fat.
8. Mix well.

Preparing the *żurek* – part 2
1. After around 30 minutes add the *zakwas*. *(Note 1, important)*
2. Mix well.

Thickening the *żurek*
1. Thicken the *żurek* right after adding the *zakwas*.
2. Add the sour cream to a cup.
3. Add small amounts of *żurek* to the cup, spoon by spoon (just the liquid), mixing constantly. *(Note 2)*
4. Add the prepared mixture to the *żurek*.
5. Mix well.
6. Add salt and pepper to taste.
7. Cook for 3 minutes.

Preparing the *żurek* – part 3
1. Turn off the hob.
2. Add the sugar, marjoram, salt and pepper to taste.
3. Mix well.

Preparing the egg
1. Put the hob on medium heat.
2. Pour the water into a small saucepan and bring to a boil.
3. Using a spoon, carefully place an egg into boiling water.
4. Boil for 8 minutes.
5. Turn off the heat.
6. Pour the hot water out and cover the egg with cold water to cool.
7. Peel the egg and rinse to get rid of any little pieces of shell.
8. Put into a soup plate and cut in half.

To serve
1. Pour the hot *żurek* over the egg.
2. Serve with a slice of rye bread.

NOTES

1. Before opening the *zakwas* take care not to shake the bottle. *Zakwas* contains gas produced by fermentation. Open the bottle slowly and pour half the contents into the pot. Replace the lid and shake the bottle to dissolve the flour sediment. When dissolved, pour the remaining liquid into the pot.
2. Adding hot liquid to the sour cream will warm it and prevent curdling. You can stop adding the *żurek* to the sour cream when the sour cream has warmed.

KITCHEN ACCESSORIES

- ☐ large pot with lid
- ☐ small saucepan
- ☐ frying pan
- ☐ cup
- ☐ knife
- ☐ chopping board
- ☐ soup plate
- ☐ tablespoon
- ☐ teaspoon
- ☐ wooden spoon

GOOD TO KNOW

contains dairy
- contains sour cream

contains pork
- contains *Silesian kiełbasa*
- contains white *kiełbasa*
- contains *boczek*

contains beef
- contains *Silesian kiełbasa*
- contains white *kiełbasa*

fridge
- for up to 2 days
- reheat before serving – heat a portion of the soup in a separate pot

kcal
- without bread
  kcal: 515 per portion, 3090 total

GOES WELL WITH

Żurek
vol 1, 2. Soups, page 41

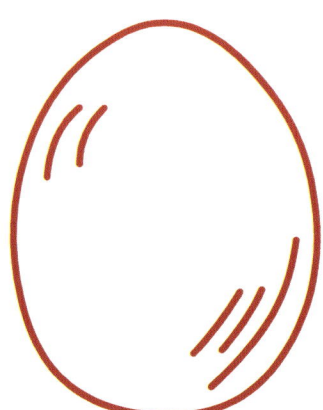

SAŁATKA JARZYNOWA (POLISH VEGETABLE SALAD)

*A traditional Polish vegetable salad served on Easter and many other occasions.
The variety of ingredients guarantees a very rich flavour.*

Difficulty	Serves	Preparation	Cooking	Resting	Total
SIMPLE	8	20 MIN	~40 MIN	1 H	~2 H

INGREDIENTS

For the vegetables
- ☐ 2 carrots (~350g)
- ☐ 2 parsnips (~350g)
- ☐ 1 celeriac (~350g)
- ☐ 1 tsp salt
- ☐ ~2 litres water *(Note 1)*

For the salad
- ☐ 6 sour gherkins (~320g) *(Note 2)*
- ☐ 1 tinned sweetcorn (340g)
- ☐ 1 tinned peas (200g)
- ☐ 10cm piece of leek (green part, ~50g) *(Note 3)*
- ☐ 3 tbsp mayonnaise
- ☐ 1½ tbsp yellow mustard

- ☐ salt to taste
- ☐ pepper to taste

For the eggs
- ☐ 6 large eggs
- ☐ ~1 litre water *(Note 4)*

To serve
- ☐ a slice of your favourite bread

 Polish products differ from the ones available locally. You will find more information about sour gherkins in the chapter "About the products" on page 328.

DIRECTIONS

Preparing the vegetables – part 1
1. Peel the carrot, parsnip and celeriac.
2. Cut each in half. *(Note 5)*
3. Put into a large pot.
4. Cover the vegetables with water by 2cm (there should be around 2 litres of water).
5. Add 1 tsp salt.
6. Put the hob on medium heat.
7. Bring the water to a boil.
8. Reduce the heat and simmer semi-covered for around 30 minutes.
9. While waiting, start preparing the other ingredients.

Preparing the eggs – part 1
1. Put the hob on medium heat.
2. Pour the water into a medium saucepan and bring to a boil.

Preparing the rest of the ingredients
1. Finely cube the sour gherkins.
2. Set a sieve over a bowl and add the gherkins. *(Note 6)*
3. Set the bowl aside.
4. Take the outer leaves off the leek and cut off any withered parts.
5. Cut 10cm off the top of the leek and rinse to remove the grit.
6. Cut the leek in half lengthwise and finely slice.
7. Put into a large bowl and set aside.

Preparing the eggs – part 2
1. The water should already be boiling.
2. Using a spoon, carefully lower the eggs into the water.
3. Boil for 8 minutes.
4. Turn off the heat.
5. Pour the hot water out and cover the eggs with cold water to cool.
6. Set the saucepan aside.

Preparing the vegetables – part 2
1. After around 30 minutes, check if the vegetables are still slightly firm. *(Note 7)*
2. When the vegetables are done, drain the water then add cold water to the saucepan to cool the vegetables.
3. Using a fork, transfer the vegetables to a large plate and leave to cool. This can take around 15 minutes.
4. Set the plate aside.

Preparing the salad
1. Squeeze the water from the sour gherkins.
2. Add to the bowl with the leek.
3. Cube the carrots, parsnips and celeriac.
4. Add to the bowl.
5. Open the tin of sweetcorn, strain and add to the bowl.
6. Open the tin of peas, strain and add to the bowl.
7. Peel the eggs.
8. Rinse the eggs to get rid of any shell.
9. Grate using a grater with large holes into the bowl.
10. Add the mayonnaise and mustard.
11. Add salt and pepper to taste.
12. Mix well.
13. Put into the fridge for around 30 minutes.

To serve
- Serve with a slice of your bread of choice.
- Alternatively, cut a few slices of tea-boiled ham and pickled peppers and place on the bread along with the salad.

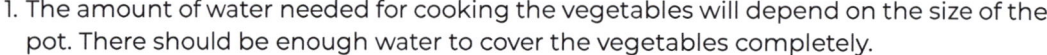

NOTES

1. The amount of water needed for cooking the vegetables will depend on the size of the pot. There should be enough water to cover the vegetables completely.
2. You can buy sour gherkins or make them yourself. You will find a recipe for ogórki kiszone (sour gherkins) in the "Pantry" chapter.
3. You can swap the leek for 1 small onion.
4. The amount of water needed for cooking the eggs will depend on the size of the saucepan. There should be enough water to cover the eggs completely.
5. You can cut the big pieces of vegetables in half and the celeriac into quarters.
6. Leave the gherkins in the sieve to drain the water.
7. Put a knife into the vegetables. If there's a slight resistance, the vegetables are ready. If not, cook for 5-10 more minutes, checking from time to time. Don't boil them too long, since it might be hard to cut them and they might fall apart in the salad.

KITCHEN ACCESSORIES

- ☐ large pot with lid
- ☐ medium saucepan with lid
- ☐ large bowl
- ☐ bowl
- ☐ knife
- ☐ peeling knife
- ☐ chopping board
- ☐ 2 tablespoons
- ☐ teaspoon
- ☐ fork
- ☐ grater
- ☐ tin opener
- ☐ sieve

GOOD TO KNOW

 vegetarian

 gluten-free option
- use gluten-free bread to serve

 fridge
- for up to 3 days

 kcal
- without bread
  210 per serving, 1680 total

GOES WELL WITH

 **Tea-Boiled Ham**
11. Pantry, page 251

 **Pickled Peppers**
11. Pantry, page 275

 ***Ogórki Kiszone* (Sour Gherkins)**
11. Pantry, page 259

STUFFED EGGS WITH SUNDRIED TOMATOES, GARLIC AND FETA CHEESE

A delicious Mediterranean-style egg starter, perfect for celebrating Easter filled with sundried tomatoes, Greek feta cheese and garlic.

Difficulty	Makes	Preparation	Cooking	Total
SIMPLE	12	~20 MIN	8 MIN	~30 MIN

INGREDIENTS

For the eggs
- ☐ 6 large eggs
- ☐ ~1 litre water *(Note 1)*

For the filling
- ☐ 50g feta cheese
- ☐ 6 sundried tomato pieces
- ☐ 3 garlic cloves
- ☐ 1 tbsp mayonnaise
- ☐ ½ bunch of chives (~10g)
- ☐ salt to taste
- ☐ pepper to taste

DIRECTIONS

Preparing the eggs – part 1
1. Put the hob on medium heat.
2. Pour the water into a medium saucepan and bring to a boil.

Preparing the garlic and tomatoes – part 1
1. Put the hob on low heat.
2. Add the garlic and sundried tomatoes to a frying pan. *(Note 2)*
3. Heat until the garlic is soft. *(Note 3)*

Pictured:
1. Stuffed Eggs with Tuna
2. Stuffed Eggs with Ham and Cheese
3. Stuffed Eggs with Mushrooms
4. Stuffed Eggs with Sundried Tomatoes, Garlic and Feta Cheese

Preparing the eggs – part 2
1. The water should already be boiling.
2. Using a spoon, carefully lower the eggs into the water.
3. Boil for 8 minutes.
4. Turn off the heat.
5. Pour the hot water out and cover the eggs with cold water to cool.
6. Set the saucepan aside.

Preparing the garlic and tomatoes – part 2
1. Put the garlic and sundried tomatoes on a chopping board to cool.

Preparing the filling
1. Peel the eggs.
2. Rinse the eggs to get rid of any shell.
3. Cut each in half.
4. Carefully remove the yolks and transfer to a bowl.
5. Transfer the egg whites to a large plate.
6. Add the feta and mayonnaise to the bowl with the yolks.
7. Use a fork to crush the yolks and feta and combine with the mayonnaise.
8. Finely chop the sundried tomatoes.
9. Peel the garlic.
10. Crush with a fork.
11. Add the tomatoes and garlic to the bowl with the filling.
12. Rinse the chives.
13. Chop finely and add to the bowl with the filling.
14. Add salt and pepper to taste.
15. Mix well.

Preparing the stuffed eggs
1. Put the filling into a piping bag. *(Note 4)*
2. Fill the egg halves.

NOTES

1. The amount of water needed for cooking the eggs will depend on the size of the saucepan. There should be enough water to cover the eggs completely.
2. Don't peel the garlic, but add whole. Tomatoes should be drained, added without any oil.
3. Check if the garlic is soft with a fork.
4. If you don't have a piping bag, you can use a resealable plastic food bag. Put one corner of the bag in a glass. Wrap the rest of the edges around the glass. Using a spoon, put the filling in the bag. Take the bag out of the glass and close it. Press all of the filling into one corner. Cut that corner (around 0.5cm) with scissors.

KITCHEN ACCESSORIES

- ☐ medium saucepan
- ☐ frying pan
- ☐ bowl
- ☐ knife
- ☐ chopping board
- ☐ large plate
- ☐ tablespoon
- ☐ fork
- ☐ piping bag (or resealable plastic food bag)

GOOD TO KNOW

 vegetarian

 gluten-free

 contains dairy
- contains feta cheese

 kcal
- 63 per half an egg, 756 total

STUFFED EGGS WITH MUSHROOMS

*Stuffed eggs filled with delicious forest mushrooms.
With the subtle heat of mustard
and the delicate earthy flavour of finely chopped parsley.*

Difficulty	Makes	Preparation	Cooking	Total
SIMPLE	12	~30 MIN	8 MIN	~40 MIN

INGREDIENTS

For the eggs
- ☐ 6 large eggs
- ☐ ~1 litre water *(Note 1)*

For the filling
- ☐ 250g mushrooms
- ☐ 1 onion (~35g)
- ☐ 1 mushroom bouillon cube
- ☐ ½ bunch of parsley (~15g)
- ☐ 1 tbsp cooking oil
- ☐ 1 tbsp mayonnaise
- ☐ 2 tsp yellow mustard
- ☐ 50ml water
- ☐ salt to taste (optional) *(Note 2)*
- ☐ pepper to taste

 Polish products differ from the ones available locally. You will find more information about mushroom stock in the chapter "About the products" on page 328.

DIRECTIONS

Preparing the eggs – part 1
1. Put the hob on medium heat.
2. Pour the water into a medium saucepan and bring to a boil.

Preparing the onion
1. Peel the onion and chop finely.
2. Put the hob on medium heat.
3. Heat the oil in a large saucepan.
4. Add the chopped onion.
5. Occasionally stir with a wooden spoon.
6. Fry until translucent.

Preparing the eggs – part 2
1. The water should already be boiling.
2. Using a spoon, carefully lower the eggs into the water.
3. Boil for 8 minutes.
4. Turn off the heat.
5. Pour the hot water out and cover the eggs with cold water to cool.
6. Set the saucepan aside.

Preparing the mushrooms
1. Rinse the mushrooms and peel if necessary.
2. Chop finely.

photo on page 170

3. When the onions become translucent, add mushrooms to the saucepan.
4. Add the water to the saucepan. *(Note 3)*
5. Add the mushroom bouillon cube.
6. Reduce the heat and simmer for around 10 minutes. *(Note 4)*
7. Stir from time to time.
8. Turn off and remove from the heat and set the saucepan aside.

Preparing the filling
1. Peel the eggs.
2. Rinse the eggs to get rid of any shell.
3. Cut each in half.
4. Carefully remove the yolks and transfer to a bowl.
5. Transfer the egg whites to a large plate.
6. Rinse the parsley.
7. Chop finely and add to the bowl with the yolks.
8. Add the mayonnaise and mustard.
9. Crush the yolks with a fork and mix everything together.
10. Add the onions and mushrooms.
11. Add salt and pepper to taste. *(Note 5)*
12. Mix well.

Preparing the stuffed eggs
1. Put the filling into a piping bag. *(Note 6)*
2. Fill the egg halves.

NOTES

1. The amount of water needed for cooking the eggs will depend on the size of the saucepan. There should be enough water to cover the eggs completely.
2. You'll need the salt if the filling is not salty enough.
3. Adding water prevents the onion from burning before the mushrooms start releasing liquid.
4. Simmer the mushrooms so that they are soft and all the water evaporates.
5. Taste the filling before adding the salt. The bouillon cube is salty, and you might not need any more salt.
6. If you don't have a piping bag, you can use a resealable plastic food bag. Put one corner of the bag in a glass. Wrap the rest of the edges around the glass. Using a spoon, put the filling in the bag. Take the bag out of the glass and close it. Press all of the filling into one corner. Cut that corner (around 0.5cm) with scissors.

KITCHEN ACCESSORIES

- ☐ large saucepan
- ☐ medium saucepan
- ☐ bowl
- ☐ knife
- ☐ chopping board
- ☐ large plate
- ☐ tablespoon
- ☐ teaspoon
- ☐ fork
- ☐ wooden spoon
- ☐ piping bag (or resealable plastic food bag)

GOOD TO KNOW

 vegetarian

 gluten-free

 contains mushrooms
- contains fresh mushrooms
- contains mushroom bouillon cube

 kcal
- 67 per half an egg, 804 total

STUFFED EGGS WITH TUNA

*Delicious stuffed eggs filled with tuna Polish gherkins,
freshly chopped parsley and chives, mayonnaise and mustard.
A delightful option, not just for Easter.
You can also make it for other occasions and gatherings!*

Difficulty	Makes	Preparation	Cooking	Total
SIMPLE	12	~20 MIN	8 MIN	~30 MIN

INGREDIENTS

For the eggs
- ☐ 6 large eggs
- ☐ ~1 litre water *(Note 1)*

For the filling
- ☐ 1 tin of tuna in spring water (~150g)
- ☐ 1 sour gherkin (or pickled) *(Note 2)*
- ☐ ½ bunch of parsley (~15g)
- ☐ ½ bunch of chives (~10g)
- ☐ 1½ tbsp mayonnaise
- ☐ 1 tsp yellow mustard
- ☐ salt to taste
- ☐ pepper to taste

 Polish products differ from the ones available locally. You will find more information about sour gherkins in the chapter "About the products" on page 328.

DIRECTIONS

Preparing the eggs – part 1
1. Put the hob on medium heat.
2. Pour the water into a medium saucepan and bring to a boil.

Preparing the sour gherkin
1. Set a sieve over a bowl.
2. Grate the gherkin using a grater with large holes into a sieve. *(Note 3)*
3. Set the bowl aside.

Preparing the eggs – part 2
1. The water should already be boiling.
2. Using a spoon, carefully lower the eggs into the water.
3. Boil for 8 minutes.
4. Turn off the heat.
5. Pour the hot water out and cover the eggs with cold water to cool.
6. Set the saucepan aside.

Preparing the filling
1. Peel the eggs.
2. Rinse the eggs to get rid of any shell.
3. Cut each in half.
4. Carefully remove the yolks and transfer to a separate bowl.
5. Transfer the egg whites to a large plate.
6. Open the tinned tuna and drain the liquid.
7. Transfer to a bowl with the yolks.
8. Add the mayonnaise and mustard.
9. Use a fork to crush and combine the ingredients.

photo on page 170

10. Squeeze the water from the gherkins.
11. Add to the bowl with the filling.
12. Rinse the parsley and chop finely.
13. Rinse the chives and chop finely.
14. Add the chives and parsley to the bowl with the filling.
15. Add salt and pepper to taste.
16. Mix well.

Preparing the stuffed eggs
1. Put the filling into a piping bag. *(Note 4)*
2. Fill the egg halves.

NOTES

1. The amount of water needed for cooking the eggs will depend on the size of the saucepan. There should be enough water to cover the eggs completely.
2. You can buy sour or pickled gherkins, or make them yourself. You will find a recipe for <u>ogórki kiszone (sour gherkins)</u> and for <u>ogórki konserwowe (pickled gherkins)</u> in the "Pantry" chapter.
3. Leave the gherkins in the sieve to drain the water.
4. If you don't have a piping bag, you can use a resealable plastic food bag. Put one corner of the bag in a glass. Wrap the rest of the edges around the glass. Using a spoon, put the filling in the bag. Take the bag out of the glass and close it. Press all of the filling into one corner. Cut that corner (around 0.5cm) with scissors.

KITCHEN ACCESSORIES

- ☐ medium saucepan
- ☐ 2 bowls
- ☐ knife
- ☐ chopping board
- ☐ large plate
- ☐ tablespoon
- ☐ teaspoon
- ☐ fork
- ☐ grater
- ☐ sieve
- ☐ piping bag (or resealable plastic food bag)

GOOD TO KNOW

 gluten-free

 contains fish
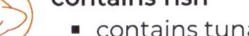
- contains tuna

 kcal
- 74 per half an egg, 888 total

GOES WELL WITH

 *Ogórki Kiszone* **(Sour Gherkins)**
11. Pantry, page 259

 *Ogórki Konserwowe* **(Pickled Gherkins)**
11. Pantry, page 263

Easter

STUFFED EGGS WITH HAM AND CHEESE

Stuffed eggs filled with finely chopped ham and cheddar cheese with the addition of peppery radish – a perfect snack for every party!

Difficulty	Makes	Preparation	Cooking	Total
SIMPLE	12	~20 MIN	8 MIN	~30 MIN

INGREDIENTS

For the eggs
- ☐ 6 large eggs
- ☐ ~1 litre water *(Note 1)*

For the filling
- ☐ 100g ham *(Note 2)*
- ☐ 100g cheddar cheese
- ☐ 2 radishes
- ☐ ½ bunch of parsley (~15g)
- ☐ ½ bunch of chives (~10g)
- ☐ 1 tbsp mayonnaise
- ☐ 1 tsp yellow mustard
- ☐ salt to taste
- ☐ pepper to taste

DIRECTIONS

Preparing the eggs – part 1
1. Put the hob on medium heat.
2. Pour the water into a medium saucepan and bring to a boil.

Preparing the rest of the ingredients
1. Finely chop the ham.
2. Add to a bowl.
3. Grate the cheese using a grater with small holes into the bowl.
4. Cut the roots and leaves from the radishes.
5. Rinse, chop finely and add to the bowl.
6. Set the bowl aside.

Preparing the eggs – part 2
1. The water should already be boiling.
2. Using a spoon, carefully lower the eggs into the water.
3. Boil for 8 minutes.
4. Turn off the heat.
5. Pour the hot water out and cover the eggs with cold water to cool.
6. Set the saucepan aside.

Preparing the filling
1. Peel the eggs.
2. Rinse the eggs to get rid of any shell.
3. Cut each in half.
4. Carefully remove the yolks and transfer to the bowl with the ham, cheese and radish.
5. Transfer the egg whites to a large plate.
6. Add the mayonnaise and mustard to the bowl.

photo on page 170

7. Crush the yolks with a fork and mix everything together.
8. Rinse the parsley and chop finely.
9. Rinse the chives and chop finely.
10. Add the chives and parsley to the bowl with the filling.
11. Add salt and pepper to taste.
12. Mix well.

Preparing the stuffed eggs
1. Put the filling into a piping bag. *(Note 3)*
2. Fill the egg halves.

NOTES

1. The amount of water needed for cooking the eggs will depend on the size of the saucepan. There should be enough water to cover the eggs completely.
2. You can buy ham or make it yourself. You will find a recipe for tea-boiled ham in the "Pantry" chapter.
3. If you don't have a piping bag, you can use a resealable plastic food bag. Put one corner of the bag in a glass. Wrap the rest of the edges around the glass. Using a spoon, put the filling in the bag. Take the bag out of the glass and close it. Press all of the filling into one corner. Cut that corner (around 0.5cm) with scissors.

KITCHEN ACCESSORIES

- ☐ medium saucepan
- ☐ bowl
- ☐ knife
- ☐ chopping board
- ☐ large plate
- ☐ tablespoon
- ☐ teaspoon
- ☐ fork
- ☐ grater
- ☐ piping bag (or resealable plastic food bag)

GOOD TO KNOW

vegetarian option
- swap the ham for a vegetarian alternative

gluten-free

contains dairy
- contains cheddar cheese

contains pork
- contains ham

pork-free option
- you can swap the ham for turkey ham

kcal
- 106 per half an egg, 1272 total

GOES WELL WITH

Tea-Boiled Ham
11. Pantry, page 251

Easter

EASTER BABKA

*Easter babka is the queen of all Easter cakes!
A delicate sponge filled with raisins and sprinkled with icing sugar,
the centrepiece of the Easter table!*

Difficulty	Serves	Preparation	Baking	Resting	Total
INTERMEDIATE	12	30 MIN	30 MIN	1 H	2 H

INGREDIENTS

For the cake batter
- ☐ 80g plain flour
- ☐ 80g potato starch
- ☐ 80g sugar
- ☐ 16g vanilla sugar
- ☐ 5 large eggs
- ☐ 2 tbsp cocoa powder
- ☐ ½ tsp baking powder

For the filling
- ☐ 100g raisins *(Note 1)*
- ☐ 1 tsp plain flour
- ☐ 500ml water

For the decoration
- ☐ 2 tbsp icing sugar

For the bundt tin
- ☐ 3-5 tbsp breadcrumbs
- ☐ 1 tbsp butter

 Polish products differ from the ones available locally. You will find more information about potato starch and vanilla sugar in the chapter "About the products" on page 328.

DIRECTIONS

Preparing the raisins
1. Put the hob on medium heat.
2. Pour the water into a medium saucepan or kettle and bring to a boil.
3. Put the raisins in a bowl.
4. Cover with boiling water (around 250ml). *(Note 2)*
5. Set aside for around 5 minutes. *(Note 3)*
6. Drain the water from the raisins.
7. Once again cover with boiling water (around 250ml).
8. Set aside for around 5 minutes.
9. Pour the water out.
10. Lay the raisins on a paper towel. *(Note 4)*
11. Transfer to a separate small bowl.
12. Add 1 tsp plain flour to the bowl.
13. Stir, so that all the raisins are covered with flour.
14. Set the bowl aside.

Preparing the bundt tin
1. Sift the breadcrumbs onto a large plate. *(Note 5)*
2. Butter the inner side of the bundt tin.
3. Pour all the breadcrumbs into the tin.
4. Gently shake the bundt tin, so that the breadcrumbs stick to the bundt tin evenly.
5. Set the bundt tin aside.

Preparing the flour and sugar
1. Sift the flour and starch into a separate bowl.
2. Add the baking powder.
3. Set the bowl aside.
4. Measure the sugar into another separate small bowl.

Preparing the egg whites
1. Separate the yolks from the whites. Put the yolks in a large bowl and the whites in the bowl of a food mixer. *(Note 6)*
2. Add 1 tbsp of prepared sugar to the egg whites. *(Note 7)*
3. Whisk the egg whites to stiff peaks. This can take around 10 minutes.
4. Set the egg whites aside.
5. While waiting, prepare the yolks.

Preparing the yolks
1. To the bowl with the yolks add vanilla sugar and the remaining sugar.
2. Using a hand mixer combine all of the ingredients. This can take around 5 minutes.
3. Set the prepared yolks aside.

Preparing the oven
1. Preheat the oven to 180°C / 350°F or gas 4.

Preparing the cake batter
1. Add the egg whites to the bowl with the yolks spoon by spoon.
2. Fold in the egg white with a spatula.
3. Add the flour gradually.
4. Mix to combine the ingredients with the hand mixer turned off. *(Note 8)*
5. Whisk thoroughly to combine all the ingredients.

Preparing the *babka*
1. Pour half of the cake batter into the prepared bundt tin.
2. Spread evenly using a spatula.
3. Add the cocoa and raisins to the batter in the bowl.
4. Use the spatula to carefully mix until a uniform consistency is formed and the raisins are completely covered.
5. Pour the cocoa batter with the raisins into the middle of the batter, in a circular motion following the shape of the bundt tin.

Baking
1. Bake for around 30 minutes. *(Note 9)*
2. Don't open the oven while baking to prevent the *babka* from sinking.
3. Take the baked *babka* out of the oven and turn out of the tin onto a cooling rack to cool completely.

To serve
- Sprinkle with icing sugar.

NOTES

1. You can swap the raisins with the same amount of dried cranberries.
2. Some dried fruit has sulphur dioxide (E220) added to it to conserve and protect the product from moisture and mould, this step helps to remove the sulphur dioxide.
3. Raisins will soften and slightly swell in hot water.
4. The paper towel will absorb excess water. Squeeze the raisins so they release as much liquid as possible.
5. It's best to use the fine breadcrumbs to prepare the bundt tin. Then, after you bake the *babka* and have taken it out of the tin, big chunks of breadcrumbs won't have stuck to the *babka*.
6. If you don't have a food mixer, you can prepare the batter in a large bowl using a hand mixer.

7. The remaining sugar will be added to the bowl with the yolks.
8. This will prevent the mixer from blowing the flour everywhere.
9. After around 30 minutes, check if the sponge is cooked inside. Be careful: the *babka* will be very hot! Insert a toothpick right to the bottom of the *babka*. If some batter is stuck to the toothpick, bake the *babka* for 5 more minutes. After this time check the *babka* again and bake for 5 additional minutes if it's not ready.

KITCHEN ACCESSORIES

- ☐ medium saucepan
- ☐ 2 large bowls
- ☐ bowl
- ☐ small bowl
- ☐ large plate
- ☐ 2 tablespoons
- ☐ 2 teaspoons
- ☐ hand mixer

- ☐ spatula
- ☐ toothpick
- ☐ sieve
- ☐ small sieve
- ☐ kitchen scale
- ☐ cooling rack
- ☐ bundt tin (diameter 20cm)
- ☐ paper towel

GOOD TO KNOW

 vegetarian

 pantry
- store in a dry place up to 4 days

 kcal
- 165 per serving, 1980 total

EASTER KEKS

Keks full of nuts and dried fruit is served on Easter. It's really delicious when covered with lemon icing and candied orange peel or sprinkled with icing sugar.

Difficulty
INTERMEDIATE

Serves
12

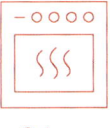
Preparation
50 MIN

Baking
50 MIN

Resting
1 H

Total
2 H 40 MIN

INGREDIENTS

For the cake batter
- 180g plain flour
- 150g sugar
- 70g potato starch
- 16g vanilla sugar
- 4 large eggs
- 1½ tsp baking powder
- ½ tsp salt
- 150ml cooking oil

For the decoration
- 2 tbsp icing sugar
- 50g candied orange peel (optional) *(Note 1)*

For the filling
- 50g walnuts
- 50g dried cranberries
- 50g dried apricots
- 50g raisins
- 1 tsp plain flour
- 500ml water

For the loaf tin
- 1 tbsp butter

For the icing (optional)
- 100g icing sugar
- 3 tbsp lemon juice (or water)

 Polish products differ from the ones available locally. You will find more information about candied orange peel, potato starch and vanilla sugar in the chapter "About the products" on page 328.

DIRECTIONS

Preparing the dried fruits and nuts
1. Put the hob on medium heat.
2. Pour the water into a medium saucepan or kettle and bring to a boil.
3. Put the cranberries, apricots and raisins in a bowl.
4. Cover with boiling water (around 250ml). *(Note 2)*
5. Set aside for around 5 minutes. *(Note 3)*
6. Finely chop the walnuts.
7. Put into a separate bowl.
8. Drain the water from the fruit.
9. Once again cover with boiling water (around 250ml).
10. Set aside for around 5 minutes.
11. Pour the water out.
12. Lay the fruit on a paper towel. *(Note 4)*
13. Put the cranberries and raisins into the bowl with the nuts.
14. Finely chop the apricots and add to the bowl with the fruit and nuts.
15. Add 1 tsp plain flour to the bowl.
16. Stir, so that all the fruit and nuts are covered with flour.
17. Set the bowl aside.

Preparing the loaf tin
1. Using scissors, cut the baking paper as a single sheet, to cover the bottom and inner sides of the loaf tin.
2. Brush the loaf tin with butter so the paper sticks.
3. Line the loaf tin with the baking paper.
4. Grease the baking paper with more butter.
5. Set the loaf tin aside.

Preparing the oven
1. Preheat the oven to 170°C / 325°F or gas 3.

Preparing the cake batter
1. Crack the eggs into a large bowl, and add the salt, sugar and vanilla sugar.
2. Whisk until the ingredients are combined.
3. Add the oil.
4. Whisk again.
5. Sift the plain flower and potato starch into the bowl.
6. Add the baking powder.
7. Mix to combine the ingredients with the hand mixer turned off. *(Note 5)*
8. Whisk thoroughly to combine all the ingredients.

Preparing the *keks*
1. Pour half of the cake batter into your prepared loaf tin.
2. Spread evenly using a spatula.
3. Add the prepared fruit and nuts to the batter in the bowl.
4. Mix thoroughly with a spatula so that the fruit and nuts are covered with batter.
5. Pour the remaining batter into the loaf tin.

Baking
1. Bake for around 50 minutes. *(Note 6)*
2. Don't open the oven while baking to prevent the *keks* from sinking.
3. Take the baked *keks* out of the oven and turn out of the tin onto a cooling rack to cool completely.
4. Remove the baking paper from the *keks*.

To serve
- Sprinkle with icing sugar.
- The *keks* can also be decorated with icing and <u>candied orange peel</u>. Prepare the icing using the recipe below and cut the orange peel with scissors and then place on the *keks* covered with fresh icing. Wait for the icing to set and the peel to stick.

Preparing the icing (optional)
1. Put the icing sugar into a small bowl.
2. Add lemon juice spoon by spoon, stirring until a yoghurt-like consistency. *(Note 7)*
3. Using a brush, spread the icing on the *keks*.
4. Cut the candied orange peel and sprinkle on top. (optional)
5. Set the *keks* aside for the icing to set.

NOTES

1. If using candied orange peel you will also need to prepare icing. In the "Pantry" chapter you will find a recipe for the perfect <u>candied orange peel</u>.
2. Some dried fruit has sulphur dioxide (E220) added to it to conserve and protect the product from moisture and mould, this step helps to remove the sulphur dioxide.
3. Dried fruits will soften and slightly swell in hot water.
4. The paper towel will absorb excess water. Squeeze the fruit so they release as much liquid as possible.

5. This will prevent the mixer from blowing the dry ingredients everywhere.
6. After around 50 minutes, check if the sponge is cooked inside. Be careful: the sponge will be very hot! Insert a toothpick right to the bottom of the sponge. If some batter is stuck to the toothpick, bake the sponge for 5 more minutes. After this time check the sponge again and bake for 5 additional minutes if it's not ready.
7. Be careful when adding the juice because it will dilute the icing. Thickening it will require adding a lot of icing sugar.

KITCHEN ACCESSORIES

- ☐ medium saucepan
- ☐ large bowl
- ☐ 2 bowls
- ☐ small bowl (optional)
- ☐ measuring jug
- ☐ knife
- ☐ chopping board
- ☐ 2 tablespoons
- ☐ 2 teaspoons
- ☐ hand mixer

- ☐ spatula
- ☐ brush
- ☐ scissors
- ☐ toothpick
- ☐ sieve
- ☐ kitchen scale
- ☐ cooling rack
- ☐ loaf tin (measured inside 23x13x7cm)
- ☐ baking paper
- ☐ paper towel

GOOD TO KNOW

 vegetarian

 contains dairy
- contains butter

 contains nuts
- contains walnuts

 pantry
- store in a dry place up to 4 days

kcal
- no additions
  305 per serving, 3660 total
- with icing sugar
  310 per serving, 3720 total
- with icing
  338 per serving, 4056 total
- with icing and candied orange peel
  351 per serving, 4212 total

GOES WELL WITH

 **Candied Orange Peel**
11. Pantry, page 321

Easter

MAKOWIEC (POPPY SEED ROLL)

A traditional yeast roulade filled with poppy seed mixture and sprinkled with icing sugar or covered with icing and decorated with candied orange peel.

				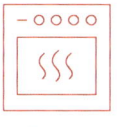		
Difficulty **INTERMEDIATE**	Makes **2**	Preparation **~1 H 15 MIN**	Proving **45 MIN**	Baking **30 MIN**	Resting **1 H**	Total **~3 H 30 MIN**

INGREDIENTS

For the dough
- ☐ 500g plain flour (+ more for dusting)
- ☐ 70g unsalted butter
- ☐ 50g sugar
- ☐ 30g fresh yeast (or 7g instant yeast)
- ☐ 3 large eggs
- ☐ ¼ tsp salt
- ☐ 250ml milk

For the filling
- ☐ 850g poppy seed mixture *(Note 1)*

For the decoration
- ☐ 2 tbsp icing sugar
- ☐ 50g candied orange peel (optional) *(Note 2)*

For preparing the baking paper
- ☐ 4 tbsp cooking oil

For the icing (optional)
- ☐ 100g icing sugar
- ☐ 3 tbsp lemon juice (or water)

 Polish products differ from the ones available locally. You will find more information about candied orange peel, masa makowa and yeast in the chapter "About the products" on page 328.

DIRECTIONS

Preparing the yeast
1. Put the hob on low heat.
2. Pour the milk into a medium saucepan.
3. Warm the milk until slightly warm but not hot.
4. Turn off and remove from the heat and set the saucepan aside.
5. Crumble the yeast into the saucepan.
6. Mix until dissolved and set aside.

Preparing the dough
1. Put the hob on low heat.
2. Add the butter to a small saucepan.
3. Melt on a low heat to prevent burning.
4. When the butter is liquid, set aside.
5. With 2 eggs, separate the yolks from the whites into two separate small bowls. Discard the egg whites.
6. Sift the flour into the bowl of a food mixer. *(Note 3)*
7. Add the sugar and salt.

8. Mix and make a well in the flour.
9. Add the yolks into the well.
10. Add 1 egg.
11. Add the prepared yeast.
12. Knead the dough for around 5 minutes, until all the ingredients are combined.
13. Add the melted butter.
14. Knead the dough until smooth and elastic. This can take around 10 mins in the food mixer and a little bit longer if kneading the dough by hand. *(Note 4)*
15. When the dough is ready, cover the bowl with a tea towel.
16. Set the bowl aside in a warm place for around 30 minutes for the dough to rise, doubling in volume. *(Note 5)*

Preparing the baking tray

1. Using scissors, cut the baking paper to fit the baking tray.
2. Line the baking tray with the baking paper.
3. Set aside.

Preparing the *makowiec*

1. After the dough has risen, sprinkle the surface with flour. Transfer the dough onto the work surface.
2. Knead the dough by hand for around 5 minutes.
3. Roll out the dough into a thick sausage shape and cut in half.
4. Put one half back into the bowl.
5. Cover the bowl with a tea towel and set aside to a warm place.
6. Roll the dough into a 4mm thick rectangle - the dimensions depend on the size of the baking tray. *(Note 6)*
7. Put half of the poppy seed mixture in the middle of the rolled-out dough.
8. Spread evenly with a spatula, leaving about 2cm of free space around the edges. *(Note 7)*
9. Start rolling the dough from the shortest side into a roulade, forming the *makowiec* by pinching in the rolled outer edges.
10. To transfer the *makowiec*, use the scissors to cut a sheet of baking paper, enough to wrap around the *makowiec* twice.
11. Using a brush, brush the baking paper with oil.
12. Transfer the *makowiec* to the baking paper and form a cylinder around the *makowiec* so that there's 1cm of free space between the *makowiec* and the baking paper on the top. *(Note 8)*
13. Put the covered *makowiec* on the prepared baking tray with the seam of the baking paper underneath the *makowiec*.
14. Prepare a second *makowiec* with the remaining dough.
15. Set the baking tray aside for around 15 minutes, so the *makowiec* can rise.

Preparing the oven

1. Preheat the oven to 180°C / 350°F or gas 4.

Baking

1. Bake for around 30 minutes, until golden.
2. When the *makowiec* are baked, place on a cooling rack to cool completely.

To serve

- Sprinkle with icing sugar.
- The *makowiec* can also be decorated with icing and candied orange peel. Prepare the icing using the recipe below and cut the orange peel with scissors and then place on the *makowiec* covered with fresh icing. Wait for the icing to set and the peel to stick.

Preparing the icing (optional)

1. Put the icing sugar into a small bowl.
2. Add lemon juice spoon by spoon, stirring until a yoghurt-like consistency. *(Note 9)*
3. Using a brush, spread the icing on the *makowiec*.
4. Cut the candied orange peel and sprinkle on top. (optional)
5. Set the *makowiec* aside for the icing to set.

NOTES

1. You can swap the ready-made poppy seed mixture for one you make yourself. You will find the ingredients and the step-by-step description in the recipe for makowiec with walnut cream and chocolate glaze in the "Christmas" chapter. If you decide to prepare it yourself, prepare the poppy seed mixture beforehand.
2. If using candied orange peel you will also need to prepare icing. In the "Pantry" chapter you will find a recipe for the perfect candied orange peel.
3. If you don't have a food mixer, you can knead the dough by hand in a large bowl. Sift the flour into the bowl instead of the food mixer.
4. If you are kneading the dough by hand in a bowl, at first it will stick to your hands a lot. Keep stretching the dough while kneading. After kneading, the dough should be smooth and only slightly sticky. It might feel slightly oily. It shouldn't stick to your hands. If it continues to stick to your hands after 10 minutes of kneading, add 1 tbsp flour and knead for 5 minutes. If it's still too sticky, add another tbsp flour and knead for 5 more minutes. I wouldn't add more than 2 tbsp flour.
5. If you can set your oven to 30°C / 90°F, you can put the bowl with the dough inside, covered with a tea towel.
6. The size of your baking tray will decide the dimensions of the rolled-out dough. Make sure one side of the rectangle is shorter than the shortest side of your baking tray by around 3 or 4cm. After the dough has been rolled out, filled and rolled up it will need to fit in the tray. My tray is 26 x 30cm, therefore I will roll out each piece of dough to be 23cm wide and about 30cm long (using up half of the dough). After rolling I get a roulade that's around 8 x 25cm.
7. The sides that are not covered with poppy seed mixture will be used for closing the *makowiec* later.
8. Wrapping *makowiec* prevents it from rising too much and cracking while it's baking.
9. Be careful when adding the juice because it will dilute the icing. Thickening it will require adding a lot of icing sugar.

KITCHEN ACCESSORIES

- ☐ medium saucepan
- ☐ small saucepan
- ☐ 2 small bowls
- ☐ measuring jug
- ☐ knife
- ☐ tablespoon
- ☐ teaspoon
- ☐ food mixer
- ☐ brush
- ☐ scissors
- ☐ sieve
- ☐ rolling pin
- ☐ pastry board
- ☐ kitchen scale
- ☐ cooling rack
- ☐ baking tray (measured inside 30x26cm)
- ☐ tea towel
- ☐ baking paper

GOOD TO KNOW

vegetarian

contains dairy
- contains butter
- contains milk

contains nuts
- check if the poppy seed mixture contains nuts

pantry
- store in a dry place up to 4 days

kcal
- without garnishes
  2360 per *makowiec*, 4720 total
- with icing sugar
  2391 per *makowiec*, 4782 total
- with icing
  2558 per *makowiec*, 5116 total
- with icing and candied orange peel
  2636 per *makowiec*, 5272 total

GOES WELL WITH

Makowiec with Walnut Cream and Chocolate Glaze
10. Christmas, page 229

Candied Orange Peel
11. Pantry, page 321

10. CHRISTMAS

Christmas is a very important Catholic holiday in Poland. Christmas traditions are very symbolic and common to most regions in Poland – in my family home they were maintained primarily by my grandmother and now by my mum.

Traditionally *Wigilia* – Christmas Eve feast – begins when the first star appears in the sky. It symbolises the star of Bethlehem which the Three Kings followed to pay tribute to the newly born Jesus. In practice, the Christmas Eve feast usually takes place in the early evening. According to Catholic tradition, before eating an excerpt of the gospel according to Saint Luke about the birth of Jesus is read. Later, household members and guests wish each other well while breaking Christmas wafers known as *opłatek*, which symbolises forgiveness and reconciliation.

You can then sit at the Christmas Eve table, covered with a white tablecloth. It symbolises purity and innocence. Under the tablecloth there is hay, referring to the stable where Jesus was born and symbolising poverty. At the Christmas Eve table there is one additional table setting, which is intended for an unexpected guest – this custom is a remnant of Slavic beliefs, according to which an untouched portion of food was left for the spirits of the dead. Nowadays the meaning of this empty chair is that on this day nobody should be alone.

According to tradition, there should be 12 dishes on the Christmas Eve table. Some dishes are characteristic of particular regions of Poland, but in most homes, we can find red borscht with *uszka* dumplings, fish – usually carp, which can be prepared in various ways, and sauerkraut with mushrooms. Among these 12 dishes there are also cakes – usually *makowiec* and gingerbread. The dishes are symbolic as well – the fish symbolises rebirth and baptism, while poppy seeds and gingerbread are connected to old folk customs according to which they should bring wealth and prosperity.

After supper everybody sings carols and opens gifts which are traditionally put under a decorated Christmas tree. *Wigilia* ends with Midnight Mass - a solemn mass celebrated around midnight. It is a greeting of the newborn Jesus by the faithful and begins the celebration of Christmas in the Catholic church.

I hope that these Christmas Eve traditions are especially interesting to readers from outside of Poland. With great pleasure I pass them along to you together with my mum's recipes for amazing dishes which each year are placed on our family Christmas Eve table.

CHRISTMAS EVE RED BORSCHT WITH USZKA

Soured red borscht served with uszka is a traditional Christmas Eve dish. To make this dish, you will need to prepare beetroot zakwas, red borscht and uszka dumplings filled with mushroom. This dish can be time-consuming, if you want to make it from scratch, including preparing your own zakwas, you will need to start a few weeks before Christmas Eve. Below I show you in which order to prepare all the elements of this dish.

Beetroot *zakwas*
You need 7-10 days to make your *zakwas*, so you need to start your preparations no later than two weeks before Christmas Eve. If you don't want to hurry, you can start making it in mid-November – it will be ready when December begins (you can keep it in the fridge for up to 4 weeks). If you don't want to make the *zakwas* yourself, you can use a store-bought version in a bottle. Beetroot *zakwas* is a key ingredient for making soured red borscht.

Soured red borscht
You don't need much time to make the borscht, if you have *zakwas* already prepared or purchased. You can make it the day before Christmas Eve, so that all flavours are combined, but it will also be fine to make on Christmas Eve morning. If you don't want to leave all the preparations to the last minute, you can make the borscht much earlier and freeze it. Pour the cooked, cold borscht into containers and add a slice of raw beetroot to each portion (this will prevent the soup from losing its colour when heated). Put it in the freezer. The day before Christmas Eve transfer the desired amount of borscht to the fridge so that the soup can defrost before being reheated. Heat before serving. You can keep the borscht in the freezer for up to 3 months.

Uszka
Preparing the filling and making the *uszka* dumplings is very time consuming, and unfortunately it cannot be done in stages (as in the case of *zakwas* and borscht). Set aside a whole day to prepare the *uszka* – you can store them frozen for up to 3 months. On Christmas Eve, you can heat a portion of frozen dumplings in salted boiling water and cook them 1 minute longer than you would fresh dumplings, the recipe for which can be found later in the chapter.

BEETROOT ZAKWAS

A homemade beetroot zakwas seasoned with bay leaves, allspice and black peppercorns which guarantee a rich, full flavour.

Difficulty
SIMPLE

Makes
400 ML

Preparation
20 MIN

Resting
7-10 DAYS

Total
7-10 DAYS

INGREDIENTS

For the *zakwas*
- ☐ 4 beetroots (~500g)
- ☐ 2 garlic cloves
- ☐ 5 allspice berries
- ☐ 5 peppercorns
- ☐ 2 bay leaves
- ☐ 1 slice rye bread (~20g)

For the brine
- ☐ 1 tsp salt
- ☐ ~500ml water

For sterilising the jar and bottle
- ☐ ~2 litres water *(Note 1)*

 Polish products differ from the ones available locally. You will find more information about allspice in the chapter "About the products" on page 328.

DIRECTIONS

Day 1: evening
Preparing the jar – part 1
1. Put the hob on medium heat.
2. Pour some water into a medium saucepan or kettle and start boiling.

Preparing the brine
1. Measure 300ml of water.
2. Add the salt.
3. Stir, so the salt dissolves.
4. Set aside.

Preparing the beetroot *(Note 2)*
1. Cut the leaves off the beetroot and trim both ends.
2. Rinse and peel the beetroot.
3. Slice the beetroot into 0.5cm slices.
4. Leave on the chopping board.

Preparing the rest of the ingredients
1. Peel the garlic.
2. Prepare a slice of bread.

Preparing the jar – part 2
1. Wash the jar and keep in an emptied sink.
2. When the water starts boiling, carefully pour the boiling water into and over the cleaned jar.
3. Pour the water out of the jar and leave to cool.

Preparing the *zakwas*
1. Put the beetroot slices in the jar alternating with garlic and bay leaves.
2. Add the spices: allspice and peppercorns.
3. Put the slice of bread on the top.

4. Cover with the brine prepared earlier.
5. Add more water to cover all the ingredients.
6. Put a clean stone in the jar. *(Note 3)*
7. Cover the jar with the edge of a tea towel and secure with a rubber band.
8. Wrap the jar in the rest of the tea towel.
9. Set aside in a warm, dark place.

Days 2-10 *(Note 4)*
1. Remove the tea towel from the jar.
2. On the second day a foam should form on the top that will disappear in the next two to three days.
3. Stir the *zakwas* with a clean, scalded spoon. Take out the stone.
4. Clean the stone and put back into the jar.
5. Cover the jar with the edge of the tea towel and secure with the rubber band again.
6. Wrap the jar in the rest of the tea towel.
7. Set aside in a warm, dark place.
8. Repeat every day.
9. On the fifth day check if the *zakwas* is both salty and sour, if the *zakwas* tastes and smells of the garlic then the *zakwas* is ready.

Last day
Preparing the bottle
1. Put the hob on medium heat.
2. Pour some water into a medium saucepan or a kettle and start boiling.
3. Wash the bottle and keep in an emptied sink.
4. When the water starts boiling, carefully pour the boiling water into and over the bottle.
5. Pour the water out of the bottle and leave to cool.

Pouring off the *zakwas*
1. Put a sieve over a large saucepan.
2. Remove the tea towel from the jar.
3. Take out the stone.
4. Sieve the *zakwas* into the saucepan.
5. The remaining beetroot and spices can be discarded.
6. Using a funnel, pour the *zakwas* in the bottle and close tightly.
7. Put the bottle in the fridge.

To serve
- Use the beetroot *zakwas* to make soured red borscht.
- Alternatively, *zakwas* can be served as a drink.

NOTES

1. You will need enough water to sterilise the inside and outside of the jar and bottle.
2. You can put on an apron and rubber gloves to prevent being stained by the beetroot – the stains are difficult to remove!
3. The stone will press the bread and beetroot to the bottom, so they are covered all the time. Instead of the stone you can use a small tin, for example with peas. If you're using a tin, take off the label, so it doesn't dissolve in the *zakwas*. Wash it thoroughly before you put it in the jar.
4. The time required to make the *zakwas* depends on how fast it begins to ferment. The fermentation process will be influenced by weather conditions, especially the temperature at which you store the jar.

KITCHEN ACCESSORIES

- ☐ large saucepan
- ☐ medium saucepan
- ☐ measuring jug
- ☐ knife
- ☐ peeling knife
- ☐ chopping board
- ☐ tablespoon
- ☐ teaspoon
- ☐ funnel
- ☐ rubber band
- ☐ apron (optional)
- ☐ rubber gloves (optional)
- ☐ sieve
- ☐ tea towel
- ☐ bottle with cap (1 litre)
- ☐ jar (900ml)
- ☐ stone (or small tin)

GOOD TO KNOW

 vegetarian

 vegan

 fridge
- for up to 4 weeks

 kcal
- 330 total

GOES WELL WITH

 **Soured Red Borscht**
10. Christmas, page 203

SOURED RED BORSCHT

Traditional Polish beetroot borscht made with beetroot zakwas, served on Christmas Eve with uszka filled with wild mushrooms. A warming soup which tastes like Christmas.

This recipe will teach you how to make the version of soured red borscht step by step. Red borscht can also be served for dinner with *krokiety*. You will find the recipe for borscht without *zakwas* in the "Sides" chapter in volume 1.

Difficulty	Serves	Preparation	Cooking	Total
SIMPLE	8	30 MIN	~1 H	~1 H 30 MIN

INGREDIENTS

- ☐ 8 beetroots (~1kg)
- ☐ 2 carrots (~270g)
- ☐ 1 parsnip (~170g)
- ☐ 1 piece of celeriac (~160g)
- ☐ 1 onion (~70g)
- ☐ 10cm piece of leek (green part, ~50g)
- ☐ 10g dried mushrooms
- ☐ 2 garlic cloves
- ☐ 3 allspice berries
- ☐ 2 bay leaves
- ☐ 2 litres water
- ☐ 400-500ml beetroot *zakwas* (Note 1)
- ☐ sugar to taste (Note 2)
- ☐ salt to taste
- ☐ pepper to taste

 Polish products differ from the ones available locally. You will find more information about allspice and beetroot zakwas in the chapter "About the products" on page 328.

DIRECTIONS

Preparing the beetroot (Note 3)
1. Cut the leaves off the beetroot and trim both ends.
2. Rinse and peel the beetroot.
3. Slice the beetroot into 0.5cm slices.
4. Put the slices from 7 beetroots into a large pot.
5. Put the remaining beetroot slices into a bowl and set aside.

Preparing the vegetables
1. Peel the carrot and cut lengthwise.
2. Peel the parsnip and cut into large pieces; leave the end whole.
3. Peel the celeriac and cut into large pieces.
4. Take the outer leaves off the leek and cut off any withered parts.
5. Cut 10cm off the top of the leek and rinse to remove the grit.
6. Slice the leek into 3 smaller pieces.
7. Peel the garlic.
8. Add the prepared vegetables to the pot with the beetroot.

Preparing the onion
1. Peel the onion and cut in half.
2. Put on the gas, cut side down and burn on the flame. This can take around 4-5 minutes. *(Note 4)*
3. Put the burnt onion into the pot with the vegetables.

Preparing the stock
1. Pour the water into the pot.
2. Add the bay leaves and allspice.
3. Add the dried mushrooms.
4. Put the hob on medium heat.
5. Bring the water to a boil.
6. Reduce the heat and simmer semi-covered for around 1 hour.
7. Check the water level when simmering and refill if too much water has evaporated. There should be enough water to cover all the ingredients.

Preparing the borscht
1. After around 1 hour of simmering the vegetables, turn off and remove from the heat and set the pot aside.
2. Using a slotted spoon, transfer all the vegetables into a bowl. *(Note 5)*
3. Sift the stock through a sieve into a separate large pot.
4. Add the beetroot *zakwas* to the stock.
5. Add the remaining sliced beetroot. *(Note 6)*
6. Add the sugar. *(Note 7)*
7. Add salt and pepper to taste.
8. Mix well.

To serve
- For the Christmas variety serve the borscht with <u>uszka</u>. Some families also add the mushroom liquid from preparing the <u>uszka</u> filling to the borscht.
- If serving without *uszka,* put a portion of the vegetables from the borscht in a soup plate and pour the borscht over.
- Borscht can also be served as a drink, either on its own or with <u>krokiety</u>. *(Note 8)*

NOTES

1. You can buy *zakwas* or make it yourself. You will find the recipe for <u>beetroot *zakwas*</u> in the "Christmas" chapter.
2. The beetroot will make the borscht quite sweet, so add the sugar at the very end, after you taste the borscht.
3. You can put on an apron and rubber gloves to prevent being stained by the beetroot – the stains are difficult to remove!
4. You can also cut the onion into very thick slices and burn them in a frying pan (without any oil) which you put on low heat. This can take around 10 minutes.
5. You won't need the onions, leek and garlic, as well as the bay leaves and allspice berries. You can either save the remaining vegetables for serving later or discard. If you're preparing the borscht for Christmas Eve, you can serve the cooked mushroom with the borscht or add them to the <u>uszka</u> filling.
6. It's important to keep fresh raw beetroot pieces in the borscht to prevent the borscht from losing its colour. To reheat a portion of borscht before serving, ensure a slice of beetroot is in the portion you are heating. This will help keep its red colour. After heating the borscht, you can throw away the beetroot slice.
7. Before you add the sugar, taste the borscht for sweetness. Add the sugar if it's not sweet enough.
8. You can buy *krokiety* or make them yourself. You will find the recipes for <u>meat *krokiety*</u> and <u>cabbage and mushroom *krokiety*</u> in the "Obiad" chapter in volume 1.

KITCHEN ACCESSORIES

- ☐ 2 large pots
- ☐ 2 bowls
- ☐ knife
- ☐ peeling knife
- ☐ chopping board
- ☐ tablespoon
- ☐ teaspoon
- ☐ slotted spoon
- ☐ apron (optional)
- ☐ rubber gloves (optional)
- ☐ sieve

GOOD TO KNOW

 vegetarian

 vegan

 gluten-free

 contains mushrooms
- contains dried mushrooms

 fridge
- for up to 3 days
- reheat before serving – heat a portion of the borscht in a separate pot with one slice of beetroot

 freezer
- for up to 3 months
- divide cold borscht into portions and put into separate containers along with a slice or raw beetroot; this will allow you to defrost and reheat the desired amount later

 kcal
- 131 per serving, 1048 total

GOES WELL WITH

 **Beetroot *Zakwas***
10. Christmas, page 199

 ***Uszka* Filling**
10. Christmas, page 207

 ***Uszka***
10. Christmas, page 215

 **Meat *Krokiety***
vol 1, 3. Obiad, page 143

 **Cabbage and Mushroom *Krokiety***
vol 1, 3. Obiad, page 147

 **Red Borscht**
vol 1, 4. Sides, page 261

USZKA FILLING

*The filling is made with dried wild mushrooms and caramelised onions, it's earthy and slightly sweet.
These delicious filled uszka dumplings are served on Christmas Eve.*

    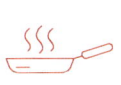 

Difficulty	Makes	Preparation	Cooking	Frying	Resting	Total
INTERMEDIATE	72	1 H	1 H	15 MIN	15 MIN	2 H 30 MIN

INGREDIENTS

- ☐ 150g dried mushrooms
- ☐ 2 onions (~270g)
- ☐ 3-4 tbsp breadcrumbs
- ☐ 2 tbsp butter
- ☐ salt to taste
- ☐ pepper to taste
- ☐ 2 litres water

DIRECTIONS

Preparing the mushrooms – part 1
1. Put the mushrooms into a large pot.
2. Put the hob on medium heat.
3. Pour the water into the pot. *(Note 1)*
4. Bring the water to a boil.
5. Reduce the heat and simmer the mushrooms semi-covered for around 1 hour or until soft.
6. Check the water level when simmering and refill if too much water has evaporated. There should be enough water to cover the mushrooms.
7. While waiting, start preparing the onion.

Preparing the onion
1. Peel the onion and chop finely.
2. Put the hob on medium heat.
3. Melt the butter in a frying pan.
4. Add the chopped onion.
5. Occasionally stir with a wooden spoon.
6. Fry until golden. This can take around 15 minutes.
7. Turn off and remove from the heat and set the pan aside.

Preparing the mushrooms – part 2
1. Set a sieve over a large bowl.
2. Transfer the cooked mushrooms into the sieve and press with a spoon to drain excess liquid.
3. Put the mushrooms on a large plate and leave to cool.
4. Set the bowl with the mushroom liquid aside. *(Note 2)*

Preparing the filling

1. Mince the mushrooms in a meat mincer with small holes into a separate large bowl.
2. Add the prepared onions to the bowl with the mushrooms.
3. Sift the breadcrumbs into the bowl with the filling. *(Note 3)*
4. Add salt and pepper to taste.
5. Mix well.
6. Check the consistency of the filling and add more breadcrumbs if needed. *(Note 4)*

Forming the filling

1. Divide the filling into two parts.
2. Put the first batch on the chopping board.
3. Set the bowl with the remaining filling aside.
4. Form into balls following the instructions in the panel.
5. Repeat for the remaining filling.

NOTES

1. The amount of water needed for cooking the mushrooms will depend on the size of the pot. There should be enough water to cover the mushrooms completely.
2. You can save the mushroom cooking liquid for <u>soured red borscht</u>.
3. It's best to use the fine breadcrumbs to prepare the filling. Larger pieces of bread will soak up the excess water becoming visible and changing the texture of the filling.
4. If the filling is still too wet, add 1 more tbsp of sifted breadcrumbs and stir everything together. Add breadcrumbs until the filling is compact and easy to form into a ball. The filling should be slightly sticky. If the filling is too dry add a little of the mushroom liquid.

INSTRUCTIONS

To fold the filling, follow the instructions:

Form the filling into a 25cm square.

Cut the square lengthwise to get 2 equal halves.

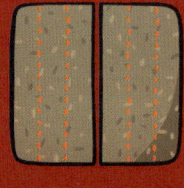

Then cut each half into 3 equal strips.

You should get 6 equal strips.

Then cut the strips crosswise to obtain equal halves.

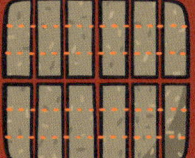
Cut each of these parts twice crosswise.

You should obtain 36 little squares.

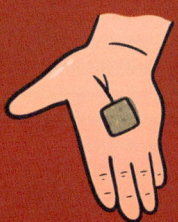
Using a teaspoon, put 1 little square in your palm.

Form into a ball.

Lay the balls on a separate chopping board.

KITCHEN ACCESSORIES

- ☐ large pot with lid
- ☐ frying pan
- ☐ 2 large bowls
- ☐ measuring jug
- ☐ knife
- ☐ 2 chopping boards
- ☐ large plate
- ☐ 2 tablespoons
- ☐ meat mincer
- ☐ wooden spoon
- ☐ sieve
- ☐ small sieve

GOOD TO KNOW

 vegetarian

 contains dairy
- contains butter

 contains mushrooms
- contains dried mushrooms

 kcal
- 464 total

GOES WELL WITH

 **Soured Red Borscht**
10. Christmas, page 203

 ***Uszka* Dough**
10. Christmas, page 211

 ***Uszka***
10. Christmas, page 215

USZKA DOUGH

*A fantastic recipe for a universal pierogi dough which is smooth, soft, elastic and does not stick to your hands.
Perfect for making Christmas uszka.*

Difficulty	Makes	Preparation	Kneading	Resting	Total
SIMPLE	72	10 MIN	20 MIN	10 MIN	40 MIN

INGREDIENTS

- 500g plain flour (+ more for dusting)
- 1 tsp salt
- 80g unsalted butter
- 200ml hot water

DIRECTIONS

1. Put the hob on low heat.
2. Add the butter to a small saucepan.
3. Melt on a low heat to prevent burning.
4. When the butter is liquid, set aside.
5. Pour hot water into a measuring jug and set aside.
6. Sift the flour onto a pastry board. *(Note 1)*
7. Add the salt.
8. Make a well in the sifted flour and add the melted butter.
9. Knead the dough with your hands for around 10 minutes. *(Note 2)*
10. Start adding water to the dough; keep kneading until smooth and elastic. This can take around 10 minutes.
11. Sprinkle one of the upper corners of your pastry board with flour.
12. Knead the dough into a ball and put onto the floured corner of the pastry board.
13. Wrap the dough in a tea towel to prevent drying out and leave to rest for around 10 minutes.

NOTES

1. The flour should be properly aerated.
2. At the beginning the flour will stick to your hands. When you take the dough into your hands, it will be slightly sticky, but will still fall apart in your fingers.

KITCHEN ACCESSORIES

- ☐ small saucepan
- ☐ measuring jug
- ☐ tablespoon
- ☐ teaspoon
- ☐ sieve
- ☐ pastry board
- ☐ tea towel

GOOD TO KNOW

 vegetarian

 kcal
- 2776 total

GOES WELL WITH

 *Uszka* **Filling**
10. Christmas, page 207

 *Uszka*
10. Christmas, page 215

USZKA

*Uszka dumplings with a mushroom filling
which are served with beetroot borscht
are almost mandatory on the Polish Christmas table.*

Difficulty	Makes	Preparation	Cooking	Total
INTERMEDIATE	72	2 H	30 MIN	2 H 30 MIN

INGREDIENTS

For the *uszka*
- *uszka* filling (page 207)
- *uszka* dough (page 211)

For making the *uszka*
- 1 tbsp plain flour

For cooking
- 1 tbsp salt
- 2-3 tsp butter
- 3 litres water

DIRECTIONS

Making the *uszka*
1. Put a separate tea towel on the kitchen counter or on a chopping board. *(Note 1)*
2. Take the dough from under the tea towel and work with one quarter of the dough per batch.
3. Cover the remaining dough with the tea towel. *(Note 2)*
4. Dust a pastry board or a clean flat surface with flour.
5. Place the piece of dough on the prepared work surface.
6. Form the *uszka*, following the instructions with the diagrams.
7. Repeat with all the *uszka*.
8. Place each on the prepared tea towel.
9. With a second tea towel, cover the *uszka* waiting to be cooked. *(Note 5)*

Cooking the *uszka*
1. Before starting to boil the *uszka*, have the bowls and a slotted spoon ready.
2. Put the hob on medium heat.
3. Pour the water into a large pot and bring to a boil.
4. When the water starts boiling, add the salt. *(Note 6)*
5. When the water boils again, stir with a wooden spoon to form a vortex in the pot. *(Note 7)*
6. Gently put a batch of eight *uszka* in the water. *(Note 8)*
7. Stir with a wooden spoon again to create a vortex so that the *uszka* begin to move with the water.
8. When the *uszka* come to the surface, start to measure a cooking time of 3 minutes.
9. When the 3 minutes are up, take the *uszka* out with a slotted spoon.
10. Place into the smaller bowl and add 1 tsp butter.
11. Roll the *uszka* in the melting butter. *(Note 9)*
12. Pour the *uszka* into the separate large bowl.
13. Repeat with all the *uszka*.

INSTRUCTIONS

To prepare and fold the uszka, follow the instructions:

 Roll out the dough into a rectangle and thickness of 3-4mm. (Notes 3 and 4)

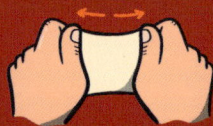 Take one square in your hand and slightly stretch it with your fingers.

 Using a pizza knife, cut the dough lengthwise into strips at 5cm intervals.

 Put a stretched square of dough on your palm, so that the side which was stuck to the work surface is on top. The part that was rolled should touch the palm.

 Put one ball of filling in the centre of the square of dough held in your hand.

 Then cut crosswise at 5cm intervals.

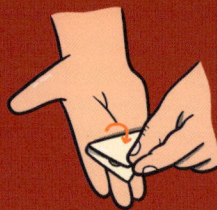 Fold and stick together two of the opposite corners of the dough to enclose the ball of stuffing in the shape of a triangle.

 After cutting, you should get 5 x 5cm squares. Collect the edges you didn't use and add to the rest of the dough wrapped in a tea towel. (Note 2)

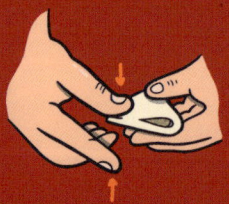 Pinch the edges of the dough to form a sealed triangle.

Put your dumpling on one palm.

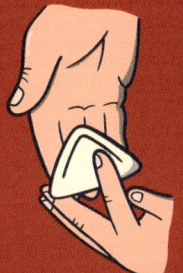

Place the index finger of your other hand on the part with the filling and your thumb and middle finger underneath on the outer edges of the dumpling.

Bring the edges at your thumb and middle finger closer together, around your index finger.

With a finger from your main hand pinch the edges of the dough that now meet so that the ends stick together.

This is how you get an "uszko" dumpling.

To serve
- Put a portion of the *uszka* in a soup plate and pour a portion of the soured red borscht over.

NOTES

1. Place your prepared *uszka* on a tea towel, where they can wait to be cooked.
2. Remember to always cover the dough you are not using with a tea towel, so it doesn't dry out.
3. Try to roll the dough out to a rectangle or a square shape. This will make it easier to cut the dough later on and reduce the amount of dough that will need to be rolled out again.
4. If a part of the dough sticks to the rolling pin, sprinkle it with flour and gently rub into the dough.
5. This will prevent the *uszka* from drying.
6. The water will stop boiling for a while after you add the salt. Wait for it to start boiling again. You should only salt the water once at the beginning – don't add more when you cook further batches.
7. The moving water will prevent your *uszka* from falling to the bottom and sticking to the pot or sticking together.
8. Don't cook too many *uszka* at once. They need to have enough space in the pot so they don't stick together.
9. The butter will prevent the *uszka* from sticking together.

KITCHEN ACCESSORIES

- ☐ large pot
- ☐ large bowl
- ☐ bowl
- ☐ knife
- ☐ pizza knife
- ☐ chopping board
- ☐ 2 tablespoons
- ☐ teaspoon
- ☐ wooden spoon
- ☐ slotted spoon
- ☐ rolling pin
- ☐ pastry board
- ☐ 3 tea towels

GOOD TO KNOW

 vegetarian

 contains dairy
- contains butter

 contains mushrooms
- contains dried mushrooms

 fridge
- for up to 3 days
- reheat before serving again – heat a portion of *uszka* in salted boiling water (1 tsp of salt). Heat them until they rise to the surface. Take them out of the water and transfer to a bowl with the butter, so they don't stick. You can also fry them in a frying pan with a little bit of butter until they are golden.

 freezer
- you can freeze the *uszka* when they are cooked and cooled down. Put them on a chopping board, so they don't touch. Put the chopping board in the freezer. When the *uszka* are frozen, transfer them to a freezer bag. Store for up to 3 months. To heat, cook the *uszka* in salted water for 4 minutes (1 minute longer than fresh *uszka*).

 kcal
- 45 per uszko, 3240 total

GOES WELL WITH

 **Soured Red Borscht**
10. Christmas, page 203

 ***Uszka* Filling**
10. Christmas, page 207

 ***Uszka* Dough**
10. Christmas, page 211

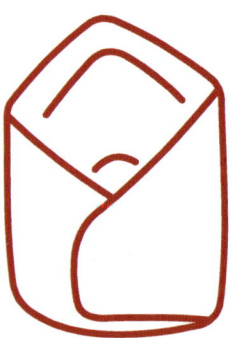

218   Christmas

CHRISTMAS EVE FRIED FISH

Marinated in milk, onion and lots of spice, this crispy battered and fried fish is an essential part of the Polish Christmas menu.

Difficulty	Serves	Preparation	Defrosting	Resting	Frying	Total
INTERMEDIATE	6	1 H 30 MIN	4 H	2-12 H	~1 H	~1,5 DAYS

INGREDIENTS

For the fish
- ☐ 500g white fish fillets *(Note 1)*
- ☐ 1 onion (~150g)
- ☐ 10g fish seasoning
- ☐ ½ lemon (or 2 tbsp lemon juice)
- ☐ 2 tsp salt
- ☐ 1 litre milk

For the breading
- ☐ 300g breadcrumbs
- ☐ 2 large eggs
- ☐ 2 tbsp plain flour

For frying
- ☐ 250ml cooking oil

DIRECTIONS

Day 1: evening *(Note 2)*
Preparing the fish (frozen)
1. Take the fish out of the freezer and rinse the ice.
2. Place on a large plate to defrost. *(Note 3)*
3. Cover the plate with aluminium foil, leaving some free space on the sides.
4. Put into the fridge. *(Note 4)*

Day 2: morning
Seasoning the fish
1. When the fish has defrosted remove any water from the plate.
2. Check for and remove any bones in the fillets.
3. Chop the fillets into smaller pieces. *(Note 5)*
4. Roll the lemon on the kitchen counter. *(Note 6)*
5. Cut the lemon in half.
6. Put the fish on a chopping board.
7. Sprinkle the fillets with lemon juice and fish seasoning on one side.
8. Put the fillets on a separate large plate, seasoned side down.
9. Sprinkle again lemon and fish seasoning.
10. Put the fillets in the fridge. *(Note 7)*

Day 2: afternoon
Soaking the fish
1. Pour the milk into a medium saucepan.
2. Add salt to the milk and stir until dissolved.
3. Take the fillets out of the fridge.
4. Peel the onion, cut in half and then into thin slices.
5. Beginning with the onion, construct layers of onion and fish in a bowl finishing with onion on top.
6. Pour milk into the bowl to cover the fish.
7. Put the bowl in the fridge for 2 hours.

Day 2: afternoon
Preparing the fillets
1. Take the fillets out of the fridge.
2. Carefully pour the contents into a sieve to remove the milk.
3. Remove the onion from the fillets, the onion can be discarded.
4. Set a sieve over a bowl and let the fillets drain.
5. Set the bowl aside.

Preparing the breading
1. Crack the eggs into a cup.
2. Add the flour.
3. Whisk with a fork. *(Note 8)*
4. Transfer the mixture to a soup plate.
5. Put the breadcrumbs into a second soup plate.

Breading the fillets
1. Transfer a fillet to the soup plate with the egg mixture.
2. Dip in the egg mixture.
3. Take out and rub the edges on the plate to get rid of excess egg mixture.
4. Then transfer to the plate with the breadcrumbs.
5. Sprinkle breadcrumbs on both sides.
6. Transfer to a separate large plate.
7. Repeat with all the fillets.
8. Set aside.

Frying
1. Put the hob on medium heat.
2. Heat the oil in a frying pan.
3. Turn the hob down to low heat.
4. Put the fillets in the pan.
5. Fry on both sides until golden. Each side can take around 6-8 minutes.
6. Put the fried fillets onto a plate lined with paper towel. *(Note 9)*

To serve
- Traditionally on Christmas Eve fish is usually served with sauerkraut with mushrooms and boiled potatoes cut into pieces. On other occasions the fish can also be served with mashed potatoes.

NOTES

1. You can use cod, blue grenadier, pollock or hake fillets.
2. If the fish is frozen, it will take longer to prepare, so it's best to begin the day before serving. If the fish is not frozen, you can start in the morning. Just rinse it and then follow the steps in the "Seasoning the fish" section.
3. Put only one layer of fish on the plate. If you have more, put them on a second plate. Don't put the fillets on top of each other because they won't defrost and might freeze together. Water will leak from the fish which you need to pour out. Don't put the fillets on a paper towel because they might stick.
4. If you are defrosting the fillets on the day you are serving them, please take into account that it may take about 4 hours.
5. We want the fillets to be of equal size and roughly 10 cm in length. It's not important to be precise. Some of the fillets can be kept at their original size if they are roughly this size already.
6. Before cutting the lemon, roll it for a while on the kitchen counter, pressing slightly with your hand. This will help you extract all the juice from the lemon.

7. If the fish is thawed and you are preparing it on the day of serving, just place the fillets in the fridge for about 2 hours after you season them.
8. The consistency should be thinner than yoghurt. If it's too thin, add another tbsp of flour.
9. The paper towel will absorb excess fat.

KITCHEN ACCESSORIES

- ☐ medium saucepan
- ☐ frying pan
- ☐ 2 bowls
- ☐ cup
- ☐ knife
- ☐ chopping board
- ☐ 2 soup plates
- ☐ 2 large plates
- ☐ plate
- ☐ tablespoon
- ☐ teaspoon
- ☐ fork
- ☐ silicone spatula
- ☐ sieve
- ☐ aluminium foil
- ☐ paper towel

GOOD TO KNOW

 gluten-free option
- swap flour for a gluten-free version
- swap breadcrumbs for a gluten-free version

 contains dairy
- contains milk

 contains fish
- contains fish fillets

 fridge
- for up to 2 days
- can be eaten hot or cold – to reheat, heat the in a frying pan and fry on each side, until the fillet is warm; you can also reheat in the oven or microwave

 kcal
- 702 per serving, 4212 total

GOES WELL WITH

 **Christmas Eve Sauerkraut with Mushrooms**
10. Christmas, page 225

 **Mashed Potatoes**
vol 1, 4. Sides, page 197

Christmas

CHRISTMAS EVE SAUERKRAUT WITH MUSHROOMS

A delicate sweet and sour composition made with sauerkraut and wild mushrooms. A traditional Polish side made with ingredients which fill the house with Christmas aromas.

Difficulty	Serves	Preparation	Frying	Cooking	Total
SIMPLE	6	30 MIN	~15 MIN	~1 H	~1 H 45 MIN

INGREDIENTS

For the mushrooms
- ☐ 20g dried mushrooms
- ☐ 1 litre water

For the cabbage
- ☐ 600g sauerkraut
- ☐ 20g butter
- ☐ 1 onion (~130g)
- ☐ 1 carrot (~100g)
- ☐ 1 parsnip (~60g)
- ☐ 1 mushroom bouillon cube
- ☐ 4 allspice berries
- ☐ 3 bay leaves
- ☐ 1½ tsp ground caraway
- ☐ pepper to taste *(Note 1)*
- ☐ ~700ml water *(Note 2)*

For the roux
- ☐ 20g butter
- ☐ 2 tbsp plain flour

 Polish products differ from the ones available locally. You will find more information about allspice, caraway, mushroom stock and sauerkraut in the chapter "About the products" on page 328.

DIRECTIONS

Preparing the mushrooms – part 1
1. Put the mushrooms into a medium saucepan. *(Note 3)*
2. Put the hob on medium heat.
3. Pour the water into the saucepan.
4. Bring the water to a boil.
5. Reduce the heat and simmer the mushrooms semi-covered for around 1 hour or until soft.
6. Check the water level when simmering and refill if too much water has evaporated. There should be enough water to cover the mushrooms.

Preparing the sauerkraut – part 1
1. Squeeze the liquid out of the sauerkraut. *(Note 4)*
2. Put on a chopping board and chop finely.
3. Transfer the sauerkraut to a large pot.
4. Add the mushroom bouillon cube.
5. Add the spices: bay leaves, allspice, caraway and pepper. *(Note 1)*
6. Put the hob on medium heat.
7. Pour the water into the pot.
8. Mix well.
9. Bring the water to a boil.

10. Reduce the heat and simmer semi-covered for around 1 hour.
11. Stir from time to time.
12. Check the water level when simmering and refill if too much water has evaporated. There should be enough water to cover the cabbage.
13. While waiting, prepare the onion and all the other ingredients.

Preparing the onion
1. Peel the onion and chop finely.
2. Put the hob on medium heat.
3. Melt the butter in a frying pan.
4. Add the chopped onion.
5. Occasionally stir with a wooden spoon.
6. Fry until golden. This can take around 15 minutes.
7. Add the fried onions to the pot with the sauerkraut.
8. Mix well.

Preparing the vegetables
1. Peel the carrots and parsnip.
2. Grate using a grater with large holes.
3. Add to the pot with the sauerkraut.
4. Mix well.

Preparing the sauerkraut – part 2
1. After around 30 minutes of boiling check the sauerkraut for sourness. *(Note 5)*
2. Take the lid off to evaporate the water to half height of the sauerkraut.
3. Stir from time to time.

Preparing the mushrooms – part 2
1. After boiling the mushrooms remove and place on a chopping board. Keep the liquid for later.
2. Chop finely.
3. Add the mushrooms to the pot with the sauerkraut.
4. When the water in the pot with the sauerkraut is reduced by half, add the mushroom cooking liquid.
5. Mix well.
6. Heat to evaporate the water to half the height of the sauerkraut again.

Preparing the roux
1. Only thicken the sauerkraut near the end when soft.
2. Put the hob on medium heat.
3. Melt the butter carefully in a frying pan to prevent burning.
4. Add the flour.
5. Stir with a wooden spoon to remove any lumps. *(Note 6)*
6. Turn off and remove from the heat and set the pan aside.
7. Add small amounts of the sauerkraut liquid to the pan, spoon by spoon (just the liquid, without sauerkraut), mixing constantly. *(Note 7)*
8. Add the roux to the sauerkraut.
9. Mix well.
10. Add pepper to taste.
11. Cook for 3 minutes.

To serve
- Traditionally on Christmas Eve sauerkraut is usually served with <u>fried fish</u> and boiled potatoes cut into pieces. On other occasions the sauerkraut can also be served with <u>mashed potatoes</u>.

NOTES

1. While simmering season the sauerkraut with pepper and then at the very end, to taste.
2. The amount of water needed for cooking the sauerkraut will depend on the size of the pot. There should be enough water to cover the sauerkraut completely.
3. If you want to prepare a double portion of mushrooms, cook them in a large saucepan, but do not increase the amount of water. The mushrooms will swell during cooking and will need more space.

4. Don't discard the liquid from the sauerkraut jar. While cooking the sauerkraut, check how it tastes. If it's not sour enough, add more liquid from the jar.
5. Check the sauerkraut for sourness. Be careful: the sauerkraut will be very hot! If it's not sour enough, add more liquid from the sauerkraut jar. Mix and boil for another 2 minutes. Check the flavour once more and decide if more liquid is needed. Add gradually – not all at once.
6. After adding the flour, quickly mix it with the butter to make a uniform golden roux with a yoghurt-like consistency.
7. Adding hot liquid to the roux helps it to dissolve, so that there are no lumps of flour and butter.

KITCHEN ACCESSORIES

- ☐ large pot
- ☐ medium saucepan
- ☐ frying pan
- ☐ knife
- ☐ peeling knife

- ☐ chopping board
- ☐ 2 tablespoons
- ☐ teaspoon
- ☐ wooden spoon
- ☐ grater

GOOD TO KNOW

 vegetarian

 contains dairy
- contains butter

 contains mushrooms
- contains dried mushrooms
- contains mushroom bouillon cube

 fridge
- for up to 3 days
- tastes better the next day
- reheat before serving – heat a portion in a frying pan or in the microwave.

 kcal
- 105 per serving, 630 total

GOES WELL WITH

 **Christmas Eve Fried Fish**
10. Christmas, page 221

 **Mashed Potatoes**
vol 1, 4. Sides, page 197

MAKOWIEC WITH WALNUT CREAM AND CHOCOLATE GLAZE

Poppy seed cake combines layers of soft sponge cake, a mixture of poppy seeds, nuts and dried fruits and a rich walnut cream.
It's covered with a chocolate glaze and will melt the hearts of all your guests!

Difficulty	Serves	Preparation	Baking	Resting	Total
CHALLENGING	30	~4 H	~25 MIN	30 MIN	~5 H

INGREDIENTS

For the sponge
- ☐ 240g plain flour
- ☐ 120g sugar
- ☐ 16g vanilla sugar
- ☐ 6 large eggs
- ☐ 1 tsp baking powder
- ☐ ½ tsp salt

For the poppy seed mixture
- ☐ 400g poppy seeds
- ☐ 400g dried cranberries
- ☐ 200g dried apricots
- ☐ 200g raisins
- ☐ 100g candied orange peel *(Note 1)*
- ☐ 80g walnuts
- ☐ 80g flaked almonds
- ☐ 35g unsalted butter
- ☐ 2 packets orange jelly (140g) *(Note 2)*
- ☐ 1 large egg
- ☐ 3 tbsp honey (~100g)
- ☐ 1 tsp almond extract
- ☐ 800ml milk
- ☐ 500ml water
- ☐ sugar (optional) *(Note 3)*

For the cream filling
- ☐ 300g unsalted butter (+ more for buttering the tin)
- ☐ 200g walnuts
- ☐ 16g vanilla sugar
- ☐ 150ml milk

For the glaze *(Note 4)*
- ☐ 300g milk chocolate
- ☐ 150g unsalted butter
- ☐ 150ml milk

 Polish products differ from the ones available locally. You will find more information about candied orange peel, jelly and vanilla sugar in the chapter "About the products" on page 328.

Christmas

DIRECTIONS

Preparing the cream filling – part 1
Preparing the butter
1. Take the butter out of the fridge.
2. Cube the butter.
3. Transfer to a large bowl.
4. Set the bowl aside. *(Note 5)*

Preparing the sponge
Preparing the baking tin
1. Using scissors, cut the baking paper as a single sheet, to cover the bottom and inner sides of the tin.
2. Brush the baking tin with butter so the paper sticks.
3. Line the baking tin with the baking paper.
4. Grease the baking paper with more butter.
5. Set the baking tin aside.

Preparing the ingredients
1. Sift the flour into a bowl.
2. Separate the yolks from the whites into two separate small bowls.
3. Measure the sugar into a separate small bowl.

Preparing the batter – part 1
1. Add the egg whites to the bowl of a food mixer. *(Note 6)*
2. Add the salt.
3. Start whisking.
4. Add the sugar and vanilla sugar.
5. Whisk to stiff peaks. This can take around 10 minutes.

Preparing the oven
1. Preheat the oven to 180°C / 350°F or gas 4.

Preparing the batter – part 2
1. Add the yolks to the whisked egg whites.
2. Whisk thoroughly.
3. Add the plain flour and baking powder.
4. Whisk until the ingredients are combined. This can take around 5 minutes.
5. Pour the mixture into the prepared baking tin.
6. Spread evenly using a spatula.

Baking
1. Bake for around 20-25 minutes, until golden.
2. Place the sponge on a cooling rack to cool.
3. While waiting, prepare the poppy seed mixture.

Preparing the poppy seed mixture
Preparing the poppy seeds
1. Put the hob on low heat.
2. Pour the milk into a large saucepan.
3. Bring to a boil. *(Note 7)*
4. Add the poppy seeds.
5. Cook for around 2 minutes from the moment of boiling.
6. Stir from time to time.
7. Turn off and remove from the heat and set the saucepan aside.
8. Set a sieve over a bowl.
9. Put the poppy seeds in the sieve and press using a spoon to remove excess milk.
10. Put the sieve with the poppy seeds on a large plate and leave until cool.
11. Set the bowl with the milk aside. *(Note 8)*
12. While waiting, prepare the nuts and dried fruits.

Preparing the dried fruits and nuts
1. Put the hob on medium heat.
2. Pour the water into a medium saucepan or kettle and bring to a boil.
3. Put the cranberries, apricots and raisins in a bowl.
4. Cover with boiling water (around 250ml). *(Note 9)*
5. Set aside for around 5 minutes. *(Note 10)*
6. Finely chop the walnuts, flaked almonds and candied orange peel.
7. Put into a separate bowl.
8. Drain the water from the fruit.
9. Once again cover with boiling water (around 250ml).
10. Set aside for around 5 minutes.

11. Pour the water out.
12. Put the cranberries and raisins into the bowl with the nuts and almond flakes.
13. Finely chop the apricots and add to the bowl with the fruit and nuts.
14. Set the bowl aside.

Preparing the poppy seed mixture
1. Mince the poppy seeds twice in a meat mincer with small holes. *(Note 11)*
2. Transfer into a large saucepan.
3. Add the honey, butter and almond extract.
4. Crack the egg into a separate bowl and whisk with a hand mixer for 1-2 minutes.
5. Add the whisked egg to the poppy seed mixture.
6. Add all the fruit and nuts.
7. Put the hob on low heat.
8. Mix the mixture thoroughly so that the honey and butter dissolve.
9. Heat the poppy seed mixture until very hot, stirring constantly.
10. Check the mixture for consistency. *(Note 12)*
11. Add the orange jelly and sugar. *(Note 3)*
12. Mix thoroughly, to combine the jelly with the mixture. *(Note 13)*
13. Turn off and remove from the heat and set the saucepan aside.

Preparing the *makowiec* – part 1
1. Remove the baking paper from the sponge.
2. Add fresh baking paper to the baking tin and set aside. *(Note 14)*
3. Remove the top crust from the sponge. *(Note 15)*
4. Put the sponge into the baking tin lined with baking paper.
5. Put the hot poppy seed mixture on top of the sponge.
6. Spread evenly using a spatula.
7. Set the poppy seed cake aside so that the mixture cools completely. *(Note 16)*
8. While waiting, prepare the walnut cream.

Preparing the cream filling – part 2
Preparing the walnut mixture
1. Grind the walnuts in a nut grinder. *(Note 17)*
2. Transfer to a small bowl.
3. Put the hob on low heat.
4. Pour the milk into a medium saucepan.
5. Bring to a boil. *(Note 7)*
6. Turn off the hob.
7. Add the vanilla sugar to the saucepan with the milk.
8. Mix well.
9. Pour the milk into the bowl with the nuts.
10. Mix thoroughly until everything is well combined and has a uniform consistency.
11. Set aside to cool completely. This can take around 30 minutes. *(Note 18)*
12. Stir from time to time.

Combining the ingredients
1. The nut mixture needs to have cooled before continuing.
2. Using a hand mixer, whip the butter in the large bowl.
3. Add the mixture spoon by spoon.
4. Whisk until the ingredients are combined.

Preparing the *makowiec* – part 2
1. Put the cream filling on the poppy seed mixture only when cooled completely.
2. Put the cream on top of the poppy seed mixture.
3. Spread evenly using a spatula.
4. Put the *makowiec* in the fridge for around 30 minutes so the cream filling can set.

Preparing the glaze

1. Pour the milk into a small saucepan.
2. Put the hob on low heat.
3. Add the butter.
4. Break the chocolate into smaller pieces and add to the saucepan.
5. Keep stirring, so that all ingredients melt and a uniform mixture forms.
6. Set the glaze aside to cool. *(Notes 19 and 20)*
7. Stir from time to time.

Preparing the *makowiec* – part 3

1. Pour the glaze on top of the cream filling.
2. Spread evenly.
3. Put the *makowiec* back in the fridge for around 30 minutes.

NOTES

1. You can buy candied orange peel or make it yourself. In the "Pantry" chapter you will find a recipe for the perfect <u>candied orange peel</u>.
2. You can swap orange jelly for lemon jelly.
3. When the mixture is ready, check it for sweetness and add sugar to taste.
4. You can make the glaze yourself or use a store-bought chocolate glaze. You will need 400g of glaze.
5. When the butter is at room temperature, it's easier to fold into the walnut cream.
6. If you don't have a food mixer, you can prepare the batter in a large bowl using a hand mixer.
7. When the milk is close to boiling, it starts to foam and bubble so watch it to ensure it does not boil over.
8. Don't pour the milk out: you might need it for the cream filling later.
9. Some dried fruit has sulphur dioxide (E220) added to it to conserve and protect the product from moisture and mould, this step helps to remove the sulphur dioxide.
10. Dried fruits will soften and slightly swell in hot water.
11. You can use a blender instead of the meat mincer.
12. If the mixture is too dry, you can add a couple tbsp of the milk you cooked the poppy seeds in. The mixture should be moist and slightly sticky.
13. Check if it's sweet enough. Be careful: the mixture will be very hot! If you want to, you can sweeten the mixture. Mix everything together and wait for the sugar to dissolve.
14. Baking paper will secure the sides of the sponge while you make more layers.
15. The mixture will not stick to the sponge crust – that's why you need to remove it. To do this, use a fork to scratch the top of the cake lengthwise and then across. Scrape the top with the side of a fork. Put the removed sponge in a separate small bowl. You can have it with a warm cup of tea.
16. The next layer will be the cream filling, therefore the poppy seed mixture needs to cool completely, so the cream doesn't melt.
17. You can use a blender instead of the nut grinder.
18. You can cool the mixture quicker by pouring cold water into the sink and resting the bowl in the cold water. The mixture should cool completely in around 10 minutes.
19. Hot glaze will melt the cream filling on the makowiec. Wait for it to cool – it can't be hot, but it still needs to remain spreadable.
20. You can cool the glaze quicker by pouring cold water into the sink and resting the saucepan in the cold water. The glaze should cool down completely in around 7 minutes.

KITCHEN ACCESSORIES

- [ ] large saucepan
- [ ] medium saucepan
- [ ] small saucepan
- [ ] large bowl
- [ ] 3 bowls
- [ ] 3 small bowls
- [ ] measuring jug
- [ ] knife
- [ ] chopping board
- [ ] large plate
- [ ] 3 tablespoons
- [ ] teaspoon
- [ ] fork
- [ ] meat mincer (or hand blender)
- [ ] nut grinder (or hand blender)
- [ ] hand mixer
- [ ] food mixer
- [ ] spatula
- [ ] scissors
- [ ] sieve
- [ ] kitchen scale
- [ ] baking tin (measured inside 35 x 20 x 7cm)
- [ ] baking paper

GOOD TO KNOW

vegetarian

contains dairy
- contains butter
- contains milk

contains nuts
- contains walnuts

contains pork
- contains jelly – check if it's made with pork gelatine

fridge
- store covered for up to 4 days

kcal
- 454 per serving, 13620 total

GOES WELL WITH

Candied Orange Peel
11. Pantry, page 321

CHRISTMAS GINGERBREAD CAKE

Absolutely exquisite Christmas gingerbread cake with a tart plum jam, a mild and sweet vanilla cream filling and covered with a rich dark chocolate glaze.

Difficulty
CHALLENGING

Serves
15

Preparation
~4 H

Baking
1 H

Resting
2 DAYS

Total
2 DAYS 5 H

INGREDIENTS

For the dough
- ☐ 500g plain flour (+ more for dusting)
- ☐ 150g honey
- ☐ 140g sugar
- ☐ 125g unsalted butter
- ☐ 20g gingerbread seasoning *(Note 1)*
- ☐ 1 large egg
- ☐ 1 tbsp cocoa powder
- ☐ 1 tsp bicarbonate of soda
- ☐ 60ml water

For the baking tin
- ☐ 1 tbsp butter

For the cream filling
- ☐ 500ml milk
- ☐ 180g unsalted butter
- ☐ 32g vanilla sugar
- ☐ 3 tbsp sugar
- ☐ 2 tbsp potato starch
- ☐ 2 tbsp plain flour

For soaking the sponge
- ☐ 1 tea bag (black tea)
- ☐ 1 tsp sugar
- ☐ 250ml hot water
- ☐ lemon juice

For layering the cake
- ☐ ~450g plum jam *(Note 2)*

For the glaze *(Note 3)*
- ☐ 150g 50-70% dark chocolate
- ☐ 75g unsalted butter
- ☐ 75ml milk

For the gingerbread seasoning (optional) *(Note 4)*
- ☐ 30g ground cinnamon
- ☐ 20g ground ginger
- ☐ 10g ground nutmeg
- ☐ 5g ground cardamom
- ☐ 3g cloves
- ☐ 2g coriander seeds
- ☐ 5 allspice berries
- ☐ 4 whole star anise

 Polish products differ from the ones available locally. You will find more information about gingerbread spice, potato starch and vanilla sugar in the chapter "About the products" on page 328.

DIRECTIONS

Preparing the gingerbread seasoning (optional)
1. Add all the ground spices to a bowl: cinnamon, ginger, nutmeg and cardamom.
2. Grind the coriander seeds and cloves in a pestle and mortar and add to the bowl with the rest of the spices.
3. Grind the allspice berries and star anise in the pestle and mortar and add to the bowl with the rest of the spices.
4. Mix well.

Preparing the pastry
Preparing the ingredients
1. Measure the honey into a small bowl.
2. Measure the sugar into a separate bowl.
3. Measure the butter into another separate bowl.
4. Cube the butter.

Preparing the gingerbread mixture
1. Add 2 tbsp of sugar to a small saucepan.
2. Set the rest of the sugar aside.
3. Put the hob on medium heat.
4. Caramelise the sugar. This can take around 5 minutes. *(Note 5)*
5. Turn off and remove from the heat and set the saucepan aside.
6. To the hot caramel add the honey, butter, gingerbread seasoning, cocoa and the remaining sugar.
7. Mix well.
8. Put the hob on medium heat again.
9. Warm all the ingredients so that they dissolve and form a uniform mixture. *(Note 6)*
10. Set aside to cool completely. This can take around 30 minutes. *(Note 7)*
11. While waiting, start preparing the flour and bicarbonate of soda.

Preparing the bicarbonate of soda
1. Pour the water into a measuring jug.
2. Add the bicarbonate of soda.
3. Stir to dissolve.

Preparing the dough – part 1
1. Sift the flour into the bowl of a food mixer. *(Note 8)*
2. Add the water with the bicarbonate of soda.
3. Crack the egg into the bowl.
4. Add the cooled gingerbread mixture.
5. Knead the dough until smooth and elastic. This can take around 10 mins in the food mixer and a little bit longer if kneading the dough by hand. *(Note 9)*

Preparing the baking tin
1. Using scissors, cut the baking paper to fit the bottom of the baking tin.
2. Brush the baking tin with butter so the paper sticks.
3. Line the baking tin with the baking paper.
4. Set the baking tin aside.

Preparing the oven
1. Preheat the oven to 180°C / 350°F or gas 4.

Preparing the dough – part 2
1. Sprinkle a work surface with flour. Transfer the dough onto the work surface.
2. Roll out the dough into a thick sausage shape and cut into 3 equal parts.
3. Roll out one part of the dough to the size of the baking tin base and to a thickness of about 3-4mm.
4. Put into the prepared baking tin.

Baking
1. Bake for around 20 minutes.

Preparing the dough – part 3
1. While baking one batch of the dough, roll out the next.
2. After baking, put the cake layer on a cooling rack.
3. Remove the baking paper from the cake. *(Note 10)*
4. Line the baking tin with fresh baking paper.
5. Put another rolled out batch of the dough into the baking tin and bake.
6. Repeat for the remaining dough, remembering to change the baking paper.
7. Leave the cake layers to cool completely.
8. After baking all the pastry layers, layer the baking tin with fresh baking paper, to cover the bottom and inner sides of the tin. *(Note 11)*
9. While waiting, start preparing the cream filling.

Preparing the cream filling
Preparing the milk and flour
1. Pour 100ml of milk into a bowl.
2. Add the plain flour and potato starch.
3. Using a hand mixer, combine all the ingredients. Whisk for around 1 minute.
4. Set the bowl aside.

Preparing the mixture
1. Put the hob on low heat.
2. Put the remaining milk in a medium saucepan (400ml).
3. Bring to a boil. *(Note 12)*
4. Add the milk with the flour to the boiling milk.
5. Keep stirring with a wooden spoon until uniform. *(Note 13)*
6. When the mixture starts bubbling, cook for 3 minutes.
7. Turn off the hob.
8. Add the sugar and vanilla sugar.
9. Mix well.
10. Set aside to cool completely. This can take around 30 minutes. *(Note 14)*
11. Stir from time to time.

Finishing the cream filling
1. The mixture needs to have cooled before continuing.
2. Cube the butter and put into a separate bowl.
3. Whisk the butter.
4. Add the mixture spoon by spoon.
5. Whisk until the ingredients are combined.

Preparing the cake
Preparing the tea (Notes 15 and 16)
1. Brew the tea in a cup.
2. Add sugar and lemon juice.
3. Stir for the sugar to dissolve.

Layering the cake
1. When the cake layers have cooled completely, start layering the cake layers with plum jam and cream filling.
2. Put one cake layer in the baking tin.
3. Sprinkle with tea. *(Note 17)*
4. Put the plum jam on the cake.
5. Spread evenly with a spatula.
6. Cover with the second cake layer.
7. Sprinkle with tea. *(Note 18)*
8. Spread the cream filling evenly.
9. Cover with the third cake layer. *(Note 19)*
10. Set the prepared cake aside.

Preparing the glaze
1. Pour the milk into a small saucepan.
2. Put the hob on low heat.
3. Add the butter.
4. Break the chocolate into smaller pieces and add to the saucepan.
5. Keep stirring, so that all ingredients melt and a uniform mixture forms.
6. Pour the glaze onto the cake.
7. Spread evenly.

To serve
- Put the cake in the fridge for 2 days. *(Note 20)*

NOTES

1. You can use a ready-made gingerbread seasoning or make your own according to the given recipe.
2. You can buy plum jam (*powidła śliwkowe*) or make it yourself. You will find a recipe for *powidła śliwkowe* in the "Pantry" chapter.
3. You can make the glaze yourself or use a store-bought chocolate glaze. You will need 200g of glaze.
4. This amount of ingredients will give you 80g of gingerbread seasoning. Add an extra 10 minutes to the total time to prepare these biscuits. Use the leftover seasoning for making traditional Christmas gingerbread biscuits.
5. The caramel should be very thick and golden.
6. Be careful not to bring the mixture to a boil.
7. You can cool the mixture quicker by pouring cold water into the sink and resting the saucepan in the cold water. The mixture should cool completely in around 10 minutes.
8. If you don't have a food mixer, you can knead the dough by hand on the work surface. Sift the flour onto the work surface. Make a well in the sifted flour and add the rest of the ingredients.
9. When kneading the dough by hand, start combining all the ingredients with a knife. Then knead the dough by hand. The dough should be smooth and brown. It can stick to your hands slightly, but not stay on them. It might feel slightly oily.
10. It is easier to remove the baking paper while the cake is warm. Removing the paper when the cake layer is cold might damage it, since the cake might stick to the paper.
11. Baking paper will secure the sides of the cake while you make more layers.
12. When the milk is close to boiling, it starts to foam and bubble so watch it to ensure it does not boil over.
13. Lumps are going to form at first, but as you keep stirring, you'll get a uniform mixture.
14. You can cool the mixture quicker by pouring cold water into the sink and resting the saucepan in the cold water. The mixture should cool completely in around 10 minutes.
15. You don't have to use all the tea to soak the cake.
16. You can prepare the tea earlier. It doesn't matter if you use hot or cold tea.
17. When the tea has soaked into the cake add the plum jam straight away. If left too long, it will become difficult to spread the plum jam over the cake.
18. When the tea has soaked into the cake add the cream filling straight away. If left too long, it will become difficult to spread the cream filling over the cake.
19. Don't sprinkle the third cake layer with tea.
20. The cake needs to wait 48 hours so the gingerbread layers can soften. If you want to speed up the process, cover the baking tin with a chopping board and place into a plastic bag. Close the bag and put it into the fridge. The cake should be ready in 24 hours.

KITCHEN ACCESSORIES

- ☐ medium saucepan
- ☐ small saucepan
- ☐ 2 bowls
- ☐ small bowl
- ☐ cup
- ☐ measuring jug
- ☐ knife
- ☐ 2 tablespoons
- ☐ 2 teaspoons
- ☐ hand mixer
- ☐ food mixer
- ☐ wooden spoon
- ☐ spatula
- ☐ pestle and mortar (optional)
- ☐ scissors
- ☐ sieve
- ☐ rolling pin
- ☐ pastry board
- ☐ kitchen scale
- ☐ cooling rack
- ☐ baking tin (measured inside 35 x 20 x 7cm)
- ☐ baking paper

GOOD TO KNOW

 vegetarian

 contains dairy
- contains butter
- contains milk

 pantry
- store covered for up to 3 days

 kcal
- 556 per serving, 8340 total

GOES WELL WITH

 **Traditional Christmas Gingerbread Biscuits**
10. Christmas, page 241

 ***Powidła Śliwkowe* (Plum Jam)**
11. Pantry, page 317

TRADITIONAL CHRISTMAS GINGERBREAD BISCUITS

Soft and fluffy Christmas biscuits spiced with a unique blend of warming winter. Just delicious!

Difficulty	Serves	Preparation	Resting	Baking	Total
INTERMEDIATE	~135 *	30 MIN	2 DAYS	~2 H	2 D 2 H 30 MIN

INGREDIENTS

For the dough
- ☐ 600g plain flour (+ more for dusting)
- ☐ 230g honey
- ☐ 230g brown sugar
- ☐ 100g unsalted butter
- ☐ 20g gingerbread seasoning *(Note 1)*
- ☐ 15g cocoa powder
- ☐ 5g bicarbonate of soda
- ☐ 3 large eggs

For the gingerbread seasoning (optional) *(Note 2)*
- ☐ 30g ground cinnamon
- ☐ 20g ground ginger
- ☐ 10g ground nutmeg
- ☐ 5g ground cardamom
- ☐ 3g cloves
- ☐ 2g coriander seeds
- ☐ 5 allspice berries
- ☐ 4 whole star anise

 Polish products differ from the ones available locally. You will find more information about allspice and gingerbread spice in the chapter "About the products" on page 328.

DIRECTIONS

Preparing the gingerbread seasoning (optional)
1. Add all the ground spices to a bowl: cinnamon, ginger, nutmeg and cardamom.
2. Grind the coriander seeds and cloves in a pestle and mortar and add to the bowl with the rest of the spices.
3. Grind the allspice berries and star anise in the pestle and mortar and add to the bowl with the rest of the spices.
4. Mix well.

Day 1
Preparing the gingerbread mixture
1. Put the hob on low heat.
2. Melt the butter and honey in a medium saucepan.
3. Add the sugar, gingerbread spice and cocoa powder.
4. Mix until the ingredients are combined.
5. Turn off and remove from the heat and set the saucepan aside.

* depends on the size of the cookie cutters

Preparing the dough
1. Sift the flour into the bowl of a food mixer. *(Note 3)*
2. Add the bicarbonate of soda.
3. Crack the eggs into the bowl.
4. Mix to combine the ingredients. This can take around 5 minutes in the food mixer and a little bit longer if kneading the dough by hand.
5. Add the gingerbread mixture.
6. Mix until a uniform consistency. This can take around 10 minutes in the food mixer and a little bit longer if kneading the dough by hand. *(Note 4)*
7. Put the dough into a large bowl.
8. Cover with cling film.
9. Put into the fridge for 2 days.

Day 3
Preparing the baking tray
1. Using scissors, cut the baking paper to fit the baking tray.
2. Line the baking tray with the baking paper.
3. Set aside.

Preparing the oven
1. Preheat the oven to 180°C / 350°F or gas 4.

Cutting the biscuits – part 1
1. Take the dough out of the fridge.
2. Cut off a piece of dough. *(Note 5)*
3. Roll the piece in your hands. *(Note 6)*
4. Sprinkle a pastry board and the dough with flour.
5. Roll out the dough to a thickness of about 3mm.
6. Sprinkle the dough with flour and then turn over and sprinkle again. *(Note 7)*
7. Use cookie cutters to cut out shapes from the dough.
8. Add the edges that are left to the remaining dough.
9. Put the prepared biscuits on the baking tray 2cm apart. *(Note 8)*

Baking
1. Bake for around 6-10 minutes. *(Note 9)*

Cutting the biscuits – part 2
1. While the first batch is baking, roll the dough and prepare the next batch.
2. When the biscuits are baked, place on a cooling rack to cool completely. *(Note 10)*

NOTES

1. You can use a ready-made gingerbread seasoning or make your own according to the given recipe.
2. This amount of ingredients will give you 80g of gingerbread seasoning. Add an extra 10 minutes to the total time to prepare the cake. Use the leftover seasoning for making <u>Christmas gingerbread cake</u>.
3. If you don't have a food mixer, you can knead the dough by hand in a large bowl. Sift the flour into the bowl and follow the remaining instructions.
4. After you knead it, the dough will be thick and sticky. Don't add more flour. It will become elastic after resting in the fridge.
5. The dough will be tough, so use a knife.
6. When you knead the dough, it will warm up, which will make it easier to roll out.
7. This will prevent the dough from sticking to the pastry board and to the rolling pin and make it easier for you to cut biscuit shapes.
8. You can lay the biscuits on the baking tray close to each other since they will only rise a little bit.

9. If the biscuits are small, bake them for 6-8 minutes, while larger ones should be baked for 8-10 minutes.
10. Transfer using a spatula while hot, as they will be very soft. Be careful: the tray and biscuits will be very hot! The biscuits will harden as they cool.

KITCHEN ACCESSORIES

- ☐ medium saucepan
- ☐ large bowl
- ☐ small bowl (optional)
- ☐ knife
- ☐ 2 tablespoons
- ☐ teaspoon
- ☐ food mixer
- ☐ spatula
- ☐ pestle and mortar (optional)
- ☐ scissors

- ☐ sieve
- ☐ rolling pin
- ☐ pastry board
- ☐ kitchen scale
- ☐ cooling rack
- ☐ baking tray (measured inside 30x26cm)
- ☐ cookie cutters of various shapes (Christmas)
- ☐ cling film / plastic wrap
- ☐ baking paper

GOOD TO KNOW

 vegetarian

 contains dairy
- contains butter

 pantry
- store in a dry place up to 5 days

 kcal
- the exact number will depend on the size of the biscuit around 35 per biscuit, 4860 total

GOES WELL WITH

 **Christmas Gingerbread Cake**
10. Christmas, page 235

PREPARING THE DECORATIONS

If you want to prepare the decoration in the photo, you will need a circle cutter with a diameter of 13.5cm. Using this cutter, cut out a large biscuit that will be the base for the decoration. Additionally, cut 3 stars of each size (large 7.5cm, medium 5.5cm, small 3.5cm). After baking, leave them to cool completely.

When the biscuits have cooled completely, prepare the icing with 1½ lemon juice (or water) and 50g icing sugar. Mix well until you get a yoghurt-like consistency. If the consistency is too thin, add more icing sugar.

Use a teaspoon to spread the icing in one spot on the round biscuit that will form the base of the Christmas tree. Put the largest star biscuit on the icing. Spread icing over its centre and place the next largest biscuit on top, so that the corners of the star are placed between the corners of the biscuit underneath. Arrange all the stars this way, using the largest biscuits first, then the medium and finally the smallest. You can add a little icing to some of the corners of the stars and decorate them with edible silver pearls. They should look like baubles on a Christmas tree.

The snowflakes on the base of the Christmas tree are made of a sugar paste using a plunger cutter. The presents are also made with sugar paste cut into rectangles and squares. The ribbons and the bow are made with sugar paste strips. Everything was sprinkled with icing sugar.

This Christmas decoration makes a great gift. Place a few biscuits on a paper plate decorated with Christmas motifs and put the prepared decoration in the centre. Place the plate on a large piece of cellophane. Pull the corners of the foil together with one hand while collecting the remaining foil with the other hand. Tie with a ribbon. Hey presto! A really attractive Christmas gift!

MULLED WINE

*A warming and aromatic drink that you can easily make at home!
A combination of cinnamon, nutmeg, cloves and citrus makes it taste rich
and deep – perfect not just for the holidays.*

Difficulty	Serves	Preparation	Cooking	Resting	Total
SIMPLE	4	5 MIN	~10 MIN	5 MIN	~20 MIN

INGREDIENTS

- ☐ 750ml red wine *(Note 1)*
- ☐ 100ml raspberry juice *(Note 2)*
- ☐ 6 cloves
- ☐ 2 allspice berries
- ☐ 1 whole star anise
- ☐ 1 orange
- ☐ 1 tbsp sugar
- ☐ 1 tbsp honey
- ☐ 1 tsp ground cinnamon
- ☐ 1 tsp ground nutmeg
- ☐ 1 tsp ground ginger *(Note 3)*

 Polish products differ from the ones available locally. You will find more information about allspice in the chapter "About the products" on page 328.

DIRECTIONS

Preparing the wine
1. Put the hob on low heat.
2. Pour the wine into a medium saucepan and heat.
3. Rinse an orange and cut into 6 segments.
4. Prick each segment with a fork. *(Note 4)*
5. Squeeze each segment to release juice into the saucepan with the wine.
6. Add the segments of orange to the wine.
7. Add the sugar, honey and spices: cloves, allspice, star anise, cinnamon, nutmeg and ginger.
8. Mix well.
9. Add the raspberry juice.
10. Keep stirring, so that the sugar and honey dissolve.
11. Warm until the wine is hot. This can take around 10 minutes. *(Note 5)*
12. Remove from the heat and set aside for around 5 minutes.

To serve
1. Put a portion of wine in a mug.
2. Add 1 segment of orange.

NOTES

1. You can use sweet or semi-sweet red wine.
2. You can swap raspberry juice for cherry juice. You will find a recipe for raspberry juice in the "Pantry" chapter.
3. Instead of ground ginger you can add 3 slices of peeled fresh ginger.
4. It will be easier to squeeze the juice from the oranges this way.
5. Be careful not to bring the wine to a boil.

KITCHEN ACCESSORIES

- ☐ medium saucepan
- ☐ knife
- ☐ chopping board
- ☐ 2 tablespoons
- ☐ 3 teaspoons
- ☐ fork

GOOD TO KNOW

 vegetarian

 gluten-free

 contains alcohol
- contains red wine

 kcal
- 307 per serving, 1228 total

GOES WELL WITH

 **Raspberry Juice**
11. Pantry, page 295

Christmas

11. PANTRY

I'm sure that in many families the kitchen is considered the heart of the home – not only because that's where the most pleasant aromas come from, but also because it is a place to spend time together and share freshly prepared meals; culinary tips and family recipes. Slightly underestimated, but no less important is the pantry - this is where we collect seasonal preserves and jars full of the flavours of summer and early autumn.

I remember grandma Emilia's pantry filled with jars of sour gherkins and sweet cherry *kompot*, which she served with *obiad*. In my family home, my mother also fills the shelves with various delicacies – just like my grandmother, she prepares sour gherkins, delicious pickled gherkins and a cucumber and carrot salad.

Right next to the vegetable preserves, there are jars filled with seasonal fruit – it would not be possible if we didn't have an orchard next to our house. The pantry is filled with sliced apples from our apple tree, which taste wonderful in apple pies, and delicious jam made from hand-picked purple plums.

In my family we work together to make preserves – there wouldn't be as many jars on our shelves if it wasn't for aunty Mary and our neighbours. We all grow vegetables and take care of fruit, and if someone has a glut of cucumbers, plums or beetroot in a given year, they share the surplus with others – this way we can all enjoy delicious, natural preserves.

Making your own preserves not only allows you to stock-up for winter – jars have become a part of Polish culture. When children move away from their parents, go to university or simply move to another city, when they come back to visit, they often receive treats from their mothers which are enclosed in jars. I receive such delicious gifts myself – even though I live in the UK, before Christmas I usually get a parcel from my mum with jars of my favourite preserves.

I hope that the recipes you find in this chapter encourage you to make your own preserves and capture the flavour of summer in jars!

TEA-BOILED HAM

A homemade, tender ham boiled in black tea with aromatic spices. Delicious on a sandwich for breakfast or as an ingredient in soups and stews.

Difficulty	Makes	Preparation	Resting	Cooking	Total
INTERMEDIATE	800 G	15 MIN	2,5 DAYS	1 H 30 MIN	4 DAYS

INGREDIENTS

For the meat
- 1kg pork loin *(Note 1)*
- 30g pickling salt *(Note 2)*
- 20g salt

For the brine
- 5 allspice berries
- 4 garlic cloves
- 4 tea bags (black tea)
- 3 bay leaves
- 1 tbsp Vegeta seasoning
- 1 tsp peppercorns
- 2 litres water

 Polish products differ from the ones available locally. You will find more information about allspice, pork and Vegeta in the chapter "About the products" on page 328.

DIRECTIONS

Day 1: evening *(Note 3)*
Preparing the pork – part 1
1. Add both salts to a small bowl.
2. Mix well.
3. Put the pork on a chopping board.
4. Rub the pork with the salt.
5. Put into a large bowl.
6. Put the bowl in the fridge for 48 hours.

Day 3: evening
Preparing the pork – part 2
1. Take the pork from the fridge.
2. Rinse well.
3. Using the instructions given in the panel, place the pork in a net.
4. Set the prepared pork aside.

Preparing the brine
1. Pour the water into a large saucepan.
2. Add the tea bags.
3. Crush the garlic and add to the saucepan. *(Note 4)*
4. Add the spices: Vegeta, allspice, bay leaves and peppercorns.

Preparing the ham – part 1
1. Put the hob on medium heat.
2. Bring the brine to a boil.
3. Put the pork into the boiling brine.
4. Reduce the heat and simmer semi-covered for around 1.5 hours.
5. Turn off the hob.
6. Leave the pork in the saucepan and set aside, allowing the brine to cool completely. *(Note 5)*

INSTRUCTIONS

To place pork into a net, follow the instructions:

Cut the net to the length of the pork plus 30cm.

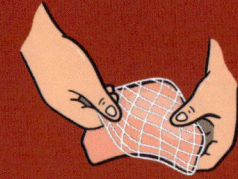

With your other hand, pull the net over the pork, removing the net from your first hand.

Tie one end of the net.

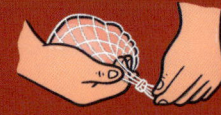

Tie the net on the other side.

Pull the net over one hand, holding the tied end in your fingers.

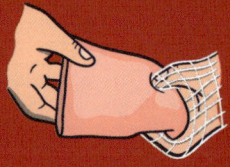

Hold the pork firmly with the hand in the net.

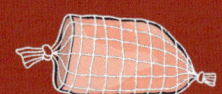

The pork is now ready for boiling.

Day 4: morning
Preparing the ham – part 2
1. Take the ham out of the brine.
2. Dry with a paper towel.
3. Remove the net from the ham.

To serve
- The ham will be perfect on sandwiches with <u>pickled peppers</u>.
- Alternatively, serve with:
  - <u>pickled mushroom salad</u>
  - <u>*sałatka jarzynowa* (Polish vegetable salad)</u>

NOTES

1. You can replace the pork loin with the same amount of pork neck or leg/ham.
2. Pickling salt can be replaced by salt without Anti-Caking Agent.
3. It is better to prepare the pork in the evening since it must remain in salt for 2 days (48 hours). After this time, it needs to be cooked and then left to cool completely overnight.
4. You don't have to peel the garlic.
5. I recommend you cover the saucepan with the lid and leave to completely cool overnight. In the morning you can take the ham out.

KITCHEN ACCESSORIES

- ☐ large saucepan with lid
- ☐ large bowl
- ☐ small bowl
- ☐ knife
- ☐ chopping board
- ☐ tablespoon
- ☐ teaspoon
- ☐ scissors
- ☐ meat net
- ☐ kitchen scale
- ☐ paper towel

GOOD TO KNOW

gluten-free

contains pork
- contains pork loin

fridge
- for up to 5 days

kcal
- 1789 total

GOES WELL WITH

Pickled Mushroom Salad
6. Party Food, page 31

***Sałatka Jarzynowa*
(Polish Vegetable Salad)**
9. Easter, page 167

Pickled Peppers
11. Pantry, page 275

Pantry

BEEF AND POULTRY PASZTET

A delicious homemade pasztet (pâté).
Perfect as an appetiser or on a sandwich in the morning.
The mixture of beef and poultry makes for a layered, yet delicate flavour.

Difficulty	Serves	Preparation	Cooking	Resting	Baking	Total
INTERMEDIATE	12	1 H	1 H 30 MIN	1 H	40 MIN	4 H 10 MIN

INGREDIENTS

For the broth
- ☐ 800g beef knuckle off the bone
- ☐ 4 chicken thighs (~800g)
- ☐ 2 parsnips (~200g)
- ☐ 2 carrots (~250g)
- ☐ 1 piece of celeriac (~300g)
- ☐ 20cm piece of leek
  (both white and green parts, ~100g)
- ☐ 1 onion (~150g)
- ☐ 4 garlic cloves
- ☐ 3 allspice berries
- ☐ 2 bay leaves
- ☐ 2 tsp salt
- ☐ ~2 litres water

For the *pasztet*
- ☐ 2 bread rolls
- ☐ 2 large eggs
- ☐ 2-3 tbsp breadcrumbs (optional) *(Note 1)*
- ☐ salt to taste
- ☐ pepper to taste

For the loaf tins
- ☐ 1 tsp butter

 Polish products differ from the ones available locally. You will find more information about allspice and beef in the chapter "About the products" on page 328.

DIRECTIONS

Preparing the meat
1. Cut the beef into smaller pieces.
2. Put into a large pot.
3. Add the chicken thighs into the pot.

Preparing the onion
1. Peel the onion and cut in half.
2. Put on the gas, cut side down and burn on the flame. This can take around 4-5 minutes. *(Note 2)*
3. Put the burnt onion into the pot with the meat.
4. While waiting, prepare the rest of the vegetables.

Preparing the vegetables
1. Peel the carrot, parsnip and piece of celeriac.
2. Cut the vegetables in half and put into the pot along with the meat and burnt onion.
3. Take the outer leaves off the leek and cut off any withered parts.
4. Cut and keep around 20cm of the middle part of the leek and rinse to remove the grit.
5. Slice the kept section of leek into 3 smaller pieces.
6. Transfer to the pot.
7. Peel the garlic and put into the pot.

Preparing the broth
1. Cover the meat and vegetables with water (around 1.5-2 litres).
2. Add the bay leaves and allspice.
3. Add the salt.
4. Put the hob on medium heat.
5. Bring the water to a boil.
6. Reduce the heat and simmer semi-covered for around 1.5 hours.
7. Check the water level when simmering and refill if too much water has evaporated. There should be enough water to cover all the ingredients.
8. After around 1.5 hours of simmering, check if the meat is soft. Be careful: the meat will be very hot! *(Note 3)*
9. After cooking the broth, strain into a separate large pot.
10. Put the boiled meat and vegetables on big plates and wait until cool enough to handle. This can take around 20 minutes. *(Note 4)*
11. Wait for the stock to cool and the fat to rise to the surface. This can take around 1 hour.

Preparing the loaf tins
1. Using scissors, cut the baking paper as a single sheet, to cover the bottom and inner sides of the loaf tins.
2. Brush the loaf tins with butter so the paper sticks.
3. Line both with the baking paper.
4. Set aside.

Preparing the *pasztet*
1. Pour the fat from the broth into a medium saucepan.
2. Cut the buns in half and add to the saucepan with the fat. *(Note 5)*
3. Using a fork, separate the meat from the bones and leave on the plate. *(Note 6)*
4. In a meat mincer with large holes, grind both types of meat together with the soaked bread. Tearing the buns into pieces helps.
5. Mix until everything is combined.
6. Grind again in a meat mincer with small holes.
7. Add salt and pepper to taste.
8. Mix well.
9. Crack the eggs into the bowl.
10. Mix thoroughly until everything is well combined and has a pâté consistency. *(Note 7)*
11. Put the mixture into the prepared tins.

Preparing the oven
1. Preheat the oven to 180°C / 350°F or gas 4.

Baking
1. Bake for around 40 minutes.
2. Place the baked *pasztet* on a cooling rack to cool down.

To serve
- Spread on a slice of your bread of choice.

NOTES

1. Only add the breadcrumbs if the filling is too loose (too watery).
2. You can also cut the onion into very thick slices and burn them in a frying pan (without any oil) which you put on low heat. This can take around 10 minutes.
3. When the meat is soft, you can turn off the heat. If not, cook it until it's tender.
4. You won't need the onions, leek and garlic, as well as the bay leaves and allspice berries. You'll need some of the broth to make the *pasztet*. You can use the rest, along with the vegetables, to prepare rosolnik. Just prepare drop noodles and chop some parsley. Alternatively use the remaining broth to make tomato soup or rosół with noodles. You can prepare a salad for 2 people with the remaining vegetables. Cube them and put into a bowl. Add 2 tablespoons of mayonnaise, a teaspoon of mustard and salt and pepper. Mix well.

5. Press the buns with a fork, so it absorbs the fat. Even if the buns are still dry, don't add more broth at this stage.
6. Warm meat falls off the bone very easily. It's going to be much more difficult when the meat is cold.
7. If the *pasztet* is too dry and doesn't stick together, gradually add a bit of broth, stirring every time. Don't add too much broth, so that the *pasztet* is not too wet. If the mixture is too watery, gradually add 1 tablespoon of breadcrumbs and mix thoroughly each time.

KITCHEN ACCESSORIES

- ☐ large pot with lid
- ☐ large pot
- ☐ medium saucepan
- ☐ bowl
- ☐ knife
- ☐ peeling knife
- ☐ chopping board
- ☐ 2 large plates
- ☐ tablespoon
- ☐ teaspoon
- ☐ fork
- ☐ meat mincer
- ☐ scissors
- ☐ sieve
- ☐ cooling rack
- ☐ 2 loaf tins (measured inside 23x13x7cm)
- ☐ baking paper

GOOD TO KNOW

contains dairy
- contains butter

contains beef
- contains boneless haunch of beef

fridge
- for up to 4 days

freezer
- for up to 3 months
- divide cold *pasztet* into portions and put into separate containers; then you can defrost the desired amount

kcal
- 379 per serving, 4548 total

GOES WELL WITH

Rosół with Noodles
vol 1, 2. Soups, page 45

Rosolnik with Drop Noodles
vol 1, 2. Soups, page 49

Tomato Soup
vol 1, 2. Soups, page 53

Drop Noodles
vol 1, 4. Sides, page 253

OGÓRKI KISZONE (SOUR GHERKINS)

These traditional horseradish, garlic and dill spiced cucumbers are delicious and a great way to preserve cucumbers for the year.

The ingredients listed here are for one large jar; however, when making *ogórki kiszone* you will usually make a large batch of jars in one go. It's a perfect recipe for using up a glut of cucumbers from the garden.

Difficulty	Makes	Preparation	Cooking	Total
SIMPLE	1 *	45 MIN	~15 MIN	~1 H **

INGREDIENTS

Proportions per one 900ml jar
For the cucumbers
- ~450g pickling cucumbers *(Notes 1 and 2)*
- 5cm piece of horseradish
- 1 sprig of dill *(Note 3)*
- 2 garlic cloves

For the brine
- 1 tbsp non-iodized salt *(Note 4)*
- water *(Note 5)*

For sterilising the jars and lids
- 2 litres water *(Note 6)*

 Polish products differ from the ones available locally. You will find more information about cucumbers, dill and horseradish in the chapter "About the products" on page 328.

DIRECTIONS

Preparing the jars – part 1
1. Put the hob on medium heat.
2. Pour the water into a medium saucepan or kettle and bring to a boil.

Preparing the ingredients – part 1
1. Transfer the cucumbers to the sink.
2. Clean and rinse. *(Note 7)*
3. Put the cucumbers into a large bowl.
4. Peel and slice the horseradish.
5. Transfer to a bowl.
6. Rinse the sprig of dill.
7. Cut into 5cm pieces.
8. Leave on the chopping board.
9. Peel the garlic.
10. Leave on the chopping board.

Preparing the jars – part 2
1. Wash the jars and lids.
2. Leave in the sink.
3. When the water starts boiling, carefully pour the boiling water into and over the cleaned jars and lids.
4. Pour the water out and allow the jars to cool.

---

* *use this recipe to calculate how many jars you will be making*
** *without the time needed for fermentation*

Preparing the ingredients – part 2
1. Place three of the dill pieces into the bottom of each jar.
2. Add the garlic and horseradish.
3. Pack the cucumbers tightly into each jar leaving around 2cm between the top of the cucumbers and top of the jar.

Preparing the brine
1. Fill and cover the cucumbers in the jars with water. Leaving about 2cm of space at the top.
2. Pour the water from each jar into a large pot. *(Note 8)*
3. Calculate and add the salt. *(Note 9)*
4. Put the hob on medium heat.
5. Bring the brine to a boil. *(Note 10)*

Preparing the sour gherkins
1. Fill and cover the cucumbers in each jar with the brine. Leaving about 2cm of space at the top.
2. Close each jar tightly. *(Note 11)*
3. Put each jar upside down. *(Note 12)*
4. Leave to cool completely.
5. Turn right way up and set aside. *(Note 13)*
6. After 2 days put into the pantry. *(Note 14)*
7. *Ogórki kiszone* are ready after around 1 month.

To serve
- *Ogórki kiszone* can be served with:
  - *oscypek* with cranberries and *boczek*
  - *kotlety schabowe*
  - minced pork patties
  - meatballs in mushroom sauce
  - egg patties
  - *zrazy*
- *Ogórki kiszone* can also be added to the following dishes:
  - pickled mushroom salad
  - *sałatka jarzynowa* (Polish vegetable salad)
  - stuffed eggs with tuna
  - sour gherkin soup
  - Polish stroganoff

NOTES

1. The number of cucumbers depends on how many can fit into each jar.
2. The best cucumbers are the young ones, since they have small seeds. They are also easier to put into jars. Big cucumbers have bigger seeds and might be hollow inside. Check your cucumbers for any damage or discoloration that could cause them to go bad. You can use damaged cucumbers for sandwiches or *mizeria*.
3. You can use any type of dill.
4. You can use iodized or non-iodized salt. Thanks to non-iodized salt, you can keep the pickles in a jar for longer than one year (even two to three years). Iodized salt accelerates the rusting of the lids from the inside. Therefore, you can only store such cucumbers for about one year. Don't use salt that has additional ingredients.
5. The amount of water will depend on the number of cucumbers you prepare. The recipe will guide you on how to calculate how much water is required.
6. You will need enough water to sterilise the inside and outside of the jars and lids.
7. Remove any wilted parts of the cucumber flowers that may be located at one end of the vegetable.
8. The pot should be large enough to contain the water from all the jars.
9. Add one tablespoon of salt per jar.
10. Hot brine will soften the cucumbers. It will speed up the fermentation process and the preserves won't need to be pasteurised.
11. When you pour hot brine into the jars, they will warm up very quickly. To avoid burns when closing them, hold them in one hand with a tea towel. This will allow you to easily twist the lids with your other hand.
12. Check if any of the jars are hissing. If they are, it means the lid is not tight. Replace the lid and check again.

13. Set aside into a warm place for 2 days to begin the fermentation process.
14. Store in a cool, dark place.

KITCHEN ACCESSORIES

- ☐ large pot
- ☐ medium saucepan
- ☐ large bowl
- ☐ bowl
- ☐ knife
- ☐ peeling knife
- ☐ chopping board
- ☐ tablespoon
- ☐ tea towel
- ☐ jars with lids (900ml)

GOOD TO KNOW

 vegetarian

 vegan

 gluten-free

 fridge
- after opening use within five days and store in the fridge

 pantry
- store for 1-3 years

 kcal
- 88 per jar (900ml)

GOES WELL WITH

 *Oscypek* with Cranberries and *Boczek*
6. Party Food, page 15

 **Pickled Mushroom Salad**
6. Party Food, page 31

 *Sałatka Jarzynowa* (Polish Vegetable Salad)
9. Easter, page 167

 **Stuffed Eggs with Tuna**
9. Easter, page 176

 **Sour Gherkin Soup**
vol 1, 2. Soups, page 61

 **Polish Stroganoff**
vol 1, 2. Soups, page 89

 *Kotlety Schabowe*
vol 1, 3. Obiad, page 99

 **Minced Pork Patties**
vol 1, 3. Obiad, page 103

 **Meatballs in Mushroom Sauce**
vol 1, 3. Obiad, page 107

 **Egg Patties**
vol 1, 3. Obiad, page 111

 *Zrazy*
vol 1, 3. Obiad, page 129

 *Mizeria*
vol 1, 4. Sides, page 211

OGÓRKI KONSERWOWE (PICKLED GHERKINS)

*Uniquely flavoured pickled gherkins with garlic, dill and spices.
The delicious spiced pickling liquid raises them to the next level!*

The ingredients listed here are for one large jar; however, when making *ogórki konserwowe* you will usually make a large batch of jars in one go. It's a perfect recipe for using up a glut of cucumbers from the garden.

Difficulty	Makes	Preparation	Cooking	Pasteurisation	Total
SIMPLE	1 *	45 MIN	~15 MIN	3 MIN	~1 H

INGREDIENTS

Proportions per one 900ml jar
For the cucumbers
- ~450g pickling cucumbers *(Notes 1 and 2)*
- 5cm piece of horseradish
- 2 garlic cloves
- 1 sprig of dill *(Note 3)*
- 6 peppercorns
- 4 allspice berries
- 2 bay leaves
- ½ tsp mustard seeds
- ½ tsp salt

Proportions per 1 litre of water *(Note 4)*
For the pickling liquid
- 220g sugar
- 1 litre water *(Note 5)*
- 250ml 10% spirit vinegar

For sterilising the jars and lids
- ~2 litres water *(Note 6)*

 Polish products differ from the ones available locally. You will find more information about allspice, cucumbers, dill and horseradish in the chapter "About the products" on page 328.

DIRECTIONS

Preparing the jars – part 1
1. Put the hob on medium heat.
2. Pour the water into a medium saucepan or kettle and bring to a boil.

Preparing the ingredients – part 1
1. Transfer the cucumbers to the sink.
2. Clean and rinse. *(Note 7)*
3. Put the cucumbers into a large bowl.
4. Peel and slice the horseradish.
5. Transfer to a bowl.
6. Rinse the sprig of dill.
7. Cut into 5cm pieces.
8. Leave on the chopping board.
9. Peel the garlic.
10. Leave on the chopping board.

Preparing the jars – part 2
1. Wash the jars and lids.
2. Leave in the sink.
3. When the water starts boiling, carefully pour the boiling water into and over the cleaned jars and lids.
4. Pour the water out and allow the jars to cool.

* *use this recipe to calculate how many jars you will be making*

Preparing the ingredients – part 2
1. Place three of the dill pieces into the bottom of each jar.
2. Add the garlic and horseradish.
3. Pack the cucumbers tightly into each jar leaving around 2cm between the top of the cucumbers and top of the jar. *(Note 8)*

Preparing the pickling liquid
1. Fill and cover the cucumbers in the jars with water. Leaving about 2cm of space at the top.
2. Pour the water from each jar via a measuring jug into a large pot. Take note of the amount of water used. *(Note 9)*
3. Calculate and add the vinegar and sugar. *(Note 10)*
4. Put the hob on medium heat.
5. Bring the pickling liquid to a boil.
6. Boil for around 3 minutes.
7. Stir from time to time to dissolve the sugar.
8. While waiting, add the spices to the jars.

Preparing the ingredients – part 3
1. To the jars add the spices: allspice berries, bay leaves, mustard seeds, peppercorns and salt.

Preparing the pickled gherkins
1. Fill and cover the cucumbers in each jar with the pickling liquid. Leaving about 2cm of space at the top.
2. Close each jar tightly. *(Note 11)*
3. Pasteurise for around 3 minutes. Information about the pasteurisation process can be found on page 342. *(Note 12)*
4. Lay a tea towel on the kitchen counter.
5. Turn off the hob after around 3 minutes of pasteurisation.
6. Put the jars on the prepared tea towel. Be careful: they will be very hot! *(Note 13)*
7. Leave to cool completely.
8. The pickled gherkins are ready to eat right after being pasteurised, but they taste best after around a week.

To serve
- Pickled gherkins can be served with:
  - minced pork patties
  - meatballs in mushroom sauce
  - egg patties
  - *zrazy*
- Pickled gherkins can also be added to the following dishes:
  - tuna salad
  - pickled mushroom salad
  - stuffed eggs with tuna
  - Polish stroganoff
  - Hungarian goulash
  - pizza

NOTES

1. The number of cucumbers depends on how many can fit into each jar.
2. The best cucumbers are the young ones, since they have small seeds. They are also easier to put into jars. Big cucumbers have bigger seeds and might be hollow inside. Check your cucumbers for any damage or discoloration that could cause them to go bad. You can use damaged cucumbers for sandwiches or *mizeria*.
3. You can use any type of dill.
4. The amount of pickling liquid needed for the cucumbers will depend on the amount of water that you will measure when filling the jars later on in the recipe.
5. The amount of water will depend on the number of cucumbers you prepare. The recipe will guide you on how to calculate how much water is required.
6. You will need enough water to sterilise the inside and outside of the jars and lids.
7. Remove any wilted parts of the cucumber flowers that may be located at one end of the vegetable.
8. Don't add the spices yet, so as to not pour them out of the jar when measuring the water.
9. The pot should be large enough to contain the water from all the jars.
10. Proportionately measure how much vinegar and sugar you will need for the obtained amount of water.

11. When you pour hot pickling liquid into the jars, they will warm up very quickly. To avoid burns when closing them, hold them in one hand with a tea towel. This will allow you to easily twist the lids with your other hand.
12. The difference to normal pasteurisation is that from the moment the water with the jars starts boiling, you should only cook it for around 3 minutes. The short pasteurisation time will allow the pickled gherkins to remain crisp.
13. When you take out the jars, it's best to use a kitchen glove so as not to get burnt.

KITCHEN ACCESSORIES

- large pot
- medium saucepan
- large bowl
- bowl
- measuring jug

- knife
- peeling knife
- chopping board
- tablespoon
- teaspoon

- kitchen glove
- tea towel
- jars with lids (900ml)

GOOD TO KNOW

 vegetarian

 vegan

 gluten-free

 fridge
- after opening use within five days and store in the fridge

 pantry
- store up to 1 year

 kcal
- 240 per jar (900ml)

GOES WELL WITH

 **Tuna Salad**
6. Party Food, page 23

 **Pickled Mushroom Salad**
6. Party Food, page 31

 **Stuffed Eggs with Tuna**
9. Easter, page 176

 **Polish Stroganoff**
vol 1, 2. Soups, page 89

 **Minced Pork Patties**
vol 1, 3. Obiad, page 103

 **Meatballs in Mushroom Sauce**
vol 1, 3. Obiad, page 107

 **Egg Patties**
vol 1, 3. Obiad, page 111

 **Hungarian Goulash**
vol 1, 3. Obiad, page 119

 *Zrazy*
vol 1, 3. Obiad, page 129

 **Michał's Pizza**
vol 1, 3. Obiad, page 191

 *Mizeria*
vol 1, 4. Sides, page 211

TOMATO PURÉE

*A great way to preserve the unique taste of fresh tomatoes in a jar.
Purée without any additives is an excellent base
for a multitude of tomato-based dishes.*

Difficulty	Makes	Preparation	Cooking	Pasteurisation	Total
SIMPLE	7 *	30 MIN	~15 MIN	15 MIN	~1 H

INGREDIENTS

For the purée
- ~1.3kg tomatoes
- 3 litres water

For sterilising the jars and lids
- ~2 litres water *(Note 1)*

DIRECTIONS

Preparing the jars
1. Put the hob on medium heat.
2. Pour the water into a medium saucepan or kettle and bring to a boil.
3. Wash the jars and lids.
4. Leave in the sink.
5. When the water starts boiling, carefully pour the boiling water into and over the cleaned jars and lids.
6. Pour the water out and allow the jars to cool.

Preparing the tomatoes
1. Put the hob on medium heat.
2. Pour the water into a large pot and bring to a boil.
3. Using a sharp knife, make a cross on top of every tomato – don't go too deep.
4. Set the tomatoes aside.
5. When the water is boiling, turn off the heat.
6. Using a spoon, carefully place the tomatoes into the pot.
7. Leave in the boiled water for 2-3 minutes.
8. Pour the hot water out of the pot and cover the tomatoes with cold water.
9. Set aside in the cold water for 2 minutes.
10. Pour the water out.
11. Peel the tomatoes.
12. Cut out the green stem.
13. Cut in half and then into quarters.
14. Put the tomatoes in a bowl.

---

* 7 jars (300ml each)

Preparing the tomato purée
1. Using a hand blender, blend the tomatoes to get a uniform consistency.
2. Pour the purée into jars. Leaving about 2cm of space at the top.
3. Close each jar tightly.
4. Pasteurise for around 15 minutes. Information about the pasteurisation process can be found on page 342. *(Note 2)*

Use as an ingredient
- Use tomato purée for various sauces, soups and pastas.
- Perfect for:
    - tomato soup
    - sauce for unrolled *gołąbki*
    - tomato sauce

NOTES

1. You will need enough water to sterilise the inside and outside of the jars and lids.
2. Pasteurising time depends on the size of the jar.

KITCHEN ACCESSORIES

- ☐ large pot
- ☐ bowl
- ☐ knife
- ☐ chopping board

- ☐ tablespoon
- ☐ hand blender
- ☐ 7 jars with lids (300ml)

GOOD TO KNOW

 vegetarian

 vegan

 gluten-free

 kcal
- 434 per jar (300ml), 238 total

 fridge
- without pasteurisation, store in the refrigerator for up to 3 days

 pantry
- transfer the purée into jars
- you can pasteurise the jars and store them in the pantry up to 1 year

GOES WELL WITH

 **Tomato Soup**
vol 1, 2. Soups, page 53

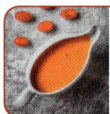 **Tomato Sauce**
vol 1, 4. Sides, page 247

 **Unrolled *Gołąbki***
vol 1, 3. Obiad, page 169

PICKLED BEETROOT

Easy marinated beetroot – just four ingredients and the pickling liquid! These are a fantastic addition to meat dishes or a cheese platter.

The ingredients listed here are for one large jar; however, when making pickled beetroot you will usually make a large batch of jars in one go. It's a perfect recipe for using up a glut of beetroot from the garden.

Difficulty	Makes	Preparation	Cooking	Resting	Pasteurisation	Total
INTERMEDIATE	1 *	20 MIN	45 MIN	~45 MIN	20 MIN	~2 H 10 MIN

INGREDIENTS

Proportions per one 900ml jar
For the beetroot
- ☐ 1kg beetroot *(Note 1)*
- ☐ 8 allspice berries
- ☐ 3 bay leaves
- ☐ 1 tsp caraway seeds
- ☐ 1 litre water *(Note 2)*

Proportions per 1 litre of water *(Note 3)*
For the pickling liquid
- ☐ 220g sugar
- ☐ 1 tbsp salt
- ☐ 250ml 10% spirit vinegar
- ☐ 1 litre water *(Note 4)*

For sterilising the jars and lids
- ☐ ~2 litres water *(Note 5)*

 Polish products differ from the ones available locally. You will find more information about allspice and caraway in the chapter "About the products" on page 328.

DIRECTIONS

Preparing the beetroot – part 1 *(Note 6)*
1. Cut the leaves off the beetroot and trim both ends.
2. Rinse the beetroot.
3. Transfer the beetroot into a large pot. *(Note 7)*
4. Put the hob on medium heat.
5. Pour the water into the pot and bring to a boil. *(Note 8)*
6. Reduce the heat and simmer semi-covered for around 45 minutes from the moment of boiling. *(Note 9)*

Preparing the jars
1. Put the hob on medium heat.
2. Pour the water into a medium saucepan or kettle and bring to a boil.
3. Wash the jars and lids.
4. Leave in the sink.
5. When the water starts boiling, carefully pour the boiling water into and over the cleaned jars and lids.
6. Pour the water out and allow the jars to cool.

* use this recipe to calculate how many jars you will be making

Preparing the beetroot – part 2
1. Check if the beetroot is soft. *(Note 10)*
2. Drain the water after the beetroot is cooked.
3. Cover with cold water.
4. Set aside for 10 minutes.
5. Pour the water out.
6. Peel when cold enough to handle.

Preparing the ingredients – part 1
1. Put the beetroot into each jar leaving around 2cm between the top of the beetroot and top of the jar. *(Note 11)*

Preparing the pickling liquid
1. Fill and cover the beetroot in the jars with water. Leaving about 2cm of space at the top.
2. Pour the water from each jar via a measuring jug into a large pot. Taking note of the amount of water used. *(Note 12)*
3. Calculate and add the vinegar, sugar and salt. *(Note 13)*
4. Put the hob on medium heat.
5. Bring the pickling liquid to a boil.
6. Boil for around 3 minutes.
7. Stir from time to time to dissolve the sugar.
8. While waiting, add the spices to the jars.

Preparing the ingredients – part 2
1. To the jars, add the spices: caraway, allspice and bay leaves.

Preparing pickled beetroot
1. Fill and cover the beetroot in each jar with the pickling liquid. Leaving about 2cm of space at the top.
2. Close each jar tightly. *(Note 14)*
3. Pasteurise for around 20 minutes. Information about the pasteurisation process can be found on page 342. *(Note 15)*
4. Beetroots are ready to eat right after being pasteurised.

Use as an ingredient
- Pickled beetroot can be added to salads, as well as to:
  - sweet beetroot ćwikła
  - beetroot and horseradish ćwikła
  - apple and caraway beetroot ćwikła
  - warm beetroot ćwikła

NOTES

1. It's best if the beetroot are medium sized, so that they fit in the jar. Then they will also cook at the same time.
2. The amount of water will depend on the size of the saucepan and beetroot. The water has to cover the beetroot completely.
3. The amount of pickling liquid needed for the beetroot will depend on the amount of water that you will measure when filling the jars later on in the recipe.
4. The amount of water will depend on the amount of beetroot you prepare. The recipe will guide you on how to calculate how much water is required.
5. You will need enough water to sterilise the inside and outside of the jars and lids.
6. You can put on an apron and rubber gloves to prevent being stained by the beetroot – the stains are difficult to remove!
7. The pot should be large enough to contain all the beetroot.
8. The amount of water will depend on the size of the pot and beetroot. The water has to cover the beetroot completely.
9. Cooking time will depend on the size of the beetroot. Small beetroot (the size of a large egg) will need around 45 minutes and bigger ones around 1 hour.

10. Put a fork in a beetroot that's boiling. If it goes in easily, the beetroot is ready. If not, cook for 5-10 more minutes, checking if they are soft from time to time.
11. Don't add the spices yet, so as to not pour them out of the jar when measuring the water.
12. The pot should be large enough to contain the water from all the jars.
13. Proportionately measure how much vinegar and sugar you will need for the obtained amount of water.
14. When you pour hot pickling liquid into the jars, they will warm up very quickly. To avoid burns when closing them, hold them in one hand with a tea towel. This will allow you to easily twist the lids with your other hand.
15. Pasteurising time depends on the size of the jar.

KITCHEN ACCESSORIES

- ☐ large pot with lid
- ☐ medium saucepan
- ☐ measuring jug
- ☐ knife
- ☐ peeling knife
- ☐ chopping board
- ☐ tablespoon
- ☐ teaspoon
- ☐ fork
- ☐ apron (optional)
- ☐ rubber gloves (optional)
- ☐ tea towel
- ☐ jars with lids (900ml)

GOOD TO KNOW

 vegetarian

 vegan

 gluten-free

 fridge
- after opening use within five days and store in the fridge

 pantry
- store up to 1 year

 kcal
- 688 per jar (900ml)

GOES WELL WITH

Sweet Beetroot *Ćwikła*
Beetroot and Horseradish *Ćwikła*
Apple and Caraway Beetroot *Ćwikła*
Warm Beetroot *Ćwikła*
vol 1, 4. Sides, pages 201-208

PICKLED PEPPERS

Homemade pickled peppers bursting with amazing flavours, with cloves, allspice, bay leaves and mustard seeds. Perfect with one pot wonders and on sandwiches.

Difficulty	Makes	Preparation	Cooking	Pasteurisation	Total
SIMPLE	5 *	45 MIN	~15 MIN	10 MIN	~1 H 10 MIN

INGREDIENTS

For the peppers
☐ 1.5kg peppers

Proportions per one 0.5 litre jar
Spices
☐ 4 cloves
☐ 4 allspice berries
☐ 2 bay leaves
☐ ½ tsp mustard seeds
☐ ½ tsp salt

Proportions per 1 litre of water *(Note 1)*
For the pickling liquid
☐ 220g sugar
☐ 1 litre water *(Note 2)*
☐ 250ml 10% spirit vinegar

For sterilising the jars and lids
☐ ~2 litres water *(Note 3)*

 Polish products differ from the ones available locally. You will find more information about allspice in the chapter "About the products" on page 328.

DIRECTIONS

Preparing the jars – part 1
1. Put the hob on medium heat.
2. Pour the water into a medium saucepan or kettle and bring to a boil.

Preparing the ingredients – part 1
1. Rinse the peppers and remove the stalks.
2. Cut in half and remove the white parts and seeds.
3. Slice into thin, 2cm wide strips.
4. Put into the bowl and set aside.

Preparing the jars – part 2
1. Wash the jars and lids.
2. Leave in the sink.
3. When the water starts boiling, carefully pour the boiling water into and over the cleaned jars and lids.
4. Pour the water out and allow the jars to cool.

Preparing the ingredients – part 2
1. Put the peppers into each jar leaving around 2cm between the top of the peppers and top of the jar. *(Note 4)*

---

* 5 jars (0.5 litre each)

Preparing the pickling liquid

1. Fill and cover the peppers in the jars with water. Leaving about 2cm of space at the top.
2. Pour the water from each jar via a measuring jug into a large pot. Take note of the amount of water used. *(Note 5)*
3. Calculate and add the vinegar and sugar. *(Note 6)*
4. Put the hob on medium heat.
5. Bring the pickling liquid to a boil.
6. Boil for around 3 minutes.
7. Stir from time to time to dissolve the sugar.
8. While waiting, add the spices to the jars.

Preparing the ingredients – part 3

1. To the jars add the spices: cloves, allspice berries, bay leaves, mustard seeds and salt.

Preparing the pickled peppers

1. Fill and cover the peppers in each jar with the pickling liquid. Leaving about 2cm of space at the top.
2. Close each jar tightly. *(Note 7)*
3. Pasteurise for around 10 minutes. Information about the pasteurisation process can be found on page 342. *(Note 8)*
4. The peppers are ready to eat right after being pasteurised.

To serve

- Pickled peppers can be served on sandwiches along with <u>tea-boiled ham</u>.
- Pickled peppers can also be added to the following dishes:
  - <u>sałatka jarzynowa (Polish vegetable salad)</u>
  - <u>Hungarian goulash</u>

NOTES

1. The amount of pickling liquid needed for the peppers will depend on the amount of water that you will measure when filling the jars later on in the recipe.
2. The amount of water will depend on the amount of peppers you prepare. The recipe will guide you on how to calculate how much water is required.
3. You will need enough water to sterilise the inside and outside of the jars and lids.
4. Don't add the spices yet, so as to not pour them out of the jar when measuring the water.
5. The pot should be large enough to contain the water from all the jars.
6. Proportionately measure how much vinegar and sugar you will need for the obtained amount of water.
7. When you pour hot pickling liquid into the jars, they will warm up very quickly. To avoid burns when closing them, hold them in one hand with a tea towel. This will allow you to easily twist the lids with your other hand.
8. Hot pickling liquid will soften the peppers; to prevent the peppers becoming too soft pasteurise the jars for 10 minutes.

KITCHEN ACCESSORIES

- ☐ large pot
- ☐ medium saucepan
- ☐ bowl
- ☐ measuring jug
- ☐ knife
- ☐ chopping board
- ☐ tablespoon
- ☐ teaspoon
- ☐ tea towel
- ☐ 5 jars with lids (500ml)

GOOD TO KNOW

 vegetarian

 vegan

 gluten-free

 fridge
- after opening use within five days and store in the fridge

 pantry
- store up to 1 year

 kcal
- 69 per jar (0.5 litre), 354 total

GOES WELL WITH

 *Sałatka Jarzynowa* **(Polish Vegetable Salad)**
9. Easter, page 167

 **Tea-Boiled Ham**
11. Pantry, page 251

 **Hungarian Goulash**
vol 1, 3. Obiad, page 119

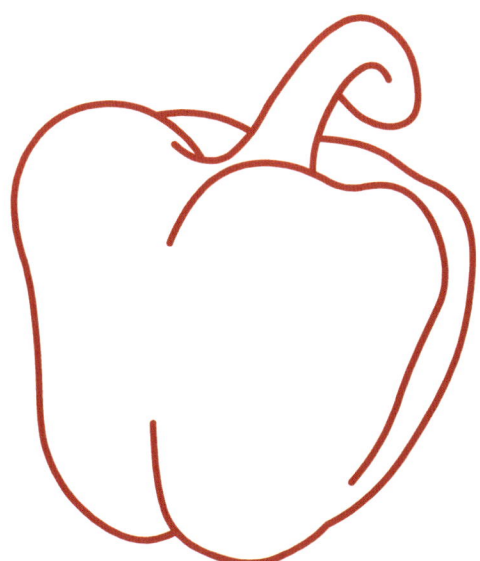

SEASONED RED CABBAGE

Seasoned red cabbage tastes delicious thanks to a combination of bay leaves, allspice berries and black peppercorns. It's a great side to many dishes.

Difficulty	Makes	Preparation	Resting	Cooking	Pasteurisation	Total
INTERMEDIATE	10 *	15 MIN	1 H	~30 MIN	15 MIN	~2 H

INGREDIENTS

For the cabbage
- ☐ 2 red cabbage (~2kg)
- ☐ 2 onions (~240g)
- ☐ 2 tbsp salt
- ☐ 1 tsp ground coriander *(Note 1)*

For the seasoning
- ☐ 220g sugar
- ☐ 6 peppercorns
- ☐ 5 allspice berries
- ☐ 3 bay leaves
- ☐ 1 litre water
- ☐ 250ml 10% spirit vinegar

For sterilising the jars and lids
- ☐ ~2 litres water *(Note 2)*

 Polish products differ from the ones available locally. You will find more information about allspice in the chapter "About the products" on page 328.

DIRECTIONS

Preparing the cabbage – part 1
1. Remove the outer leaves from the cabbage.
2. Cut in half and then into quarters.
3. Remove the core and finely chop the leaves. *(Note 3)*
4. Transfer the chopped cabbage to a large bowl.
5. Add the salt.
6. Mix well.
7. Set aside for around 1 hour.

Preparing the jars
1. Put the hob on medium heat.
2. Pour the water into a medium saucepan or kettle and bring to a boil.
3. Wash the jars and lids.
4. Leave in the sink.
5. When the water starts boiling, carefully pour the boiling water into and over the cleaned jars and lids.
6. Pour the water out and allow the jars to cool.

Preparing the onion
1. Peel the onion, cut in half and then into thin slices.
2. Leave on the chopping board and set aside.

---

* 10 jars (280ml each)

Preparing the cabbage – part 2
1. Squeeze the liquid out of the cabbage.
2. Transfer the cabbage to a separate large bowl.
3. Set the bowl aside.

Preparing seasoned red cabbage
1. Put the hob on medium heat.
2. Pour the water into a large pot and bring to a boil.
3. Add the vinegar and sugar.
4. Bring the seasoned liquid to a boil.
5. Boil for around 3 minutes.
6. Stir from time to time to dissolve the sugar.
7. Add the chopped onion.
8. Simmer for around 5 minutes.
9. Add the prepared cabbage and spices: peppercorns, allspice and bay leaves.
10. Simmer the cabbage semi-covered on medium heat for 15-20 minutes. *(Note 4)*
11. Stir from time to time.
12. After around 10 minutes add the coriander.
13. Mix well.
14. When the vegetables are ready, turn off and remove from the heat and set the pot aside.
15. Set aside to cool; the cabbage should remain warm. This can take around 30 minutes.
16. Put the cabbage into jars along with the seasoned liquid. Leaving about 2cm of space at the top.
17. Close each jar tightly.
18. Pasteurise for around 15 minutes. Information about the pasteurisation process can be found on page 342. *(Note 5)*
19. Cabbage is ready to eat right after being made. Using jars and pasteurising will allow the cabbage to be stored for longer.

To serve
- Red cabbage can be served with:
  - *kotlety schabowe*
  - minced pork patties
  - meatballs in mushroom sauce
  - egg patties
  - pork neck stew
  - *zrazy*
  - honey roast pork

NOTES
1. You can use coriander seeds, ground coriander or coriander leaves.
2. You will need enough water to sterilise the inside and outside of the jars and lids.
3. It's easier to do this step using a food processor, remove the core and cut the cabbage into smaller pieces before processing.
4. The cabbage should be crunchy, not overcooked. If it's not ready, cook for 5 more minutes and then taste it again. Be careful: the cabbage will be very hot!
5. Pasteurising time depends on the size of the jar.

KITCHEN ACCESSORIES
- ☐ large pot with lid
- ☐ medium saucepan
- ☐ 2 large bowls
- ☐ knife
- ☐ chopping board
- ☐ tablespoon
- ☐ teaspoon
- ☐ 10 jars with lids (280ml)

GOOD TO KNOW

 vegetarian

 vegan

 gluten-free

 fridge
- after opening use within five days and store in the fridge

 pantry
- store up to 1 year

 kcal
- 178 per jar (280ml), 1780 total

GOES WELL WITH

 **Kotlety Schabowe**
vol 1, 3. Obiad, page 99

 **Minced Pork Patties**
vol 1, 3. Obiad, page 103

 **Meatballs in Mushroom Sauce**
vol 1, 3. Obiad, page 107

 **Egg Patties**
vol 1, 3. Obiad, page 111

 **Pork Neck Stew**
vol 1, 3. Obiad, page 125

 **Zrazy**
vol 1, 3. Obiad, page 129

 **Honey Pork Roast**
vol 1, 3. Obiad, page 135

CUCUMBER AND CARROT SALAD

*A flavourful salad made with cucumbers,
carrots and onions with allspice berries and bay leaves.
A great way of preserving vegetables which can enrich every meal.*

Difficulty	Makes	Preparation	Resting	Cooking	Pasteurisation	Total
INTERMEDIATE	10 *	40 MIN	13 H	~30 MIN	20 MIN	~14 H 30 MIN

INGREDIENTS

For the salad
- ☐ 3kg pickling cucumbers
- ☐ 4 onions (~450g)
- ☐ 3 carrots (~400g)
- ☐ 2 tbsp salt
- ☐ 1 litre water

For the seasoning
- ☐ 220g sugar
- ☐ 5 allspice berries
- ☐ 4 bay leaves
- ☐ 1 litre water
- ☐ 250ml 10% spirit vinegar

For sterilising the jars and lids
- ☐ ~2 litres water *(Note 1)*

 Polish products differ from the ones available locally. You will find more information about allspice and cucumbers in the chapter "About the products" on page 328.

DIRECTIONS

The day before pouring the salad into jars: evening *(Note 2)*

Preparing the cucumbers and onions – part 1
1. Transfer the cucumbers to the sink.
2. Clean and rinse. *(Note 3)*
3. Cut the ends on both sides and slice into 2-3mm slices. *(Note 4)*
4. Transfer the sliced cucumbers into a large bowl.
5. Add the salt.
6. Mix well.
7. Check if the cucumbers are slightly too salty.
8. Set the bowl aside.
9. Peel the onion, cut in half and then into thin slices.
10. Add to the bowl with the cucumbers.
11. Mix well.
12. Put the bowl in the fridge for around 12 hours.

Preparation day

Preparing the jars – part 1
1. Put the hob on medium heat.
2. Pour the water into a medium saucepan or kettle and bring to a boil.

---

* 10 jars (300ml each)

Preparing the carrots
1. Put the hob on medium heat.
2. Pour the water into a large saucepan and bring to a boil.
3. Peel the carrots and cut into 2mm slices.
4. Put into the saucepan.
5. When the water starts boiling, boil the carrots for around 5 minutes. *(Note 5)*
6. Drain the cooked carrots and place into a separate large bowl.
7. Set aside.

Preparing the jars – part 2
1. Wash the jars and lids.
2. Leave in the sink.
3. When the water starts boiling, carefully pour the boiling water into and over the cleaned jars and lids.
4. Pour the water out and allow the jars to cool.

Preparing the cucumbers and onions – part 2
1. Take the cucumbers and onions from the fridge.
2. Squeeze the water out.
3. Transfer into the bowl with the carrots.
4. Set the bowl aside.

Preparing the salad
1. Put the hob on medium heat.
2. Pour the water into a large pot and bring to a boil.
3. Add the vinegar and sugar.
4. Bring the seasoned liquid to a boil.
5. Boil for around 3 minutes.
6. Stir from time to time to dissolve the sugar.
7. Add the sliced cucumbers with carrots and onions.
8. Add the bay leaves and allspice.
9. Simmer everything together for around 15 minutes.
10. Stir from time to time.
11. When the vegetables are ready, turn off and remove from the heat and set the pot aside.
12. Set aside to cool; the salad should remain warm. This can take around 30 minutes.
13. Put the salad into jars along with the seasoned liquid. Leaving about 2cm of space at the top.
14. Close each jar tightly.
15. Pasteurise for around 15 minutes. Information about the pasteurisation process can be found on page 342. *(Note 6)*
16. The salad is ready to eat right after being made. Using jars and pasteurising will allow the salad to be stored for longer.

To serve
- Cucumber and carrot salad is a great side for meat dishes as well as:
  - *kopytka (szagłówki)*
  - *leniwe*

NOTES
1. You will need enough water to sterilise the inside and outside of the jars and lids.
2. It's best to prepare the cucumbers and onions in the evening, so they can rest overnight (around 12 hours).
3. Remove any wilted parts of the cucumber flowers that may be located at one end of the vegetable.
4. Don't peel them.
5. The carrots should remain crunchy, as they keep cooking in the seasoned liquid.
6. Pasteurising time depends on the size of the jar.

KITCHEN ACCESSORIES

- ☐ large pot
- ☐ large saucepan
- ☐ medium saucepan
- ☐ 2 large bowls
- ☐ knife
- ☐ peeling knife
- ☐ chopping board
- ☐ tablespoon
- ☐ 10 jars with lids (300ml)

GOOD TO KNOW

 vegetarian

 vegan

 gluten-free

 fridge
- after opening use within five days and store in the fridge

 pantry
- store up to 1 year

 kcal
- 171 per jar (300ml), 1710 total

GOES WELL WITH

 *Kopytka (Szagłówki)*
v. 1, 5. Pierogi Festival, page 325

 *Leniwe*
v. 1, 5. Pierogi Festival, page 329

PICKLED VEGETABLE SALAD

*Traditional pickled gherkins with peppers, onions and carrots, seasoned with garlic, dill and horseradish.
A delicious addition to meat and vegetarian dishes.*

The ingredients listed here are for one large jar; however, when making pickled vegetable salad you will usually make a large batch of jars in one go. It's a perfect recipe for using up a glut of vegetables from the garden.

Difficulty	Makes	Preparation	Cooking	Pasteurisation	Total
SIMPLE	1 *	55 MIN	~5 MIN	20 MIN	~1 H 20 MIN

INGREDIENTS

Proportions per one 900ml jar
For the salad
- ☐ ~340g pickling cucumbers *(Notes 1 and 2)*
- ☐ 250g peppers
- ☐ 2 carrots (~250g)
- ☐ 1 onion (~150g)
- ☐ 1 garlic clove
- ☐ 1 sprig of dill
- ☐ 5cm piece of horseradish
- ☐ 1 litre water

Proportions per one 900ml jar
For the pickling liquid
- ☐ 5 tbsp 10% spirit vinegar
- ☐ 2 tbsp sugar
- ☐ 1 tsp salt
- ☐ ~500ml water *(Note 3)*

For sterilising the jars and lids
- ☐ ~2 litres water *(Note 4)*

 Polish products differ from the ones available locally. You will find more information about cucumbers, dill and horseradish in the chapter "About the products" on page 328.

DIRECTIONS

Preparing the carrots
1. Put the hob on medium heat.
2. Pour the water into a medium saucepan and bring to a boil.
3. Peel the carrots and cut into 2mm slices.
4. Put into the saucepan.
5. When the water starts boiling, cook the carrots for around 5 minutes. *(Note 5)*
6. Drain the cooked carrots and place in a bowl.
7. Set aside.

---

* use this recipe to calculate how many jars you will be making

Preparing the jars
1. Put the hob on medium heat.
2. Pour the water into a medium saucepan or kettle and bring to a boil.
3. Wash the jars and lids.
4. Leave in the sink.
5. When the water starts boiling, carefully pour the boiling water into and over the cleaned jars and lids.
6. Pour the water out and allow the jars to cool.

Preparing the rest of the ingredients
1. Transfer the cucumbers to the sink.
2. Clean and rinse.
3. Peel and slice the cucumbers into 4mm slices.
4. Put into a separate bowl and set aside.
5. Peel the onion, cut in half and then into thin slices.
6. Put into a separate bowl and set aside.
7. Rinse the peppers and remove the stalks.
8. Cut in half and remove the white parts and seeds.
9. Cut into small, 1cm cubes.
10. Put into a separate bowl and set aside.
11. Peel and slice the horseradish.
12. Leave on the chopping board.
13. Peel the garlic.
14. Leave on the chopping board.
15. Rinse the sprig of dill.
16. Cut into 5cm pieces.
17. Leave on the chopping board.

Preparing the salad
1. Put the garlic in the jar.
2. Put the dill and horseradish on the bottom of the jar.
3. Layer the vegetables (each layer should be around 2-3cm thick): cucumbers, onions, peppers, carrots.
4. Press down hard.
5. If there's still space in the jar, add more layers, leaving around 2cm between the top of the vegetables and top of the jar.
6. Add the vinegar, sugar and salt to the jar.
7. Fill and cover the vegetables in the jars with water. Leaving about 2cm of space at the top.
8. Close each jar tightly.
9. Pasteurise for around 20 minutes. Information about the pasteurisation process can be found on page 342. *(Note 6)*
10. The salad is ready to eat right after being pasteurised.

To serve
- This salad is a great side for:
  - *kotlety schabowe*
  - minced pork patties

NOTES

1. The number of cucumbers depends on how many can fit into each jar.
2. The best cucumbers are the young ones, since they have small seeds. They are also easier to put into jars. Big cucumbers have bigger seeds and might be hollow inside. Check your cucumbers for any damage or discoloration that could cause them to go bad. You can use damaged cucumbers for sandwiches or *mizeria*.
3. The amount of water will depend on the number of vegetables in the jar.
4. You will need enough water to sterilise the inside and outside of the jars and lids.
5. The carrots should remain crunchy.
6. Pasteurising time depends on the size of the jar.

KITCHEN ACCESSORIES

- ☐ medium saucepan
- ☐ 4 bowls
- ☐ knife
- ☐ peeling knife
- ☐ chopping board
- ☐ 2 tablespoons
- ☐ teaspoon
- ☐ jars with lids (900ml)

GOOD TO KNOW

 vegetarian

 vegan

 gluten-free

 fridge
- after opening use within five days and store in the fridge

 pantry
- store up to 1 year

 kalorie
- 88 per jar (900ml)

GOES WELL WITH

 **Kotlety Schabowe**
vol 1, 3. Obiad, page 99

 **Minced Pork Patties**
vol 1, 3. Obiad, page 103

 **Mizeria**
vol 1, 4. Sides, page 211

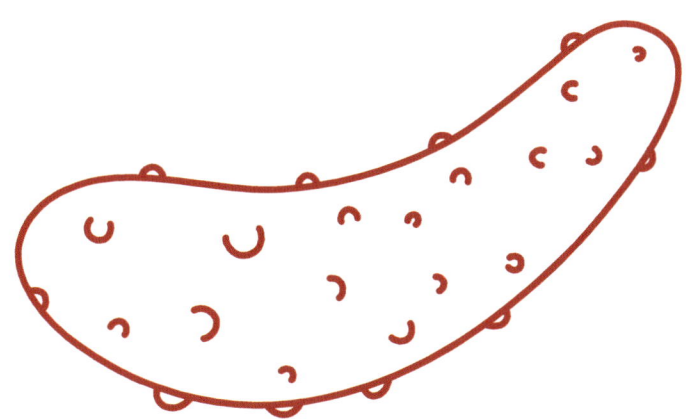

COURGETTE LECZO

Leczo is an easy dish that is great for using up a seasonal glut of courgettes. On a busy day you can just open a jar and enjoy a delicious, quick meal.

Difficulty	Makes	Preparation	Resting	Cooking	Pasteurisation	Total
INTERMEDIATE	4 *	1 H	2 H	~40 MIN	20 MIN	~4 H

INGREDIENTS

For the *leczo*
- 750g courgette
- 500g peppers
- 4 onions (~300g)
- 3 garlic cloves
- 1 chilli pepper (optional)
- 5 allspice berries
- 3 bay leaves
- 1 tbsp sugar (+ more to taste)
- 1 tsp ground black pepper
- 1 tbsp salt (+ more to taste)
- 120ml cooking oil
- 120ml 10% spirit vinegar

For the tomatoes
- 1.5kg tomatoes
- 3 litres water

For sterilising the jars and lids
- ~2 litres water *(Note 1)*

 Polish products differ from the ones available locally. You will find more information about allspice and kiełbasa in the chapter "About the products" on page 328.

DIRECTIONS

Preparing the courgette
1. Rinse the courgette and remove the ends.
2. If the courgette is large, peel and remove the seeds.
3. Cut into 1cm cubes.
4. Put into a bowl.
5. Add 1 tbsp salt.
6. Mix well.
7. Set the bowl aside for around 2 hours. *(Note 2)*
8. While waiting, prepare all the other ingredients.

Preparing the peppers
1. Rinse the peppers and remove the stalks.
2. Cut in half and remove the white parts and seeds.
3. Cut into small, 1cm cubes.
4. Put the peppers into a separate bowl and set aside.
5. Rinse the chilli pepper and cut off the green stem.
6. Chop finely and transfer to the bowl with the peppers. *(Note 3, important)*

---

* 4 jars (900ml each)

Preparing the onion
1. Peel the onion and chop finely.
2. Put into a separate bowl and set aside.

Preparing the tomatoes
1. Put the hob on medium heat.
2. Pour the water into a large pot and bring to a boil.
3. Using a sharp knife, make a cross on top of every tomato – don't go too deep.
4. Set the tomatoes aside.
5. When the water is boiling, turn off the heat.
6. Using a spoon, carefully place the tomatoes into the pot.
7. Leave in the boiled water for 2-3 minutes.
8. Pour the hot water out of the pot and cover the tomatoes with cold water.
9. Set aside in the cold water for 2 minutes.
10. Pour the water out.
11. Peel the tomatoes.
12. Cut out the green stem.
13. Thickly slice the tomatoes and then cube.
14. Put into a separate large bowl.

Preparing the jars
1. Put the hob on medium heat.
2. Pour the water into a medium saucepan or kettle and bring to a boil.
3. Wash the jars and lids.
4. Leave in the sink.
5. When the water starts boiling, carefully pour the boiling water into and over the cleaned jars and lids.
6. Pour the water out and allow the jars to cool.

Preparing the *leczo*
1. Put the hob on medium heat.
2. Heat half the oil (around 60ml) in a separate large pot.
3. Add the chopped onion.
4. Occasionally stir with a wooden spoon.
5. Fry until translucent.
6. Peel the garlic.
7. Crush the garlic into the pot.
8. Mix well.
9. Fry the garlic with the onion for around 1 minute.
10. Add the tomatoes.
11. Mix well.
12. Boil for around 10 minutes to evaporate the liquid. *(Note 4)*
13. Occasionally stir with a wooden spoon.
14. Add the rest of the oil and vinegar.
15. Add the spices: pepper, allspice and bay leaves.
16. Mix well.
17. Squeeze the liquid out of the courgette.
18. Add the courgette to the pot with the tomatoes.
19. Add the peppers.
20. Mix well.
21. Reduce the heat and simmer for around 20 minutes.
22. Season with salt and sugar.
23. Put the *leczo* into jars. Leaving about 2cm of space at the top.
24. Close each jar tightly. *(Note 5)*
25. Pasteurise for around 20 minutes. Information about the pasteurisation process can be found on page 342. *(Note 6)*
26. *Leczo* is ready to eat right after being made. Using jars and pasteurising will allow the *leczo* to be stored for longer.

To serve
- After opening the jar, heat the *leczo* in a pot.
- Serve with bread or boiled potatoes.
- Alternatively, serve with sliced *kiełbasa* added to the *leczo* on the hob. Fry the *kiełbasa* before adding to the dish.

NOTES

1. You will need enough water to sterilise the inside and outside of the jars and lids.
2. While waiting, the courgette will release its liquid.
3. Chilli peppers contain capsaicin, which irritates the skin. Rubber gloves can be worn when chopping the chilli. If not using gloves, wash your hands thoroughly after chopping. Do not touch your face or eyes (even after washing your hands) because it may well still burn.
4. The tomatoes should thicken, so that the consistency is close to a tomato paste.
5. When you put hot *leczo* into the jars, they will warm up very quickly. To avoid burns when closing them, hold them in one hand with a tea towel. This will allow you to easily twist the lids with your other hand.
6. Pasteurising time depends on the size of the jar.

KITCHEN ACCESSORIES

- ☐ 2 large pots
- ☐ medium saucepan
- ☐ large bowl
- ☐ 3 bowls
- ☐ measuring jug
- ☐ knife
- ☐ chopping board
- ☐ tablespoon
- ☐ teaspoon
- ☐ wooden spoon
- ☐ garlic crusher (press)
- ☐ rubber gloves (optional)
- ☐ 4 jars with lids (900ml)

GOOD TO KNOW

 vegetarian

 vegan

 gluten-free

 pantry
- store up to 1 year

 kalorie
- 763 per jar (900ml), 3052 total

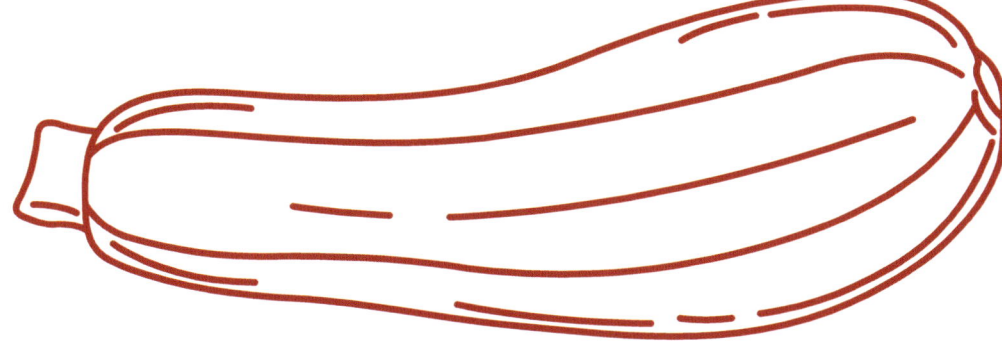

Pantry 293

RASPBERRY JUICE

*Natural raspberry juice made with a steam juicer without any preservatives – a taste of summer that you can also enjoy in the winter.
Add to water, tea or mulled wine.*

You will need a steam juicer for this recipe.
Its use is described in the Accessories chapter on page 340.

Difficulty	Makes	Preparation	Cooking	Pasteurisation	Total
SIMPLE	3 *	15 MIN	~1 H	15 MIN	~1 H 30 MIN

INGREDIENTS

For the juice
- [ ] 1kg raspberries *(Note 1)*
- [ ] 2 tbsp sugar (+ more to taste)
- [ ] water *(Note 2)*

For sterilising the jars and lids
- [ ] ~2 litres water *(Note 3)*

DIRECTIONS

Preparing the raspberries
1. Go through the raspberries and remove any spoilt fruit.
2. Remove any stalks.
3. Put the raspberries into a bowl and set aside.

Preparing the steam juicer – part 1
1. Pour the water into the bottom vessel of the juicer. Leaving about 2cm of space at the top.
2. Put the middle vessel with the hose in the bottom vessel. *(Note 4)*
3. In the middle vessel put the top vessel with the holes.
4. Put the raspberries in the top vessel.
5. Cover with sugar.
6. Place the lid on the steam juicer.
7. Put the hob on medium heat.
8. Bring the water in the bottom vessel to a boil.
9. Reduce the heat to a simmer.
10. Place a large pot on a stool next to the hob.
11. Put the hose into the pot. *(Note 5)*

Preparing the jars
1. Put the hob on medium heat.
2. Pour the water into a medium saucepan or kettle and bring to a boil.
3. Wash the jars and lids.
4. Leave in the sink.
5. When the water starts boiling, carefully pour the boiling water into and over the cleaned jars and lids.
6. Pour the water out and allow the jars to cool.

---

* 3 jars (280ml each)

Preparing the steam juicer – part 2

1. When the juice slowly begins to gather in the hose, release the clamp to pour the juice into the pot.
2. While simmering, refill if too much water has evaporated.
3. If the juice stops gathering in the hose, turn off the hob and finish working with the steam juicer.
4. Remove the lid from the top vessel.
5. Put the remaining raspberries into a container and set aside. *(Note 6)*
6. Pour the juice from the middle vessel into the pot with the juice.
7. Pour away the water from the bottom vessel as this is no longer needed.

Preparing the juice

1. Add sugar to taste. *(Note 7)*
2. Mix well.
3. Pour the juice into each jar. Leaving about 2cm of space at the top.
4. Close each jar tightly.
5. Pasteurise for around 15 minutes. Information about the pasteurisation process can be found on page 342. *(Note 8)*
6. The juice is ready to drink right after being made. Using jars and pasteurising will allow the juice to be stored for longer.

Use as an ingredient

- Pour a small amount of juice into a glass and fill the glass with water to make a drink.
- Alternatively, add raspberry juice to mulled wine or tea.

NOTES

1. You can substitute the raspberries with other fruit such as strawberries or peaches. On page 340 you will find more information about the steam juicer as well as a list of fruit you can use.
2. The amount of water depends on the capacity of the bottom vessel of the steam juicer. After you pour the water into the vessel, there should be approximately 2cm of free space at the top.
3. You will need enough water to sterilise the inside and outside of the jars and lids.
4. Make sure the clamp is on the hose that drains the juice. Read the manufacturer's instructions for how to use the steam juicer safely. You will find all the general information on page 340.
5. It is best if the juicer hose is always above the pot or inserted into it. If the clamp does not close the hose tightly, the juice will flow into the pot and not onto the floor.
6. You can freeze the fruit and eat them as a sorbet. You can serve the sorbet with oponki or faworki.
7. Check if the juice in the pot is sweet enough. Be careful: the juice will be very hot!
8. Pasteurising time depends on the size of the jar.

KITCHEN ACCESSORIES

- ☐ steam juicer (5-litre)
- ☐ large pot
- ☐ medium saucepan
- ☐ bowl
- ☐ tablespoon
- ☐ food container
- ☐ 3 jars with lids (280ml)

GOOD TO KNOW

 vegetarian

 vegan

 gluten-free

 fridge
- after opening use within five days and store in the fridge

 pantry
- store up to 1 year

 kcal
- 205 per jar (280ml)

GOES WELL WITH

 *Oponki*
8. Fat Thursday, page 151

 *Mulled Wine*
10. Christmas, page 245

 *Faworki*
8. Fat Thursday, page 155

Pantry

STRAWBERRY SYRUP

A rich and tasty natural syrup made with fresh strawberries. It's so universal that you can use it to make a refreshing drink, as a mixer for cocktails or to serve with ice cream.

 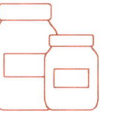    

Difficulty	Makes	Preparation	Resting	Cooking	Pasteurisation	Total
SIMPLE	2 *	15 MIN	12 H	~10 MIN	15 MIN	~12 H 40 MIN

INGREDIENTS

For the syrup
- 1kg strawberries *(Note 1)*
- 250g sugar (+ more to taste)

For sterilising the jars and lids
- ~2 litres water *(Note 2)*

DIRECTIONS

The day before pouring the syrup into jars: evening *(Note 3)*
Preparing the strawberries
1. Rinse the strawberries and cut out the stems.
2. Cut in half or if large, into quarters.
3. Put the strawberries in a large pot.
4. Cover with sugar.
5. Mix well.
6. Put into the fridge for around 12 hours.

Preparation day
Cooking the strawberries
1. Put the hob on low heat.
2. Heat the strawberries in the pot to dissolve the sugar.
3. Stir from time to time. *(Note 4)*
4. Turn off and remove from the heat and set the pot aside.
5. Set aside to cool, so that the strawberries remain warm and absorb the dissolved sugar. This can take around 15 minutes.

Preparing the jars
1. Put the hob on medium heat.
2. Pour the water into a medium saucepan or kettle and bring to a boil.
3. Wash the jars and lids.
4. Leave in the sink.
5. When the water starts boiling, carefully pour the boiling water into and over the cleaned jars and lids.
6. Pour the water out and allow the jars to cool.

Preparing the syrup
1. Set a sieve over a bowl.
2. Put the strawberries in the sieve.
3. Slightly press the strawberries with a spoon, to extract the juice.
4. Pour the syrup into each jar. Leaving about 2cm of space at the top.
5. Put the rest of the fruit into separate jars. Leaving about 2cm of space at the top.
6. Close each jar tightly.

---

* 2 jars (280ml each)

7. Pasteurise all the jars for around 15 minutes. Information about the pasteurisation process can be found on page 342. *(Note 5)*
8. The syrup is ready to drink right after being made. Using jars and pasteurising will allow the syrup to be stored for longer.

Use as an ingredient
- Pour a small amount of syrup into a glass and fill the glass with water to make a drink.
- Use the fruit in desserts or to make jam.

NOTES

1. You can swap the strawberries for the same amount of cherries. Remember to remove the pits before covering with sugar.
2. You will need enough water to sterilise the inside and outside of the jars and lids.
3. It's best to prepare the strawberries in the evening, so they can rest overnight (around 12 hours).
4. Check the strawberries for sweetness. If you want them to be sweeter, add more sugar.
5. Pasteurising time depends on the size of the jar.
6. You will need two jars to make the syrup and two jars for the juice.

KITCHEN ACCESSORIES

- ☐ large pot
- ☐ medium saucepan
- ☐ bowl
- ☐ knife
- ☐ peeling knife
- ☐ chopping board
- ☐ tablespoon
- ☐ sieve
- ☐ 4 jars with lids (280ml) *(Note 6)*

GOOD TO KNOW

 vegetarian

 vegan

 gluten-free

 fridge
- after opening use within five days and store in the fridge

 pantry
- store up to 1 year

 kcal
- syrup
  354 per jar (280ml)
- fruit
  290 per jar (280ml)

Pantry

SWEET CHERRY KOMPOT

*A delicious drink made with sweet cherries.
A great way to capture the flavour of summer
and bring back warm holiday memories in the middle of winter.*

Difficulty	Makes	Preparation	Pasteurisation	Total
SIMPLE	2 *	20 MIN	20 MIN	40 MIN

INGREDIENTS

Proportions per two 900ml jars
For the sweet cherry kompot
- 1kg sweet cherries
- 8 tbsp sugar *(Note 1)*
- 1-1.5 litres water

For sterilising the jars and lids
- ~2 litres water *(Note 2)*

 Polish products differ from the ones available locally. You will find more information about sweet cherries in the chapter "About the products" on page 328.

DIRECTIONS

Preparing the jars
1. Put the hob on medium heat.
2. Pour the water into a medium saucepan or kettle and bring to a boil.
3. Wash the jars and lids.
4. Leave in the sink.
5. When the water starts boiling, carefully pour the boiling water into and over the cleaned jars and lids.
6. Pour the water out and allow the jars to cool.

Preparing the sweet cherry *kompot*
1. Rinse the cherries and remove any stems.
2. Remove any bruised, damaged fruit. *(Note 3)*
3. Put the cherries into each jar. Leaving about 2cm of space at the top.
4. Cover with sugar (4 tbsp for 1 jar).
5. Cover the fruit with water. Leaving about 2cm of space at the top.
6. Close each jar tightly.
7. Pasteurise for around 20 minutes. Information about the pasteurisation process can be found on page 342. *(Note 4)*
8. *Kompot* is ready to drink right after being pasteurised.

* 2 jars (900ml each)

To serve
1. Pour the content of the jar into a large pot.
2. Add around 1.5 litres of water to dilute the *kompot*. *(Note 5)*
3. The fruit can be eaten or added to desserts.

Use as an ingredient
- Use the cherries from the *kompot* to make sweet cherry *pierogi*. *(Note 6)*

NOTES

1. You need 4 tbsp sugar for one 900ml jar. If you are preparing the *kompot* with a different amount of fruit, measure the amount of sugar proportionally.
2. You will need enough water to sterilise the inside and outside of the jars and lids.
3. The cherries should not be pitted for the *kompot*, so they are not damaged.
4. Pasteurising time depends on the size of the jar.
5. You can dilute the *kompot* with cold or hot water. If you want to sweeten it, add warm water – the sugar will dissolve faster.
6. You will find a recipe for sweet cherry *pierogi* in the "*Pierogi* Festival" chapter in Volume 1.

KITCHEN ACCESSORIES

☐ medium saucepan
☐ tablespoon
☐ 2 jars with lids (900ml)

GOOD TO KNOW

 vegetarian

 vegan

 gluten-free

 pantry
- store up to 1 year

 fridge
- after opening use within five days and store in the fridge

 kalorie
- 501 per jar (900ml)

GOES WELL WITH

 **Sweet Cherry *Pierogi***
v. 1, 5. Pierogi Festival, page 307

PEAR KOMPOT

A sweet pear drink that does not take much time to prepare. It goes perfectly with obiad, and the leftover fruit is great for desserts.

Difficulty	Makes	Preparation	Pasteurisation	Total
SIMPLE	2 *	20 MIN	20 MIN	40 MIN

INGREDIENTS

Proportions per two 900ml jars
For the pear kompot
- 1kg pears
- 8 tbsp sugar *(Note 1)*
- 1-1.5 litres water

For sterilising the jars and lids
- ~2 litres water *(Note 2)*

DIRECTIONS

Preparing the jars
1. Put the hob on medium heat.
2. Pour the water into a medium saucepan or kettle and bring to a boil.
3. Wash the jars and lids.
4. Leave in the sink.
5. When the water starts boiling, carefully pour the boiling water into and over the cleaned jars and lids.
6. Pour the water out and allow the jars to cool.

Preparing the pear *kompot*
1. Peel the pears and cut into quarters.
2. Remove the pips and stems.
3. Put the pears into each jar. Leaving about 2cm of space at the top.
4. Cover with sugar (4 tbsp for 1 jar).
5. Fill and cover the fruit in the jars with water. Leaving about 2cm of space at the top.
6. Close each jar tightly.
7. Pasteurise for around 20 minutes. Information about the pasteurisation process can be found on page 342. *(Note 3)*
8. *Kompot* is ready to drink right after being pasteurised.

---

* 2 jars (900ml each)
photo on page 302

To serve
1. Pour the content of the jar into a large pot.
2. Add around 1.5 litres of water to dilute the *kompot*. (Note 4)
3. The fruit can be eaten or added to desserts.

NOTES

1. You need 4 tbsp sugar for one 900ml jar. If you are preparing the *kompot* with a different amount of fruit, measure the amount of sugar proportionally.
2. You will need enough water to sterilise the inside and outside of the jars and lids.
3. Pasteurising time depends on the size of the jar.
4. You can dilute the *kompot* with cold or hot water. If you want to sweeten it, add warm water – the sugar will dissolve faster.

KITCHEN ACCESSORIES

☐ medium saucepan
☐ knife
☐ peeling knife
☐ chopping board
☐ tablespoon
☐ 2 jars with lids (900ml)

GOOD TO KNOW

 vegetarian

 vegan

 gluten-free

 pantry
- store up to 1 year

 fridge
- after opening use within five days and store in the fridge

 kalorie
- 471 per jar (900ml)

PRESERVED APPLE SLICES

*A simple method to preserve a glut of apples.
Sliced apples are a delightful, sweet addition to desserts,
cakes as well as savoury dishes.*

Difficulty	Makes	Preparation	Resting	Pasteurisation	Total
SIMPLE	6 *	45 MIN	~12 H	15 MIN	~13 H

INGREDIENTS

For the apples
- ☐ 1.5kg apples *(Note 1)*
- ☐ 6 tbsp sugar
- ☐ ½ lemon

For sterilising the jars and lids
- ☐ ~2 litres water *(Note 2)*

DIRECTIONS

The day before putting apples into jars: evening
Preparing the apples – part 1
1. Peel the apples and cut into quarters.
2. Remove the pips and stems.
3. Finely slice the apples into 2mm slices.
4. Put into a large bowl.
5. Roll the lemon on the kitchen counter. *(Note 3)*
6. Cut in half.
7. Juice one half into the bowl. *(Note 4)*
8. Gradually add the sugar to the bowl.
9. Mix well.
10. Put the bowl in the fridge for around 12 hours.

Preparation day
Preparing the jars
1. Put the hob on medium heat.
2. Pour the water into a medium saucepan or kettle and bring to a boil.
3. Wash the jars and lids.
4. Leave in the sink.
5. When the water starts boiling, carefully pour the boiling water into and over the cleaned jars and lids.
6. Pour the water out and allow the jars to cool.

Preparing the apples – part 2
1. Pour the collected juice into a separate bowl.
2. Put the apples into each jar. Leaving about 2cm of space at the top. *(Note 5)*
3. Pour the juice into a separate jar. *(Note 6)*
4. Close each jar tightly.
5. Pasteurise all the jars for around 15 minutes. Information about the pasteurisation process can be found on page 342. *(Note 7)*
6. The apples are ready to use right after being pasteurised.

---

* 6 jars (280ml each)

Use as an ingredient
- Use the sliced apples to make:
  - apple pie
  - baked rice with apples and cinnamon
- Pour a small amount of juice into a glass and fill the glass with water to make a drink.

NOTES

1. The apples should be hard, so that they don't overcook when pasteurised. Varieties I would choose for this are; *Malinówka Oberlandzka*, Rubin, Kosztela, McIntosh, Reinette, Antonovka, Champion.
2. You will need enough water to sterilise the inside and outside of the jars and lids.
3. Before cutting the lemon, roll it for a while on the kitchen counter, pressing slightly with your hand. This will help you extract all the juice from the lemon.
4. Adding lemon juice will keep the apples from getting dark.
5. Don't press the apples in the jar. The apples will swell during the pasteurisation process, they might loosen the lid or even open it.
6. If there's a lot of juice, you can pasteurise it as well. If not, put it in the fridge and use it for drinking.
7. Pasteurising time depends on the size of the jar.
8. You will need six jars to make the apples and one jar for the juice.

KITCHEN ACCESSORIES

- ☐ medium saucepan
- ☐ large bowl
- ☐ bowl
- ☐ knife
- ☐ peeling knife
- ☐ chopping board
- ☐ tablespoon
- ☐ 7 jars with lids (280ml) *(Note 8)*

GOOD TO KNOW

 vegetarian

 vegan

 gluten-free

 fridge
- after opening use within five days and store in the fridge

 pantry
- store up to 1 year

 kalorie
- 178 per jar (280ml)

GOES WELL WITH

Apple Pie
7. Cakes and Desserts, page 71

Baked Rice with Apples and Cinnamon
vol 1, 3. Obiad, page 157

APPLE SAUCE

Stewed apple sauce is a great combination of sweet and sharp flavours. A delicious addition to naleśniki, crêpes, waffles, cakes and desserts, without any preservatives.

Difficulty	Makes	Preparation	Frying	Pasteurisation	Total
SIMPLE	4 *	45 MIN	40-60 MIN	15 MIN	~2 H

INGREDIENTS

For the apples
- ☐ 2kg apples
- ☐ 4 tbsp sugar
- ☐ 200ml water

For sterilising the jars and lids
- ☐ ~2 litres water *(Note 1)*

DIRECTIONS

Preparing the apples – part 1
1. Peel the apples and cut into quarters.
2. Remove the pips and stems.
3. Cut the apples into 0.5cm cubes. *(Note 2)*
4. Put into a large pot.
5. Pour the water into the pot. *(Note 3)*
6. Put the hob on low heat.
7. Bring the water to a boil.
8. Reduce the heat and simmer semi-covered for 40-60 minutes. *(Note 4)*
9. Occasionally stir with a wooden spoon.

Preparing the jars
1. Put the hob on medium heat.
2. Pour the water into a medium saucepan or kettle and bring to a boil.
3. Wash the jars and lids.
4. Leave in the sink.
5. When the water starts boiling, carefully pour the boiling water into and over the cleaned jars and lids.
6. Pour the water out and allow the jars to cool.

Preparing the apples – part 2
1. After the water evaporates, keep stirring the apples to prevent burning. *(Note 5)*
2. The apples should be soft and mushy. *(Note 6)*
3. Turn off and remove from the heat and set the pot aside.
4. Add the sugar. *(Note 7)*
5. Stir for the sugar to dissolve.
6. Set aside to cool completely. This can take around 1 hour. *(Note 8)*
7. Using a hand blender, blend to get a uniform consistency.
8. Put the apples into each jar. Leaving about 2cm of space at the top.
9. Close each jar tightly.
10. Pasteurise for around 15 minutes. Information about the pasteurisation process can be found on page 342. *(Note 9)*
11. The apples are ready to eat right after being prepared. Using jars and pasteurising will allow the sauce to be stored for longer.

---

* 4 jars (280ml each)

Use as an ingredient
- Use apple sauce to make:
  - apple and *twaróg* cake
  - *naleśniki* (crêpes)

NOTES

1. You will need enough water to sterilise the inside and outside of the jars and lids.
2. Cubed apples will cook faster.
3. Adding water will prevent the apples from burning before they start releasing their juice.
4. The time you need to soften the apples depends on the variety you use.
5. If they start sticking to the bottom and burning, transfer them to another pot and keep simmering and stirring.
6. Check if they are soft. Be careful: they will be very hot!
7. The amount of sugar will depend on the sweetness of the apples and on your preference.
8. You can cool the apples quicker by pouring cold water into the sink and placing the pot in the cold water. The apples should cool completely after around 30 minutes.
9. Pasteurising time depends on the size of the jar.

KITCHEN ACCESSORIES

- ☐ large pot with lid
- ☐ medium saucepan
- ☐ knife
- ☐ peeling knife
- ☐ chopping board
- ☐ tablespoon
- ☐ hand blender
- ☐ wooden spoon
- ☐ tea towel
- ☐ 4 jars with lids (280ml)

GOOD TO KNOW

 vegetarian

 vegan

 gluten-free

 fridge
- after opening use within five days and store in the fridge

 pantry
- store up to 1 year

 kcal
- 307 per jar (280ml)

GOES WELL WITH

 **Apple and *Twaróg* Cake**
7. Cakes and Desserts, page 97

 ***Naleśniki* (Crêpes)**
vol 1, 3. Obiad, page 139

RASPBERRY JAM

A fantastic way of turning fresh raspberries into a homemade jam. It's delicious taste and vibrant colour will raise your toast, pancakes and desserts to the next level!

Difficulty	Makes	Preparation	Frying	Pasteurisation	Total
INTERMEDIATE	3 *	10 MIN	25-35 MIN	15 MIN	~1 H

INGREDIENTS

For the lemon *(Note 1)*
- 1 lemon
- 1 tbsp citric acid *(Note 2)*
- ½ tbsp bicarbonate of soda *(Note 3)*
- 1 litre warm water

For the jam
- 1kg raspberries
- 500g sugar

For sterilising the jars and lids
- ~2 litres water *(Note 4)*

 Polish products differ from the ones available locally. You will find more information about culinary citric acid in the chapter "About the products" on page 328.

DIRECTIONS

Preparing the raspberries
1. Go through the raspberries and remove any spoilt fruit.
2. Remove any stalks.
3. Transfer half of the raspberries into a large pot.
4. Cover with half of the sugar.
5. Add the second half of the raspberries and cover with the remaining sugar.
6. Set aside for around 2 hours.

Preparing the lemon – acidic solution
1. Pour 0.5 litre of warm water into a bowl.
2. Add the citric acid.
3. Stir, so the acid dissolves.
4. Put a whole lemon into the bowl.
5. Leave in the solution for around 3 minutes.
6. Take the lemon out of the solution and rinse under running water.
7. Set the lemon aside.
8. Pour the solution out from the bowl.

Preparing the lemon – alkaline solution
1. Pour 0.5 litre of warm water into the bowl.
2. Add the bicarbonate of soda.
3. Stir so that the soda dissolves.
4. Put the whole lemon into the bowl.
5. Leave in the solution for around 3 minutes.
6. Take the lemon out of the solution and rinse under running water.
7. Set the lemon aside.
8. Pour the solution out from the bowl.

---

* 3 jars (300ml each)

Preparing the jars
1. Put the hob on medium heat.
2. Pour the water into a medium saucepan or kettle and bring to a boil.
3. Wash the jars and lids.
4. Leave in the sink.
5. When the water starts boiling, carefully pour the boiling water into and over the cleaned jars and lids.
6. Pour the water out and allow the jars to cool.

Preparing the jam
1. Before making the jam, put a small plate in the fridge.
2. Put the hob on low heat.
3. Heat the raspberries in the pot to dissolve the sugar.
4. Occasionally stir with a wooden spoon.
5. Cut the lemon in half and then into quarters. *(Note 5)*
6. Add the lemon (skin on) to the raspberries.
7. When the sugar dissolves, turn the hob to high.
8. Bring the raspberries to a boil.
9. Reduce the heat and simmer for 25-35 minutes until thickened.
10. Stir the raspberries frequently with a wooden spoon to prevent burning.
11. After around 20 minutes check the consistency. *(Note 6)*
12. When the right consistency is achieved, turn off and remove from the heat and set the pot aside.
13. Remove the lemon peel from the jam.
14. Put the jam into each jar. Leaving about 2cm of space at the top.
15. Close each jar tightly. *(Note 7)*
16. Pasteurise for around 15 minutes. Information about the pasteurisation process can be found on page 342. *(Note 8)*
17. The jam is ready to eat right after being made. Using jars and pasteurising will allow the jam to be stored for longer.

Use as an ingredient
- Use the raspberry jam to prepare:
  - Victoria sponge
  - *kocie oczka*
  - *pączki*
- Alternatively, serve:
  - on a bun with milk soup
  - on *naleśniki* (crêpes) with vanilla cream cheese for crêpes or with pastry cream

NOTES

1. Citrus fruits are treated before transporting to prevent spoiling. The skins are covered with preservatives and fungicides. Additionally, they are polished and waxed to look nice. When using the whole fruit in cooking; for their peel, pectin and flavour, they must be properly cleaned. Using a weak acid and alkali is very effective in cleaning the outside of citrus fruits.
2. You need 1 tbsp of citric acid for 0.5 litre of water. If you are preparing the solution with a different amount of water, adjust the amount of citric acid proportionally. You can substitute citric acid for the same amount of distilled vinegar (10%).
3. You need ½ tbsp of bicarbonate of soda for 0.5 litre of water. If you are preparing the solution with a different amount of water, adjust the amount of bicarbonate of soda proportionally.
4. You will need enough water to sterilise the inside and outside of the jars and lids.
5. Check if there are no pips in the lemon. Remove them if there are.
6. Put 1 tsp of jam on a cold plate. The cold plate helps to cool the jam quickly to test the consistency. Push the jam with your finger, it should wrinkle but retain its shape. If the consistency is too thin, you can turn the hob to high and continue reducing to obtain a thicker jam. Check it for consistency again.

7. When you put hot jam into the jars, they will warm up very quickly. To avoid burns when closing them, hold them in one hand with a tea towel. This will allow you to easily twist the lids with your other hand.
8. Pasteurising time depends on the size of the jar.

KITCHEN ACCESSORIES

- ☐ large pot
- ☐ medium saucepan
- ☐ bowl
- ☐ knife
- ☐ chopping board
- ☐ small plate

- ☐ 2 tablespoons
- ☐ teaspoon
- ☐ wooden spoon
- ☐ tea towel
- ☐ 3 jars with lids (300ml)

GOOD TO KNOW

 vegetarian

 vegan

 gluten-free

 fridge
- after opening use within five days and store in the fridge

 pantry
- store up to 1 year

 kcal
- 824 per jar (300ml)

GOES WELL WITH

 **Victoria Sponge**
7. Cakes and Desserts, page 49

 **Kocie Oczka**
7. Cakes and Desserts, page 109

 **Pączki**
8. Fat Thursday, page 145

 **Milk Soup**
vol 1, 1. Breakfast, page 21

 **Naleśniki (Crêpes)**
vol 1, 3. Obiad, page 139

 **Vanilla Cream Cheese for Crêpes**
vol 1, 4. Sides, page 265

 **Pastry Cream**
vol 1, 4. Sides, page 267

POWIDŁA ŚLIWKOWE (PLUM JAM)

Homemade plum jam with a unique, delicious taste. The deep, rich, plum aroma goes perfectly with meat and is also used in sweet dishes and cakes.

Difficulty	Makes	Preparation	Frying	Pasteurisation	Total
INTERMEDIATE	5 *	15 MIN	3-4 H	15 MIN	~4 H 30 MIN

INGREDIENTS

For the jam
- ☐ 2kg purple (common) plums *(Note 1)*
- ☐ 5 tbsp sugar (optional) *(Note 2)*
- ☐ 150ml water

For sterilising the jars and lids
- ☐ ~2 litres water *(Note 3)*

 Polish products differ from the ones available locally. You will find more information about purple plums in the chapter "About the products" on page 328.

DIRECTIONS

Preparing the jam – part 1
1. Rinse the plums.
2. Halve lengthwise and remove the stones.
3. Cut the plums into quarters. *(Note 4)*
4. Put into a large pot.
5. Pour 150ml of water into the pot. *(Note 5)*
6. Put the hob on medium heat.
7. Bring the water with the plums to a boil.
8. Boil for around 15 minutes.
9. Stir the plums frequently with a wooden spoon to prevent burning.
10. Turn off the hob and stir from time to time. *(Note 6)*
11. After around 10 minutes, put the hob on medium heat again.
12. Bring the plums to a boil.
13. Boil for around 5 minutes, stirring constantly with the wooden spoon.
14. Turn off the hob and stir from time to time.
15. Heat and cool again, remembering to stir. This can take 3-4 hours. *(Note 7)*

Preparing the jars
1. Put the hob on medium heat.
2. Pour the water into a medium saucepan or kettle and bring to a boil.
3. Wash the jars and lids.
4. Leave in the sink.
5. When the water starts boiling, carefully pour the boiling water into and over the cleaned jars and lids.
6. Pour the water out and allow the jars to cool.

---

* 5 jars (200ml each)

Preparing the jam – part 2

1. After some of the liquid has evaporated, the jam will have thickened. *(Note 8)*
2. Add the sugar. *(Note 9)*
3. Stir for the sugar to dissolve.
4. Put the jam into each jar. Leaving about 2cm of space at the top.
5. Close each jar tightly. *(Note 10)*
6. Pasteurise for around 15 minutes. Information about the pasteurisation process can be found on page 342. *(Note 11)*
7. The jam is ready to eat right after being made. Using jars and pasteurising will allow the jam to be stored for longer.

Use as an ingredient

- Use plum jam to prepare:
  - coconut pie with plum jam
  - walnut pie
  - *kocie oczka*
  - marmalade biscuits
  - *pączki*
  - Christmas gingerbread cake
  - *bigos*
  - plum jam *pierogi*
- Can also be served with:
  - pastry cream with *naleśniki* (crêpes)

NOTES

1. You can swap the purple plums for the president variety.
2. You can omit the sugar if you want to preserve the natural sweet and sour flavour of the plums.
3. You will need enough water to sterilise the inside and outside of the jars and lids.
4. If you cut the plums into smaller pieces, they will soften quicker.
5. Adding water will prevent the plums from burning before they start releasing their juice.
6. You don't need to heat the plums continuously, since the water will evaporate anyway.
7. Heating the plums will allow excess liquid to evaporate. By turning off the hob, the fruit will not burn or lose its colour.
8. The plums should lose around three quarters of their volume.
9. The amount of sugar will depend on how sweet you want your jam to be.
10. When you put hot jam into the jars, they will warm up very quickly. To avoid burns when closing them, hold them in one hand with a tea towel. This will allow you to easily twist the lids with your other hand.
11. Pasteurising time depends on the size of the jar.

KITCHEN ACCESSORIES

- ☐ large pot
- ☐ medium saucepan
- ☐ knife
- ☐ chopping board
- ☐ tablespoon
- ☐ wooden spoon
- ☐ tea towel
- ☐ 5 jars with lids (200ml)

GOOD TO KNOW

 vegetarian

 vegan

 gluten-free

 fridge
- after opening use within five days and store in the fridge

 pantry
- store up to 1 year

 kcal
- no sugar
184 per jar (200ml)
- with sugar
231 per jar (200ml)

GOES WELL WITH

Coconut Cream Pie with Plum Jam
7. Cakes and Desserts, page 85

Kocie Oczka
7. Cakes and Desserts, page 109

Walnut Pie
7. Cakes and Desserts, page 113

Marmalade Biscuits
7. Cakes and Desserts, page 127

Pączki
8. Fat Thursday, page 145

Christmas Gingerbread Cake
10. Christmas, page 235

Naleśniki (Crêpes)
vol 1, 3. Obiad, page 139

Bigos
vol 1, 3. Obiad, page 173

Pastry Cream
vol 1, 4. Sides, page 267

Plum Jam *Pierogi*
v. 1, 5. Pierogi Festival, page 311

CANDIED ORANGE PEEL

*Aromatic and delightful candied orange peel.
Perfect for adding a distinctive touch to cakes and desserts
that you can share with your loved ones.*

Difficulty
INTERMEDIATE

Makes
1 *

Preparation
30 MIN

Cooking
~15 MIN

Frying
~30 MIN

Resting
~1 H 30 MIN

Total
~2 H 45 MIN

INGREDIENTS

For the peel
☐ 5 oranges
☐ water *(Note 1)*

For cleaning the oranges *(Note 2)*
☐ 2 tbsp citric acid *(Note 3)*
☐ 1 tbsp bicarbonate of soda *(Note 4)*
☐ 2 litres warm water

Proportions per 100g orange peel
☐ 100g orange juice *(Note 5)*
☐ 150g sugar *(Note 6)*

 Polish products differ from the ones available locally. You will find more information about culinary citric acid in the chapter "About the products" on page 328.

DIRECTIONS

Preparing the water
1. Put the oranges into a large pot.
2. Cover with water. *(Note 7)*
3. Take the oranges from the pot and transfer into the sink.
4. Put the hob on medium heat.
5. Bring the water to a boil.
6. While waiting, prepare the oranges.

Preparing the oranges – acidic solution
1. Pour 1 litre of warm water into a large bowl.
2. Add the citric acid.
3. Stir, so the acid dissolves.
4. Put the whole oranges into the bowl.
5. Leave in the solution for around 3 minutes.
6. Take the oranges out of the solution and rinse under running water.
7. Set the oranges aside.
8. Pour the solution out from the bowl.

*1 jar (900ml)

Preparing the oranges – alkaline solution
1. Pour 1 litre of warm water into the large bowl.
2. Add the bicarbonate of soda.
3. Stir so that the soda dissolves.
4. Put the whole oranges into the bowl.
5. Leave in the solution for around 3 minutes.
6. Take the oranges out of the solution and rinse under running water.
7. Set the oranges aside.
8. Pour the solution out from the bowl.

Cooking the oranges
1. The water should already be boiling.
2. Using a slotted spoon, transfer the prepared oranges into the pot.
3. When the water boils again, cook the oranges for around 3 minutes. *(Note 8)*
4. Turn off the hob.
5. Take the oranges out with a slotted spoon.
6. Put into the sink and rinse under running water.
7. Pour the water out of the pot and add 2 litres of fresh water.
8. Put the hob on medium heat again.
9. Bring the water to a boil.
10. While waiting, prepare the orange peel.

Preparing the peel
1. Cut off the ends of the orange on both sides.
2. Cut the skin along the length of the fruit and remove. *(Note 9)*
3. Weigh the orange peel. *(Note 10)*
4. Add the peel to the boiling water.
5. Cook, covered for around 10 minutes.
6. Take the peel out with a slotted spoon.
7. Transfer to a bowl and allow to cool. This can take around 10 minutes.
8. Cut the peel into 4mm strips. *(Note 11)*
9. Leave on the chopping board and set aside.

Preparing the juice and sugar
1. Juice the oranges into a glass.
2. Weigh the juice into a small bowl. *(Note 12)*
3. Weigh the sugar into a separate small bowl. *(Note 13)*

Preparing the candied peel
1. Put the hob on medium heat.
2. Add the juice to a frying pan.
3. Dissolve the sugar in the juice.
4. Occasionally stir with a wooden spoon.
5. Add the orange peel.
6. Simmer until the juice reduces completely. This can take around 25-30 minutes.
7. At first stir from time to time, and then continuously, so that the sugar doesn't burn.
8. Turn off and remove from the heat and set the pan aside.
9. Roll out the baking paper on the kitchen counter.
10. Using 2 forks, transfer the peels to the paper, separating them from each other and leaving some space between. Be careful: the peel will be very hot! *(Note 14)*
11. Leave the peel to cool completely. This can take around 1 hour and 30 minutes.
12. The peel is ready to eat right after being made. Putting the peel in a jar will allow the peel to be stored for longer.

Storing
- Place the cold peel in a jar with a rubber band and close tightly to prevent moisture from entering.
- The peel can be frozen in a container.

Cleaning the frying pan
1. Pour water into the frying pan.
2. Put the hob on medium heat.
3. Stir with a wooden spoon, touching the bottom of the pan, so that the warm water dissolves the thick juice and sugar.
4. After dissolving the juice and sugar, pour the water out and clean the pan.

Use as an ingredient
- Use candied orange peel to prepare:
  - *pączki*
  - blueberry and *twaróg* yeast buns
- They are also a great addition to drinks, desserts and cakes such as:
  - Viennese cheesecake
  - Easter *keks*
  - *makowiec*
- Can be eaten as a snack.

NOTES

1. The amount of water will depend on the pot size and the amount of oranges. It should cover the oranges in the pot. Additionally, you will need 2 more litres to cook the peel.
2. Citrus fruits are treated before transporting to prevent spoiling. The skins are covered with preservatives and fungicides. Additionally, they are polished and waxed to look nice. When using the whole fruit in cooking; for their peel, pectin and flavour, they must be properly cleaned. Using a weak acid and alkali is very effective in cleaning the outside of citrus fruits.
3. You need 2 tbsp of citric acid for 1 litre of water. If you are preparing the solution with a different amount of water, adjust the amount of citric acid proportionally. You can substitute citric acid for the same amount of distilled vinegar (10%).
4. You need 1 tbsp of bicarbonate of soda for 1 litre of water. If you are preparing the solution with a different amount of water, adjust the amount of bicarbonate of soda proportionally.
5. I used 190g of juice to prepare the peel from 5 oranges.
6. I used 285g of sugar to prepare the peel from 5 oranges.
7. That's how you measure the water needed to cook them.
8. By cooking the oranges, they are further cleansed. It's also easier to peel them.
9. After you peel the orange, don't remove its inner white part, that is called albedo. Many people remove it, claiming that it is bitter, while actually it's the outer, orange part of the peel, which contains essential oils, that is responsible for the bitter taste of oranges. This part of the orange is called exocarp.
10. You must choose the right proportions of juice and sugar depending on the weight of the peels. For example: peel from 5 oranges weighed 190g. On average, the peel of 1 orange weighs 40g.
11. You can also cut the orange peel into squares. I recommend you cut it into strips, as it's easier to transfer to the baking paper later on. You can chop the strips later, before decorating cakes and desserts.
12. You need 100g of juice for 100g of orange peel. If you prepare peels from a different number of oranges, adjust the amount of juice proportionally.
13. You need 150g of sugar for 100g of orange peel. If you prepare peels from a different number of oranges, adjust the amount of sugar proportionally.
14. It's very easy to separate hot peels. It's much harder after they have cooled.

KITCHEN ACCESSORIES

- ☐ large pot with lid
- ☐ frying pan
- ☐ large bowl
- ☐ bowl
- ☐ small bowl
- ☐ measuring jug
- ☐ glass
- ☐ knife
- ☐ chopping board
- ☐ 2 tablespoons
- ☐ 2 forks
- ☐ citrus juicer
- ☐ wooden spoon
- ☐ slotted spoon
- ☐ scissors
- ☐ kitchen scale
- ☐ baking paper
- ☐ jar with a rubber band (900ml)

GOOD TO KNOW

 vegetarian

 vegan

 gluten-free

 freezer
- store in the freezer until you use all the peel

 pantry
- store in an airtight jar in a dry place
- store in the pantry until you use all the peel

 kcal
- 1485 total

GOES WELL WITH

 **Viennese Cheesecake**
7. Cakes and Desserts, page 93

 ***Pączki***
8. Fat Thursday, page 145

 **Easter *Keks***
9. Easter, page 185

 ***Makowiec* (Poppy Seed Roll)**
9. Easter, page 189

 ***Makowiec* with Walnut Cream and Chocolate Glaze**
10. Christmas, page 229

 **Blueberry and *Twaróg* Yeast Buns**
vol 1, 1. Breakfast, page 33

WEIGHTS AND MEASURES

Conversion of measures, weights and baking temperatures to allow easy calculation and preparation of your favourite dishes. The given values have been rounded.

BAKING TEMPERATURES

Degrees Celsius	Degrees Celsius + fan	Degrees Fahrenheit	Gas oven
110°C	90°C	225°F	¼
130°C	110°C	250°F	½
140°C	120°C	275°F	1
150°C	130°C	300°F	2
170°C	150°C	325°F	3
180°C	160°C	350°F	4
190°C	170°C	375°F	5
200°C	180°C	400°F	6
220°C	200°C	425°F	7
230°C	210°C	450°F	8
240°C	220°C	475°F	9

WEIGHT CONVERSION

Metric system	Imperial system	Metric system	Imperial system
5g	¼oz	300g	11oz
15g	½oz	350g	12oz
20g	¾oz	375g	13oz
25g	1oz	400g	14oz
40g	1½oz	425g	15oz
50g	2oz	450g	16oz / 1lb
75g	3oz	550g	1¼lb
100g	4oz	675g	1½lb
150g	5oz	800g	1¾lb
175g	6oz	900g	2lb
200g	7oz	1,3kg	3lb
225g	8oz	1,8kg	4lb
250g	9oz	2,2kg	5lb
275g	10oz		

VOLUME CONVERSION

Metric system	Imperial system
1.25ml	¼ tsp
2.5ml	½ tsp
3.75ml	¾ tsp
5ml	1 tsp
3.75ml	¼ tbs
7.5ml	½ tbs
11.25ml	¾ tbs
15ml	1 tbs
60ml	¼ cup
80ml	⅓ cup
120ml	½ cup
160ml	⅔ cup
180ml	¾ cup
240ml	1 cup

Metric system	Imperial system
25ml	1fl oz
50ml	2fl oz
85ml	3fl oz
125ml	4fl oz
150ml	5fl oz / ¼ pint
175ml	6fl oz
200ml	7fl oz
225ml	8fl oz
250ml	9fl oz
300ml	10fl oz / ½ pint
425ml	15fl oz / ¾ pint
600ml	20fl oz / 1 pint
700ml	1¼ pints
900ml	1½ pints
1 litre	1¾ pints
1.2 litres	2 pints
1.3 litres	2¼ pints
1.5 litres	2½ pints
1.6 litres	2¾ pints
1.7 litres	3 pints
1.8 litres	3¼ pints
2 litres	3½ pints
3 litres	5½ pints
4 litres	7 pints
5 litres	8¾ pints

Weights and Measures

ABOUT THE PRODUCTS

Some Polish ingredients might be difficult to find locally. Here are descriptions of some Polish products and what they contain which may help you find the right equivalent.

Allspice

With a flavour profile that is a combination of cinnamon, pepper, cloves and nutmeg, this spice had been named allspice by the English. Allspice comes from Mexico and Central America. In the 16th century it arrived in Europe and became popular a century later. From England it travelled to Poland where it gained the name "*ziele angielskie*" – "English herb". This spice is widely used as an addition to marinades, fish, meat and cured meat, such as *kiełbasa* (sausage) or ham, as well as soups, sauces, vegetables and rice. It's very intense, so use it in moderation. If you are using whole berries, add them at the beginning. In Poland it is more common to find allspice berries rather than ground allspice.

Almond sugar

Sugar infused with the flavour of almonds used mainly in baked goods and desserts. It sweetens them and gives an almond taste and aroma.

Beef

Beef is one of the most popular meats eaten in the world. Many cuts of beef are slightly different between countries. The following cuts are most similar to common Polish cuts of beef:

1. <u>Rump/round</u> – a very lean cut of beef, which you can use to prepare goulash, roulades or steak tartare. Beef knuckle can be found here.

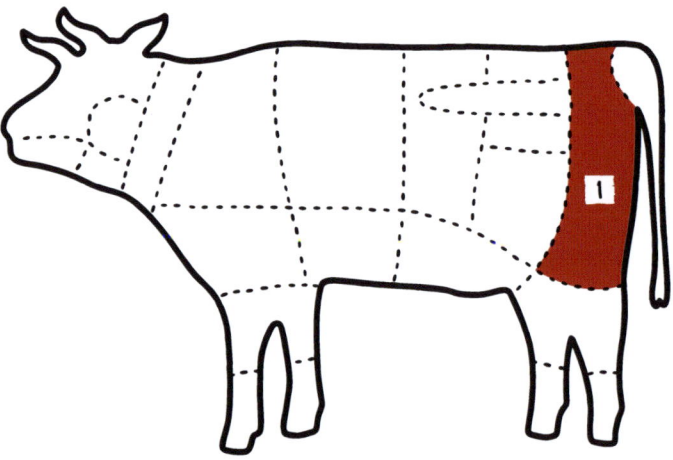

Beetroot *zakwas*

A fermented liquid made from beetroot and rye bread. The colour of beetroot *zakwas* is deep red and tastes slightly sour. Beetroot *zakwas* can be enriched by adding garlic and bay leaves. The time needed to make beetroot *zakwas* is around 7-10 days. It can be used as a drink or used to make red borscht. Traditionally soured red borscht is served on Christmas Eve. Beetroot *zakwas* can be purchased from stores that specialise in Polish products.

Budyń

Budyń is a cream with similar consistency to custard. *Budyń* comes in a range of colours and flavours. The most popular are sweet cream, vanilla and chocolate. *Budyń* is made with cream, milk, egg yolks, sugar and potato starch. Its most common version is available in shops as a powder you add to boiling milk along with the sugar. It can be eaten on its own or with some fruit. It can also be used to layer cakes and cookies or to fill various baked goods such as *pączki* and yeast buns.

Vanilla and chocolate budyń are shown here.

Candied orange peel

In Poland we usually buy it ready-made; however, if not available locally you can prepare it yourself. It's a perfect addition to cakes, desserts, and ice cream. Candied orange peel can be substituted with Italian Mixed Peel.

Caraway

Caraway seed has a very strong, aromatic flavour, so you need to use it sparingly. Caraway is a carminative, so it is used as a seasoning for dishes that are harder to digest – fatty meats, boiled and fresh cabbage – and in soups. It can be also used in slaws. You can buy it either whole or ground.

Cucumbers

Cucumbers are found in a lot of Polish recipes and are an important vegetable in Polish cooking. Cucumbers belong to the gourd family which consists of more than 50 varieties. Cucumbers are mostly eaten because of their taste since their nutrition value is minimal. Over 90% of the composition of cucumber is water, and the remaining few percent contain vitamins and minerals. When cucumbers are fermented, their chemical composition changes – the amount of lactic acid, B vitamins (B1, B2, B3, B6) and sodium rises significantly.
Cucumis sativus is widespread in all climatic zones. The fruit of cucumbers are usually eaten raw. Perfect for pickling and fermenting. The Polish cultivars I recommend are *Cezar, Hermes, Julian, Odys, Parys, Polan*.

Culinary citric acid

A white powder which enhances the taste of dishes, jams and juices, while also preserving the colour of fruit and vegetables. The culinary version is usually available in Polish stores.

Dill

Dill (Anethum graveolens) – The leaves, stems and umbels are used in a variety of Polish dishes. Fresh, chopped dill leaves can be added to salads, potatoes, soups, egg and fish dishes. You can also use dill to make dill sauce which is a great addition to meat, poultry, fish or snails. Its shoots and umbels are used to make pickles. Lukullus is the cultivar I recommend.

Gingerbread spice

A Polish blend of spices which includes cloves, cinnamon, cardamom, nutmeg, ginger, allspice and anise. It can be enriched with grated lemon or orange peel. You can buy the spice blend or make it yourself. It's mostly used for gingerbread cakes and cookies made for Christmas.

Herbatniki

Herbatniki are small and hard cookies, whose most popular shape resembles a postage stamp - they are rectangular, with small teeth on the edges. Being rich in butter, they gain their characteristic buttery taste. The Polish name *herbatniki* comes from these biscuits usually being served with tea (*herbata*).

Horseradish

Fresh horseradish has a stinging taste and a very strong aroma. Therefore, you should use less of it than you would shop-bought horseradish from a jar. Used as a seasoning. The root should be peeled and cleaned. You can grate it and use it as a condiment. In the shops, you can usually find little jars of grated, creamed horseradish.

Jelly

Jellies are eaten for dessert, often with whipped cream and fruits. It can also be used in cakes. The most popular jelly flavours are raspberry, strawberry, lemon, orange, cherry and gooseberry. Created from gelling agents such as gelatin, pectin or agar, which give it a solid gelatinous consistency. Polish products named "*galaretka*" are a combination of gelatin, sugar, colourings and flavourings. Most usually in a variety of different fruit flavours. These products must be dissolved in hot water and cooled to solidify and achieve the right consistency.

Ketchup

Regular ketchup is available pretty much everywhere. In Poland you can buy a wide variety of different ketchups, ranging from spicy, to those flavoured with herbs such as basil and oregano, and even fruit such as plums and strawberries.

Kiełbasa

Kiełbasa translates to sausage; however, these are a little different to sausages found in the UK. In Poland, *kiełbasa* are traditionally made with spiced pork, and sometimes pork and beef. *Kiełbasa* are usually cured and smoked. Therefore, they can be eaten cold and don't require cooking. They can also be cooked, baked, fried or grilled.

Maggi

Maggi is a liquid seasoning brand similar in look, taste and consistency to soy sauce. It's composed of water, salt, vinegar and lovage essence. It is used to add a savoury flavour to soups, sauces, meats, and vegetable-based dishes.

Mąka krupczatka

A light, coarse-grained wheat flour with the consistency of porridge. In Poland it can be found as flour type 450. It's mostly used to make shortcrust pastry. It might also be used for breading and making pasta.

Marmalade

Polish marmalade is much thicker than marmalade found in the UK and USA and comes in a variety of different flavours, rather than the usual orange found elsewhere. Jam or marmalade can be substituted for Polish marmalade; however, it would be better to try and find Polish marmalade where possible. Polish marmalade is prepared from puréed fresh fruit with a lot of sugar. The production mainly uses apples, which are rich in pectin. To obtain intense colour, blueberries or chokeberry are added. The flavour is enhanced by adding cherries, strawberries or gooseberries. During processing, a concentrate is created, which is thickened and then pasteurised. The marmalade should not be too hard or gelatinous. It should be easy to cut and spread, e.g. on bread. Polish marmalade is used to fill *pączki*, yeast buns and used between layers of biscuits.

Masa makowa

A mixture made from poppy seeds, cranberries and candied orange peel. Some versions can also contain raisins, apricots, walnuts and flaked almonds. The base of the mixture is prepared from boiled and then ground poppy seeds. Then the fruit and nuts are added. It's sweetened with honey and sugar. In Poland it's mostly used on Christmas and Easter to make poppy seed cakes.

Mushroom stock

Usually available as a bouillon cube. Polish mushroom stock contains: oil, potato starch, dried vegetables, dried mushrooms, black pepper and sugar. It's a good addition to soups, sauces and goulash. You can use the broth from rehydrating dried mushrooms as a substitute.

Oscypek

A hard, smoked cheese made with sheep's milk. After the cheese is made, it is left to mature and smoked e.g., with pine or spruce wood. *Oscypek* is a Polish product protected by the EU law, which determines its parameters and composition, process, and place of production. The original *oscypek* is shaped like a cylinder. Due to its popularity, dairy companies produce similar cheeses in various shapes and sizes, yet they cannot be called *oscypek* due to the legal protection of the name. You can find them under the label "*ser górski*" ("mountain cheese").

Pickled mushrooms

Pickled mushrooms are small mushrooms marinated in water, 10% spirit vinegar and sugar. Some versions may contain spices such as bay leaves, allspice and cinnamon. Pickled mushrooms are used mainly for salads; however, they can also be added to *zrazy* or used as a *pierogi* filling.

Pork

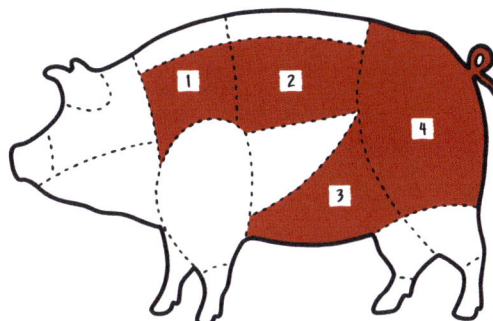

In Poland pork is a very popular meat, used in many dishes.
1. Neck/shoulder – this cut is great for braising and grilling. You can also use it to make collar bacon.
2. Loin – the most valuable part of the pig. Mostly used for frying, roasting and smoking. Sirloin and back bacon can be found here. You can also use it to make cured meats such as *polędwica sopocka* and roasted pork loin (*schab pieczony*).
3. Belly – it can be braised, roasted or boiled. Often used for Polish bacon (*boczek*), it's also added to pâtés and roulades.
4. Leg/ham – the most universal cut of pork consists of succulent and firm muscles. It is used to make smoked or boiled hams. Pork hip can also be found here.

Potato starch

Potato flour consists of 84% starch, which makes it a great thickening agent. It's perfect for thickening soups and stews. It doesn't change the taste or the colour of the dish. It can be substituted with cornstarch.

Purple plums (Common plums)

Purple plums probably travelled to Poland from Hungary – and therefore in Polish they are named Hungarian plums (*śliwki węgierki*). The fruit is of small or medium size (20-30g). Its peel is dark blue, and the pulp, ranging from dark yellow to orange, very easily comes away from the stone. Purple plums are very juicy, sweet and slightly tart. In Poland, plum season begins in mid-September and lasts until the end of October. They taste great when eaten fresh, but also with desserts and pancakes. You can dry them or make plum jam. You can also add them to meat dishes and sauces.

Sauerkraut

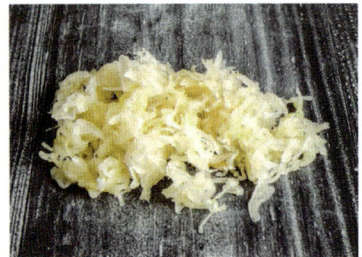

Finely chopped cabbage, fermented with salt. When fermented, the cabbage has a distinct aroma and a sour flavour. You can use it in many recipes such as *bigos*, *kapuśniak* and *pierogi*. Polish *kiszona kapusta* can be easily substituted with German sauerkraut.

Sour cream (*śmietana* and *śmietanka*)

Śmietana is a sour cream made with cow's milk which has a thick consistency. Its flavour is acidic, slightly salty and cheesy. In Poland, a few different types of *śmietana* are available. They are usually divided based on their fat content and their purpose. 12% sour cream is used in salads, sauces, and soups, while the 18% sour cream – mostly in soups.
Śmietanka is sweet and is higher in fat. It corresponds to cream. In Poland two versions can be found – 30% – for whipping and for soups – and 36% – for desserts.

Sour gherkins

Sour gherkins are made with pickling cucumbers with the addition of garlic cloves, horseradish root, as well as dill stems and their umbel flower heads. They are covered with water and salt and left to ferment. Sour gherkins can be eaten on sandwiches or as a side to hot dishes. You can also make a sour gherkin soup. They are a great side to goulash.

Sweet cherries

Sweet cherries are very popular in Poland. The season lasts from the beginning of June until the end of July. Depending on the cultivar, sweet cherries have different colours – they might be yellow, pink, red, dark red or even black. Their pulp is sweet and can be used in many ways. They can be eaten fresh or used in preserves. They give a great flavour to cakes and desserts. They are also used to make spirits.

Twaróg

White cheese made with soured milk. *Twaróg* belongs to the "fresh" group of cheeses. The consistency is crumbly, and it breaks up when cut into slices. Three versions are available in the shops: low-fat, semi-skimmed and full-fat cheese. The fattier the *twaróg* is, the creamier it is as well. Depending on the region, it's also called "white cheese", while the names "*twaróg*" and "*twarożek*" are used for dishes which consist of white cheese with sour cream, chives and radishes.

Vanillin / Vanilla Sugar

Vanilla sugar is used as a flavouring for cakes and desserts. Vanillin sugar is a cheaper substitute for vanilla sugar. You can make your own natural vanilla sugar, adding a chopped vanilla pod to a jar of sugar. You can store it in an airtight jar for several weeks. Depending on the recipe, vanillin / vanilla sugar can be substituted with a vanilla pod or vanilla extract.

Vegeta

Dried vegetable mix brand made with iodised salt, dried vegetables such as carrots, parsnips, potatoes, onion, celeriac, parsley as well as sugar, cornstarch and flavour enhancers. It's a perfect addition to boiled, fried, roasted, braised and grilled dishes.

Wafers

A confectionery product which, depending on its intended use, may be in the form of a flat, thin piece of wafer, a cone or a tube. A popular type in Poland are thin, chequered wafers called *andruty*. They are used, among other things, for making pischinger – layers of wafers and a sweet cream filling. Cones and tubes can be used in desserts, filled with ice cream or whipped cream.

White *kiełbasa*

White *kiełbasa* (sausage), unlike other Polish sausages, is a type of sausage which needs to be either cooked or baked before serving. It has a characteristic brighter colour than most Polish sausages. The sausage is mostly made with pork, sometimes with the addition of beef. It's traditionally served with *żurek* on Easter. It can also be eaten on its own with horseradish.

Yeast

Yeast is a natural raising agent. Before adding it to the dough it's best to dissolve it in milk warmed up to 37°C / 100°F. After adding it to the dough, the process of alcoholic fermentation takes place, during which carbon dioxide is released. The gas makes the dough rise and loosen. You cannot freeze nor heat the yeast too much since it stops reproducing and loses its rising properties. You can buy packets of powdered yeast. In Poland you can also buy fresh yeast in the form of a 100g block.

Zakwas for white borscht and *żurek*

A tangy fermented liquid made using flour and warm water. Depending on the flour you can prepare two versions which can be used to make borscht or *żurek*. To prepare a milder version for borscht use wheat flour. A tangier version made with rye is used to make *żurek*. Both versions required 3 days of fermentation. These two versions of *zakwas* are available in Polish stores.

ABOUT THE ACCESSORIES

You might not be familiar with some tools and gadgets used in a Polish kitchen. For my version of raspberry juice we are going to use a steam juicer, here I explain what it is and how to use it.

Steam juicer

Description
Using a steam juicer, you can make juice from fresh fruit and some vegetables. It works by exposing the fruit to steam, breaking down the cell walls of the fruit, releasing their juice. What remains, can be used to prepare jams.

This process is convenient and very safe. The resulting steam is not kept under pressure.

To the fruit you can add sugar, which acts as a preservative. It will dissolve and combine with the juice.

Construction
Depending on the model, the steam juicer can have different sizes which are given in litres. The juicer consists of three vessels that are put one on top of the other. List of vessels, starting from the top:

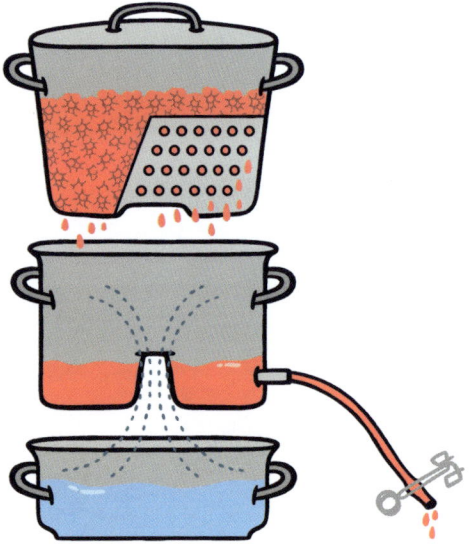

- An upper vessel (colander) equipped with a lid, with holes at the bottom that allow steam to flow and juice to be drained into the centre vessel. The holes are small enough to prevent fruit pulp, peel and seeds from entering the juice kettle.

- The centre vessel gathers the juice (juice kettle). It contains a hole which allows the flow of steam and a hose with a clamp for draining the juice.

- The bottom vessel (steam pot) warms up the water that creates the steam.

How it works
1. Water heated in the bottom vessel evaporates and passes into the middle vessel through a hole.
2. The hot steam collected in the middle vessel (juice kettle) heats the fruit via the holes in the colander.
3. Due to the steam, the juice from the fruit starts to exude and gather in the middle vessel.
4. When there's enough juice, it flows into a hose with a clamp.
5. By releasing the clamp, you can pour the hot juice into a separate pot and then pour it into jars using a funnel.
6. The jars with the juice can be pasteurised. You can find all the information about the pasteurisation process on page 342.

Use
You can make juice from various fruits in the steam juicer:
- soft fruit, such as strawberries, raspberries, bilberries, currants, grapes, cherries, mirabelle plums. Clean the fruit and remove any pits or stones. The time needed to collect the juice is around 30 minutes.
- semi-soft fruit, cut into smaller pieces, such as apples, peaches, mangoes. Clean the fruit and remove any pips or stones. The time needed to collect the juice is 30-40 minutes.
- hard fruit, such as gooseberries and pears cut into pieces; the time needed to collect the juice is 40-60 minutes.

You can also mix and match – for example, try the combination of raspberries and apples!

Vegetable scraps can also be used to make a vegetable broth as a base for soups.

Safety
- When using the steam juicer, pay special attention to position it correctly on the hob so that it does not tip over.
- Place a stool with a pot next to the hob so that the hose coming out of the vessel with the juice is always in the pot. If the clamp is leaking, the juice will flow directly into the pot. Also be careful not to tip over the stool with the pot. If you have pets or children make sure they are kept away from the stool and pot.
- When you use the steam juicer, the clamp must always be placed on the hose – even when the hose is in the pot. Only release the clamp when you want to drain the juice from the hose into the pot. Be careful not to burn yourself with hot juice.

PASTEURISATION

Thanks to pasteurisation, fruit and vegetables and their nutritional values can be preserved for a long time and enjoyed all year without losing their taste.

About pasteurisation
Pasteurisation is a method of preserving produce, which helps to retain the nutrients and flavour in vegetables and fruit. Pasteurisation destroys microbes and therefore extends the product durability.

Pasteurisation consists of heating closed jars in water or in the oven. Pasteurisation time depends on a few factors:
- the size of the jar – the bigger the jar, the longer the pasteurisation process,
- the product you are pasteurising – fruit needs less time than vegetables,
- the contents of the jar – jams and purées need less time than pieces of fruit and vegetables.

What can we pasteurise?
The most pasteurised vegetables are cucumbers, beetroots, carrots, peppers, zucchini, pumpkin and mushrooms. Popular fruits include strawberries, cherries and plums, which can be pasteurised whole, in pieces, in the form of compotes, juices or purées.

How to prepare the jars?
There are a few important rules when it comes to pasteurisation:
- jars – their edges cannot be broken nor jagged,
- the lid cannot be deformed and must adhere tightly to the jar,
- jars and lids should be thoroughly washed with hot water and dried before use.

Only put freshly made, hot preserves into the jars, leaving 2-3cm of space at the top of the jar. Carefully wipe the edge of the jar, so that it's clean and dry. Close the jar with a clean lid.

Not all types of jars can be pasteurised in the same manner. Jars with rubber seals can only be pasteurised in pots filled with water ("wet" pasteurisation), while twist-off jars can be pasteurised both in water and in the oven.

"Wet" Pasteurisation
1. Put a tea towel on the bottom of a large pot to prevent the wobbling jars from hitting it during cooking.
2. Place the jars in the pot, leaving some space between them. The jars should all be the same size.
3. You can put an additional tea towel in between the jars to dampen vibrations.
4. Pour the water up to ¾ of the height of the jars. If the jars are cold, fill the pot with cold water, and if the jars are hot use warm water.
5. Bring the water to a boil. Cook the jars for 15-30 minutes. The smaller the jar, the less time it needs. Pasteurisation time should not exceed 30 minutes.
6. After this time, take the jars out of the pot using a tea towel so as not to burn your hands, and check if they're tightly sealed. It's a good sign when the lids are slightly concave – the jar is closed well. Be careful: the jars will be very hot!
7. Place the jars on a counter or a table covered with a towel, turning them upside down. If the jar makes a hissing sound, it means it is leaking. You can either eat the contents of such a jar right away or put into a new, air-tight jar and pasteurise again.
8. Leave the jars to cool completely.

Oven pasteurisation
1. Put the jars in a high-rimmed baking tray, leaving some space between them. If one of the jars breaks during pasteurisation, the contents will spill out into the tray.
2. Put the tray in a cold oven.
3. Set the temperature to 130°C / 250°F or gas 1 for around 1 hour.
4. Turn off the oven and leave the jars until they cool completely.
5. Place the jars on a counter or a table turning them upside down. If the jar makes a hissing sound, it means it is leaking. You can either eat the contents of such a jar right away or put into a new, air-tight jar and pasteurise again.

Storing your preserves
You should store your preserves in a cool, dark place such as a pantry or a basement. It's best to store them for no more than a year. After that time, preserves change colour, oxidise and lose their nutrients. It's a good idea to put a label with the preparation date and the content of the given preserve on every jar. This helps to organise them. Nobody wants to find unlabelled and undated jars in the back of their cupboard!

INDEX

A

allspice, berries
    Beef and Poultry Pasztet 255
    Beetroot Zakwas 199
    Chicken Jelly 43
    Christmas Eve Sauerkraut with Mushrooms 225
    Christmas Gingerbread Cake 235
    Courgette Leczo 291
    Cucumber and Carrot Salad 283
    Easter Żurek 163
    „Greek" Fish (Ryba po grecku) 39
    Mulled Wine 245
    Ogórki Konserwowe (Pickled Gherkins) 263
    Pickled Beetroot 271
    Pickled Peppers 275
    Seasoned Red Cabbage 279
    Soured Red Borscht 203
    Tea-Boiled Ham 251
    Traditional Christmas Gingerbread Biscuits 241

allspice, ground
    Kebab Salad 27

almond, extract
    Makowiec with Walnut Cream and Chocolate Glaze 229

almonds, flaked
    Makowiec with Walnut Cream and Chocolate Glaze 229

amaretto
    Tiramisu 59

apple
    Apple and Twaróg Cake 97
    Apple Pie 71
    Apple Sauce 309
    Chocolate Cake with Apples, Dried Fruit and Nuts 67
    Preserved Apple Slices 307

apricots, dried
    Chocolate Cake with Apples, Dried Fruit and Nuts 67
    Easter Keks 185
    Makowiec with Walnut Cream and Chocolate Glaze 229

avocado
    Spinach, Feta and Boczek Salad 35

B

back bacon, smoked
    Easter Żurek 163
    Oscypek with Cranberries and Boczek 15
    Spinach, Feta and Boczek Salad 35

baguette
    Zapiekanka 21

baking powder
    Apple and Twaróg Cake 97
    Apple Pie 71
    Cherry and Custard Pie 79
    Chocolate Cake with Apples, Dried Fruit and Nuts 67
    Coconut Cream Pie with Plum Jam 85
    Dewdrop Cheesecake 89
    Easter Babka 181
    Easter Keks 185
    Karpatka 135
    Kocie Oczka 109
    Makowiec with Walnut Cream and Chocolate Glaze 229
    Napoleon 103
    Plum Pie 75
    Rhubarb Cake 63
    Victoria Sponge 49

bay leaf
    Beef and Poultry Pasztet 255
    Beetroot Zakwas 199
    Chicken Jelly 43
    Christmas Eve Sauerkraut with Mushrooms 225
    Courgette Leczo 291
    Cucumber and Carrot Salad 283
    Easter Żurek 163
    „Greek" Fish (Ryba po grecku) 39
    Ogórki Konserwowe (Pickled Gherkins) 263
    Pickled Beetroot 271
    Pickled Peppers 275
    Seasoned Red Cabbage 279
    Soured Red Borscht 203
    Tea-Boiled Ham 251

beef knuckle off the bone
    Beef and Poultry Pasztet 255

beetroot
    Beetroot Zakwas 199
    Pickled Beetroot 271
    Soured Red Borscht 203

bicarbonate of soda
- Candied Orange Peel 321
- Chocolate Cake with Apples, Dried Fruit and Nuts 67
- Christmas Gingerbread Cake 235
- Oponki 151
- Raspberry Jam 313
- Rhubarb Cake 63
- Traditional Christmas Gingerbread Biscuits 241

black pepper
- Beef and Poultry Pasztet 255
- Christmas Eve Sauerkraut with Mushrooms 225
- Easter Żurek 163
- „Greek" Fish (Ryba po grecku) 39
- Kebab Salad 27
- Pickled Mushroom Salad 31
- Sałatka Jarzynowa (Polish Vegetable Salad) 167
- Soured Red Borscht 203
- Spinach, Feta and Boczek Salad 35
- Stuffed Eggs with Ham and Cheese 178
- Stuffed Eggs with Mushrooms 174
- Stuffed Eggs with Sundried Tomatoes, Garlic and Feta Cheese 171
- Stuffed Eggs with Tuna 176
- Tuna Salad 23
- Uszka Filling 207

black pepper, ground
- Barbecued Kiełbaski 17
- Courgette Leczo 291
- Kebab Salad 27

boczek, smoked
- Easter Żurek 163
- Oscypek with Cranberries and Boczek 15
- Spinach, Feta and Boczek Salad 35

bread
- Barbecued Kiełbaski 17
- Chicken Jelly 43
- „Greek" Fish (Ryba po grecku) 39
- Kebab Salad 27
- Pickled Mushroom Salad 31
- Sałatka Jarzynowa (Polish Vegetable Salad) 167
- Spinach, Feta and Boczek Salad 35
- Tuna Salad 23

breadcrumbs
- Apple Pie 71
- Beef and Poultry Pasztet 255
- Cherry and Custard Pie 79
- Christmas Eve Fried Fish 221
- Easter Babka 181
- Plum Pie 75
- Uszka Filling 207

bread rolls
- Beef and Poultry Pasztet 255

bread, rye
- Beetroot Zakwas 199
- Easter Żurek 163

budyń, sweet cream
- Apple and Twaróg Cake 97

budyń, vanilla
- Cherry and Custard Pie 79
- Dewdrop Cheesecake 89
- Karpatka 135

butter
- Beef and Poultry Pasztet 255
- Chocolate Cake with Apples, Dried Fruit and Nuts 67
- Christmas Eve Sauerkraut with Mushrooms 225
- Easter Babka 181
- Easter Keks 185
- Rhubarb Cake 63
- Uszka 215
- Uszka Filling 207
- Zapiekanka 21

butter, unsalted
- Apple and Twaróg Cake 97
- Apple Pie 71
- Cherry and Custard Pie 79
- Christmas Gingerbread Cake 235
- Coconut Cream Pie with Plum Jam 85
- Cream Horns 121
- Dewdrop Cheesecake 89
- Easy Kremówka 117
- Kajmak Pischinger 139
- Karpatka 135
- Kocie Oczka 109
- Makowiec (Poppy Seed Roll) 189
- Makowiec with Walnut Cream and Chocolate Glaze 229
- Marmalade Biscuits 127
- Napoleon 103
- Pączki 145
- Plum Pie 75
- Sweet Twaróg Biscuits 131
- Traditional Christmas Gingerbread Biscuits 241
- Uszka Dough 211
- Victoria Sponge 49
- Viennese Cheesecake 93
- Walnut Pie 113
- Walnut Sponge with Almond Cream 53

C

cabbage, Chinese
  Kebab Salad 27
cabbage, red
  Seasoned Red Cabbage 279
caraway, ground
  Christmas Eve Sauerkraut with Mushrooms 225
caraway seeds
  Pickled Beetroot 271
cardamom, ground
  Christmas Gingerbread Cake 235
  Traditional Christmas Gingerbread Biscuits 241
carrot
  Beef and Poultry Pasztet 255
  Chicken Jelly 43
  Christmas Eve Sauerkraut with Mushrooms 225
  Cucumber and Carrot Salad 283
  „Greek" Fish (Ryba po grecku) 39
  Pickled Vegetable Salad 287
  Sałatka Jarzynowa (Polish Vegetable Salad) 167
  Soured Red Borscht 203
celeriac
  Beef and Poultry Pasztet 255
  Chicken Jelly 43
  „Greek" Fish (Ryba po grecku) 39
  Sałatka Jarzynowa (Polish Vegetable Salad) 167
  Soured Red Borscht 203
cheese, cheddar
  Pickled Mushroom Salad 31
  Stuffed Eggs with Ham and Cheese 178
  Tuna Salad 23
  Zapiekanka 21
cheese, feta
  Spinach, Feta and Boczek Salad 35
  Stuffed Eggs with Sundried Tomatoes, Garlic and Feta Cheese 171
cheese, mascarpone
  Tiramisu 59
cheese, twaróg (low-fat)
  Apple and Twaróg Cake 97
  Dewdrop Cheesecake 89
  Oponki 151
  Sweet Twaróg Biscuits 131
cheese, twaróg (semi-skimmed)
  Viennese Cheesecake 93
cherries
  Cherry and Custard Pie 79
cherries, sweet
  Sweet Cherry Kompot 301
chicken bouillon cube
  Easter Żurek 163
chicken fillets
  Kebab Salad 27
chicken thighs
  Beef and Poultry Pasztet 255
  Chicken Jelly 43

chilli flakes
  Barbecued Kiełbaski 17
  Kebab Salad 27
chilli pepper
  Courgette Leczo 291
chives
  Stuffed Eggs with Ham and Cheese 178
  Stuffed Eggs with Sundried Tomatoes, Garlic and Feta Cheese 171
  Stuffed Eggs with Tuna 176
  Zapiekanka 21
chocolate, dark
  Christmas Gingerbread Cake 235
chocolate, milk
  Makowiec with Walnut Cream and Chocolate Glaze 229
  Viennese Cheesecake 93
cinnamon, ground
  Apple Pie 71
  Chocolate Cake with Apples, Dried Fruit and Nuts 67
  Christmas Gingerbread Cake 235
  Mulled Wine 245
  Plum Pie 75
  Traditional Christmas Gingerbread Biscuits 241
citric acid
  Candied Orange Peel 321
  Raspberry Jam 313
clove
  Christmas Gingerbread Cake 235
  Kebab Salad 27
  Mulled Wine 245
  Pickled Peppers 275
  Traditional Christmas Gingerbread Biscuits 241
cocoa powder
  Apple and Twaróg Cake 97
  Chocolate Cake with Apples, Dried Fruit and Nuts 67
  Christmas Gingerbread Cake 235
  Coconut Cream Pie with Plum Jam 85
  Easter Babka 181
  Tiramisu 59
  Traditional Christmas Gingerbread Biscuits 241
coconut, desiccated
  Coconut Cream Pie with Plum Jam 85
coffee, espresso (instant)
  Tiramisu 59
coriander, ground
  Kebab Salad 27
  Seasoned Red Cabbage 279
coriander seeds
  Christmas Gingerbread Cake 235
  Traditional Christmas Gingerbread Biscuits 241

courgette
    Courgette Leczo 291
cranberries, dried
    Chocolate Cake with Apples, Dried Fruit and
        Nuts 67
    Easter Keks 185
    Makowiec with Walnut Cream and
        Chocolate Glaze 229
cranberry, jam
    Oscypek with Cranberries and Boczek 15
cream, double
    Kajmak Pischinger 139
cream, sour
    Apple and Twaróg Cake 97
    Apple Pie 71
    Cherry and Custard Pie 79
    Coconut Cream Pie with Plum Jam 85
    Cream Horns 121
    Dewdrop Cheesecake 89
    Easter Żurek 163
    Faworki 155
    Kocie Oczka 109
    Marmalade Biscuits 127
    Napoleon 103
    Plum Pie 75
cucumber
    Zapiekanka 21
cucumber, pickling
    Cucumber and Carrot Salad 283
    Ogórki Kiszone (Sour Gherkins) 259
    Ogórki Konserwowe (Pickled Gherkins) 263
    Pickled Vegetable Salad 287

D

dill
    Ogórki Kiszone (Sour Gherkins) 259
    Ogórki Konserwowe (Pickled Gherkins) 263
    Pickled Vegetable Salad 287

E

egg
    Apple and Twaróg Cake 97
    Apple Pie 71
    Beef and Poultry Pasztet 255
    Cherry and Custard Pie 79
    Chicken Jelly 43
    Chocolate Cake with Apples, Dried Fruit and
        Nuts 67
    Christmas Eve Fried Fish 221
    Christmas Gingerbread Cake 235
    Coconut Cream Pie with Plum Jam 85
    Dewdrop Cheesecake 89
    Easter Babka 181
    Easter Keks 185
    Easter Żurek 163
    Easy Kremówka 117
    Faworki 155
    Karpatka 135
    Kocie Oczka 109
    Makowiec (Poppy Seed Roll) 189
    Makowiec with Walnut Cream and
        Chocolate Glaze 229
    Napoleon 103
    Oponki 151
    Pączki 145
    Pickled Mushroom Salad 31
    Plum Pie 75
    Rhubarb Cake 63
    Sałatka Jarzynowa (Polish Vegetable Salad)
        167
    Stuffed Eggs with Ham and Cheese 178
    Stuffed Eggs with Mushrooms 174
    Stuffed Eggs with Sundried Tomatoes,
        Garlic and Feta Cheese 171
    Stuffed Eggs with Tuna 176
    Sweet Twaróg Biscuits 131
    Tiramisu 59
    Traditional Christmas Gingerbread Biscuits
        241
    Tuna Salad 23
    Victoria Sponge 49
    Viennese Cheesecake 93
    Walnut Pie 113
    Walnut Sponge with Almond Cream 53
egg white
    Cream Horns 121
    Dewdrop Cheesecake 89
egg yolk
    Cream Horns 121
    Dewdrop Cheesecake 89
    Easy Kremówka 117

F

fish fillets, white
    Christmas Eve Fried Fish 221
    „Greek" Fish (Ryba po grecku) 39
fish seasoning
    Christmas Eve Fried Fish 221
flour, oarsely milled wheat
    Walnut Sponge with Almond Cream 53
flour, plain
    Apple and Twaróg Cake 97
    Apple Pie 71
    Cherry and Custard Pie 79
    Chocolate Cake with Apples, Dried Fruit and Nuts 67
    Christmas Eve Fried Fish 221
    Christmas Eve Sauerkraut with Mushrooms 225
    Christmas Gingerbread Cake 235
    Coconut Cream Pie with Plum Jam 85
    Cream Horns 121
    Dewdrop Cheesecake 89
    Easter Babka 181
    Easter Keks 185
    Easy Kremówka 117
    Faworki 155
    „Greek" Fish (Ryba po grecku) 39
    Karpatka 135
    Kocie Oczka 109
    Makowiec (Poppy Seed Roll) 189
    Makowiec with Walnut Cream and Chocolate Glaze 229
    Marmalade Biscuits 127
    Napoleon 103
    Oponki 151
    Pączki 145
    Plum Pie 75
    Rhubarb Cake 63
    Sweet Twaróg Biscuits 131
    Traditional Christmas Gingerbread Biscuits 241
    Uszka 215
    Uszka Dough 211
    Victoria Sponge 49
    Viennese Cheesecake 93
    Walnut Pie 113
    Walnut Sponge with Almond Cream 53

G

garlic clove
    Barbecued Kiełbaski 17
    Beef and Poultry Pasztet 255
    Beetroot Zakwas 199
    Chicken Jelly 43
    Courgette Leczo 291
    Easter Żurek 163
    Kebab Salad 27
    Ogórki Kiszone (Sour Gherkins) 259
    Ogórki Konserwowe (Pickled Gherkins) 263
    Pickled Vegetable Salad 287
    Soured Red Borscht 203
    Spinach, Feta and Boczek Salad 35
    Stuffed Eggs with Sundried Tomatoes, Garlic and Feta Cheese 171
    Tea-Boiled Ham 251
garlic powder
    Barbecued Kiełbaski 17
    Chicken Jelly 43
    Kebab Salad 27
    Spinach, Feta and Boczek Salad 35
gelatine
    Chicken Jelly 43
gherkins, pickled
    Kebab Salad 27
    Pickled Mushroom Salad 31
    Stuffed Eggs with Tuna 176
    Tuna Salad 23
gherkins, sour
    Kebab Salad 27
    Pickled Mushroom Salad 31
    Sałatka Jarzynowa (Polish Vegetable Salad) 167
    Stuffed Eggs with Tuna 176
gingerbread seasoning
    Christmas Gingerbread Cake 235
    Traditional Christmas Gingerbread Biscuits 241
ginger, ground
    Christmas Gingerbread Cake 235
    Mulled Wine 245
    Traditional Christmas Gingerbread Biscuits 241

H

ham
    Stuffed Eggs with Ham and Cheese 178
herbes de Provence
    Barbecued Kiełbaski 17
honey
    Christmas Gingerbread Cake 235
    Makowiec with Walnut Cream and Chocolate Glaze 229
    Mulled Wine 245
    Traditional Christmas Gingerbread Biscuits 241
horseradish, piece
    Ogórki Kiszone (Sour Gherkins) 259
    Ogórki Konserwowe (Pickled Gherkins) 263
    Pickled Vegetable Salad 287

J

jam
    Pączki 145
juniper berries
    Kebab Salad 27

K

kebab seasoning
    Kebab Salad 27
ketchup
    Barbecued Kiełbaski 17
    Kebab Salad 27
    Tuna Salad 23
    Zapiekanka 21
kiełbasa, Silesian
    Barbecued Kiełbaski 17
    Easter Żurek 163
kiełbasa, white
    Easter Żurek 163

L

leek
    Beef and Poultry Pasztet 255
    Chicken Jelly 43
    Sałatka Jarzynowa (Polish Vegetable Salad) 167
    Soured Red Borscht 203
lemon
    Apple Pie 71
    Christmas Eve Fried Fish 221
    Preserved Apple Slices 307
    Raspberry Jam 313
lemon juice
    Christmas Eve Fried Fish 221
    Christmas Gingerbread Cake 235
    Easter Keks 185
    Makowiec (Poppy Seed Roll) 189
    Pączki 145
    Victoria Sponge 49
    Walnut Sponge with Almond Cream 53

M

marjoram
    Barbecued Kiełbaski 17
    Easter Żurek 163
marmalade
    Marmalade Biscuits 127
mayonnaise
    Kebab Salad 27
    Pickled Mushroom Salad 31
    Sałatka Jarzynowa (Polish Vegetable Salad) 167
    Spinach, Feta and Boczek Salad 35
    Stuffed Eggs with Ham and Cheese 178
    Stuffed Eggs with Mushrooms 174
    Stuffed Eggs with Sundried Tomatoes, Garlic and Feta Cheese 171
    Stuffed Eggs with Tuna 176
    Tuna Salad 23
    Zapiekanka 21

milk
    Apple and Twaróg Cake 97
    Cherry and Custard Pie 79
    Christmas Eve Fried Fish 221
    Christmas Gingerbread Cake 235
    Cream Horns 121
    Dewdrop Cheesecake 89
    Easy Kremówka 117
    „Greek" Fish (Ryba po grecku) 39
    Karpatka 135
    Makowiec (Poppy Seed Roll) 189
    Makowiec with Walnut Cream and Chocolate Glaze 229
    Napoleon 103
    Pączki 145
    Victoria Sponge 49
    Viennese Cheesecake 93
    Walnut Sponge with Almond Cream 53
milk, full-fat
    Kajmak Pischinger 139
mushroom bouillon cube
    Christmas Eve Sauerkraut with Mushrooms 225
    Stuffed Eggs with Mushrooms 174
mushrooms
    Stuffed Eggs with Mushrooms 174
    Zapiekanka 21
mushrooms, dried
    Christmas Eve Sauerkraut with Mushrooms 225
    Soured Red Borscht 203
    Uszka Filling 207
mushrooms, pickled
    Pickled Mushroom Salad 31
mustard
    Barbecued Kiełbaski 17
mustard seeds
    Kebab Salad 27
    Ogórki Konserwowe (Pickled Gherkins) 263
    Pickled Peppers 275
mustard, yellow
    Pickled Mushroom Salad 31
    Sałatka Jarzynowa (Polish Vegetable Salad) 167
    Stuffed Eggs with Ham and Cheese 178
    Stuffed Eggs with Mushrooms 174
    Stuffed Eggs with Tuna 176
    Tuna Salad 23

N

nutmeg, ground
    Christmas Gingerbread Cake 235
    Mulled Wine 245
    Traditional Christmas Gingerbread Biscuits 241

O

oil, cooking
    Chocolate Cake with Apples, Dried Fruit and Nuts 67
    Christmas Eve Fried Fish 221
    Courgette Leczo 291
    Cream Horns 121
    Dewdrop Cheesecake 89
    Easter Keks 185
    „Greek" Fish (Ryba po grecku) 39
    Makowiec (Poppy Seed Roll) 189
    Rhubarb Cake 63
    Stuffed Eggs with Mushrooms 174

oil, olive
    Barbecued Kiełbaski 17
    Kebab Salad 27

oil, rapeseed
    Faworki 155
    Oponki 151
    Pączki 145

onion
    Beef and Poultry Pasztet 255
    Chicken Jelly 43
    Christmas Eve Fried Fish 221
    Christmas Eve Sauerkraut with Mushrooms 225
    Courgette Leczo 291
    Cucumber and Carrot Salad 283
    „Greek" Fish (Ryba po grecku) 39
    Pickled Vegetable Salad 287
    Seasoned Red Cabbage 279
    Soured Red Borscht 203
    Stuffed Eggs with Mushrooms 174
    Tuna Salad 23
    Uszka Filling 207
    Zapiekanka 21

onion, red
    Kebab Salad 27
    Spinach, Feta and Boczek Salad 35

orange
    Candied Orange Peel 321
    Mulled Wine 245

orange, candied peel
    Easter Keks 185
    Makowiec (Poppy Seed Roll) 189
    Makowiec with Walnut Cream and Chocolate Glaze 229
    Pączki 145
    Viennese Cheesecake 93

orange, jelly
    Apple and Twaróg Cake 97
    Makowiec with Walnut Cream and Chocolate Glaze 229

orange juice
    Candied Orange Peel 321

oregano, dried
    Kebab Salad 27

oscypek
    Oscypek with Cranberries and Boczek 15

P

paprika
    Barbecued Kiełbaski 17
    Kebab Salad 27

paprika, hot
    Barbecued Kiełbaski 17
    Kebab Salad 27

paprika, smoked
    Barbecued Kiełbaski 17

parsley
    Chicken Jelly 43
    Stuffed Eggs with Ham and Cheese 178
    Stuffed Eggs with Mushrooms 174
    Stuffed Eggs with Tuna 176

parsnip
    Beef and Poultry Pasztet 255
    Chicken Jelly 43
    Christmas Eve Sauerkraut with Mushrooms 225
    „Greek" Fish (Ryba po grecku) 39
    Sałatka Jarzynowa (Polish Vegetable Salad) 167
    Soured Red Borscht 203

pears
    Pear Kompot 304

peas
    Chicken Jelly 43
    Sałatka Jarzynowa (Polish Vegetable Salad) 167
    Tuna Salad 23

peppercorns
    Beetroot Zakwas 199
    Chicken Jelly 43
    Ogórki Konserwowe (Pickled Gherkins) 263
    Seasoned Red Cabbage 279
    Tea-Boiled Ham 251

peppers
    Courgette Leczo 291
    Pickled Peppers 275
    Pickled Vegetable Salad 287

plum, jam
    Christmas Gingerbread Cake 235
    Coconut Cream Pie with Plum Jam 85
    Kocie Oczka 109
    Walnut Pie 113

plum, purple (common)
    Plum Pie 75
    Powidła śliwkowe (Plum Jam) 317

poppy seed mixture
    Makowiec (Poppy Seed Roll) 189

poppy seeds
    Makowiec with Walnut Cream and Chocolate Glaze 229

pork loin
    Tea-Boiled Ham 251

potato starch
  Christmas Gingerbread Cake 235
  Coconut Cream Pie with Plum Jam 85
  Cream Horns 121
  Easter Babka 181
  Easter Keks 185
  Easy Kremówka 117
  Napoleon 103
  Victoria Sponge 49
  Viennese Cheesecake 93
  Walnut Sponge with Almond Cream 53

R

radish
  Stuffed Eggs with Ham and Cheese 178
raisins
  Chocolate Cake with Apples, Dried Fruit and Nuts 67
  Easter Babka 181
  Easter Keks 185
  Makowiec with Walnut Cream and Chocolate Glaze 229
  Viennese Cheesecake 93
raspberry
  Raspberry Jam 313
  Raspberry Juice 295
raspberry, juice
  Mulled Wine 245
red wine
  Mulled Wine 245
rhubarb, fresh
  Rhubarb Cake 63
rosemary, dried
  Kebab Salad 27

S

salt
  Beef and Poultry Pasztet 255
  Beetroot Zakwas 199
  Chicken Jelly 43
  Christmas Eve Fried Fish 221
  Courgette Leczo 291
  Cream Horns 121
  Cucumber and Carrot Salad 283
  Easter Keks 185
  Easter Żurek 163
  Faworki 155
  „Greek" Fish (Ryba po grecku) 39
  Karpatka 135
  Kebab Salad 27
  Makowiec (Poppy Seed Roll) 189
  Makowiec with Walnut Cream and Chocolate Glaze 229
  Ogórki Konserwowe (Pickled Gherkins) 263
  Pączki 145
  Pickled Beetroot 271
  Pickled Mushroom Salad 31
  Pickled Peppers 275
  Pickled Vegetable Salad 287
  Sałatka Jarzynowa (Polish Vegetable Salad) 167
  Seasoned Red Cabbage 279
  Soured Red Borscht 203
  Stuffed Eggs with Ham and Cheese 178
  Stuffed Eggs with Mushrooms 174
  Stuffed Eggs with Sundried Tomatoes, Garlic and Feta Cheese 171
  Stuffed Eggs with Tuna 176
  Tea-Boiled Ham 251
  Tuna Salad 23
  Uszka 215
  Uszka Dough 211
  Uszka Filling 207
  Viennese Cheesecake 93
salt, non-iodized
  Ogórki Kiszone (Sour Gherkins) 259
salt, pickling
  Tea-Boiled Ham 251
sauerkraut
  Christmas Eve Sauerkraut with Mushrooms 225
spinach, fresh
  Spinach, Feta and Boczek Salad 35
sponge fingers
  Tiramisu 59
star anise, whole
  Christmas Gingerbread Cake 235
  Mulled Wine 245
  Traditional Christmas Gingerbread Biscuits 241
strawberry
  Strawberry Syrup 299
strawberry, jam
  Victoria Sponge 49

sugar
- Apple and Twaróg Cake 97
- Apple Pie 71
- Apple Sauce 309
- Candied Orange Peel 321
- Cherry and Custard Pie 79
- Chocolate Cake with Apples, Dried Fruit and Nuts 67
- Christmas Gingerbread Cake 235
- Coconut Cream Pie with Plum Jam 85
- Courgette Leczo 291
- Cream Horns 121
- Cucumber and Carrot Salad 283
- Dewdrop Cheesecake 89
- Easter Babka 181
- Easter Keks 185
- Easter Żurek 163
- Easy Kremówka 117
- Karpatka 135
- Kebab Salad 27
- Makowiec (Poppy Seed Roll) 189
- Makowiec with Walnut Cream and Chocolate Glaze 229
- Mulled Wine 245
- Napoleon 103
- Ogórki Konserwowe (Pickled Gherkins) 263
- Oponki 151
- Pączki 145
- Pear Kompot 304
- Pickled Beetroot 271
- Pickled Peppers 275
- Pickled Vegetable Salad 287
- Plum Pie 75
- Powidła śliwkowe (Plum Jam) 317
- Preserved Apple Slices 307
- Raspberry Jam 313
- Raspberry Juice 295
- Rhubarb Cake 63
- Seasoned Red Cabbage 279
- Soured Red Borscht 203
- Strawberry Syrup 299
- Sweet Cherry Kompot 301
- Sweet Twaróg Biscuits 131
- Tiramisu 59
- Victoria Sponge 49
- Viennese Cheesecake 93
- Walnut Sponge with Almond Cream 53

sugar, almond
- Walnut Pie 113
- Walnut Sponge with Almond Cream 53

sugar, brown
- Traditional Christmas Gingerbread Biscuits 241

sugar, cane
- Kajmak Pischinger 139

sugar, icing
- Apple and Twaróg Cake 97
- Apple Pie 71
- Cherry and Custard Pie 79
- Chocolate Cake with Apples, Dried Fruit and Nuts 67
- Easter Babka 181
- Easter Keks 185
- Easy Kremówka 117
- Faworki 155
- Karpatka 135
- Kocie Oczka 109
- Makowiec (Poppy Seed Roll) 189
- Marmalade Biscuits 127
- Oponki 151
- Pączki 145
- Plum Pie 75
- Rhubarb Cake 63
- Victoria Sponge 49
- Viennese Cheesecake 93
- Walnut Pie 113
- Walnut Sponge with Almond Cream 53

sugar, vanilla
- Apple and Twaróg Cake 97
- Apple Pie 71
- Cherry and Custard Pie 79
- Chocolate Cake with Apples, Dried Fruit and Nuts 67
- Christmas Gingerbread Cake 235
- Cream Horns 121
- Dewdrop Cheesecake 89
- Easter Babka 181
- Easter Keks 185
- Easy Kremówka 117
- Kocie Oczka 109
- Makowiec with Walnut Cream and Chocolate Glaze 229
- Napoleon 103
- Oponki 151
- Pączki 145
- Plum Pie 75
- Rhubarb Cake 63
- Victoria Sponge 49
- Viennese Cheesecake 93
- Walnut Sponge with Almond Cream 53

sunflower seeds
- Spinach, Feta and Boczek Salad 35

sweetcorn
- Chicken Jelly 43
- Kebab Salad 27
- Pickled Mushroom Salad 31
- Sałatka Jarzynowa (Polish Vegetable Salad) 167
- Tuna Salad 23
- Zapiekanka 21

T

tarragon
  Barbecued Kiełbaski 17
tea, black
  Christmas Gingerbread Cake 235
  Tea-Boiled Ham 251
  Victoria Sponge 49
  Walnut Sponge with Almond Cream 53
thyme, dried
  Kebab Salad 27
tomato
  Courgette Leczo 291
  Tomato Puree 267
  Tuna Salad 23
  Zapiekanka 21
tomatoes, cherry
  Spinach, Feta and Boczek Salad 35
tomato paste
  „Greek" Fish (Ryba po grecku) 39
tomato, sundried oil
  Spinach, Feta and Boczek Salad 35
tomato, sundried pieces
  Spinach, Feta and Boczek Salad 35
  Stuffed Eggs with Sundried Tomatoes, Garlic and Feta Cheese 171
tuna (in spring water)
  Stuffed Eggs with Tuna 176
  Tuna Salad 23
turmeric, ground
  Kebab Salad 27

V

vanilla pod
  Kajmak Pischinger 139
vegetable bouillon cube
  Easter Żurek 163
Vegeta seasoning
  Tea-Boiled Ham 251
vinegar, spirit 10%
  Courgette Leczo 291
  Cucumber and Carrot Salad 283
  Ogórki Konserwowe (Pickled Gherkins) 263
  Pickled Beetroot 271
  Pickled Peppers 275
  Pickled Vegetable Salad 287
  Seasoned Red Cabbage 279
vodka
  Oponki 151
  Pączki 145

W

wafers
  Kajmak Pischinger 139
walnuts
  Chocolate Cake with Apples, Dried Fruit and Nuts 67
  Easter Keks 185
  Makowiec with Walnut Cream and Chocolate Glaze 229
  Walnut Pie 113
  Walnut Sponge with Almond Cream 53
water
  Apple and Twaróg Cake 97
  Apple Sauce 309
  Beef and Poultry Pasztet 255
  Beetroot Zakwas 199
  Candied Orange Peel 321
  Chicken Jelly 43
  Chocolate Cake with Apples, Dried Fruit and Nuts 67
  Christmas Eve Sauerkraut with Mushrooms 225
  Christmas Gingerbread Cake 235
  Courgette Leczo 291
  Cucumber and Carrot Salad 283
  Easter Babka 181
  Easter Keks 185
  Easter Żurek 163
  „Greek" Fish (Ryba po grecku) 39
  Karpatka 135
  Makowiec (Poppy Seed Roll) 189
  Makowiec with Walnut Cream and Chocolate Glaze 229
  Ogórki Kiszone (Sour Gherkins) 259
  Ogórki Konserwowe (Pickled Gherkins) 263
  Pear Kompot 304
  Pickled Beetroot 271
  Pickled Mushroom Salad 31
  Pickled Peppers 275
  Pickled Vegetable Salad 287
  Powidła śliwkowe (Plum Jam) 317
  Preserved Apple Slices 307
  Raspberry Jam 313
  Raspberry Juice 295
  Sałatka Jarzynowa (Polish Vegetable Salad) 167
  Seasoned Red Cabbage 279
  Soured Red Borscht 203
  Strawberry Syrup 299
  Stuffed Eggs with Ham and Cheese 178
  Stuffed Eggs with Mushrooms 174
  Stuffed Eggs with Sundried Tomatoes, Garlic and Feta Cheese 171
  Stuffed Eggs with Tuna 176
  Sweet Cherry Kompot 301
  Tea-Boiled Ham 251
  Tiramisu 59
  Tomato Puree 267
  Tuna Salad 23
  Uszka 215
  Uszka Filling 207
  Viennese Cheesecake 93

water, boiling
    Tuna Salad 23
water, cold
    Dewdrop Cheesecake 89
    Easy Kremówka 117
    Walnut Pie 113
water, hot
    Christmas Gingerbread Cake 235
    Uszka Dough 211
    Victoria Sponge 49
    Walnut Sponge with Almond Cream 53
water, warm
    Candied Orange Peel 321
    Raspberry Jam 313

Y

yeast, fresh
    Makowiec (Poppy Seed Roll) 189
    Marmalade Biscuits 127
    Pączki 145
yeast, instant
    Makowiec (Poppy Seed Roll) 189
    Marmalade Biscuits 127
    Pączki 145
yoghurt, natural
    Kebab Salad 27
    Spinach, Feta and Boczek Salad 35

Z

zakwas, beetroot
    Soured Red Borscht 203
zakwas, rye
    Easter Żurek 163

GOOD TO KNOW

The recipes contain additional information about possible allergens or types of diets. Here is their list and description.

 total time
- total preparation time of the dish

 difficulty

★ simple

★★ intermediate

★★★ challenging

 vegetarian

 vegetarian option
- this section suggests changes to help you make the dish vegetarian

 **vegan**

 **gluten-free**

 gluten-free option
- this section suggests changes to help you make the dish gluten-free

 **contains dairy**

 **contains nuts**

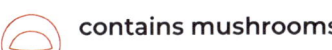 **contains mushrooms**

 **contains alcohol**

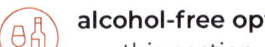 **alcohol-free option**
- this section suggests changes to help you make the dish without using alcohol

 contains pork

 pork-free option
- this section suggests changes to help you make the dish without using pork

 contains beef

 beef-free option
- this section suggests changes to help you make the dish without using beef

 contains fish

 fridge
- if the dish can be stored in the fridge

 freezer
- if the dish can be stored in the freezer

 pantry
- if the dish can be stored in the pantry

 kcal
- average calories per serving and total calories

	🕐	★	🍃	🍃	🍃	🌾	🌾
Party Food							
Oscypek with Cranberries and *Boczek* (15)	~40 min	★		✓		✓	
Barbecued *Kiełbaski* (17)	~1 h	★					✓
Zapiekanka (21)	~30 min	★	✓				✓
Tuna Salad (23)	~1 h	★					✓
Kebab Salad (27)	~2 h 5 min	★					✓
Pickled Mushroom Salad (31)	~1 h 10 min	★	✓				✓
Spinach, Feta and *Boczek* Salad (35)	~1 h 55 min	★		✓			✓
"Greek" Fish (*Ryba po grecku*) (39)	~8 h	★★					✓
Chicken Jelly (43)	~6 h	★★					✓
Cakes and Desserts							
Victoria Sponge (49)	2 h	★★	✓				
Walnut Sponge with Almond Cream (53)	2 h 30 min	★★	✓				
Tiramisu (59)	3 h	★	✓				
Rhubarb Cake (63)	3 h 30 min	★★	✓				
Chocolate Cake with Apples, Dried Fruit and Nuts (67)	3 h 30 min	★★	✓				
Apple Pie (71)	~4 h 40 min	★	✓				
Plum Pie (75)	~3 h 50 min	★	✓				
Cherry and Custard Pie (79)	~14 h	★★	✓				
Coconut Cream Pie with Plum Jam (85)	3 h 40 min	★★	✓				
Dewdrop Cheesecake (89)	4 h 10 min	★★	✓				
Viennese Cheesecake (93)	~3 h 20 min	★★	✓				
Apple and *Twaróg* Cake (97)	~5 h	★★	✓				
Napoleon (103)	5 h	★★	✓				
Kocie Oczka (109)	~2 h 30 min	★★	✓				
Walnut Pie (113)	~4 h	★★	✓				
Easy *Kremówka* (117)	3 h	★★	✓				
Cream Horns (121)	3 h	★★	✓				
Marmalade Biscuits (127)	2 h 20 min	★	✓				
Sweet *Twaróg* Biscuits (131)	3 h	★	✓				
Karpatka (135)	3 h 30 min	★★	✓				
Kajmak Pischinger (139)	~1 h 25 min	★	✓				

🥛	🌾	🍄	🍷	🍷+	🐟	🐟+	🐄	🐄+	🐖	🌡️	❄️	🥫
✓					✓	✓						
					✓		✓			✓		
✓		✓										
✓									✓	✓		
✓										✓		
✓		✓								✓		
✓					✓	✓				✓		
✓									✓	✓		
					✓	✓	✓	✓		✓		
✓										✓		
✓	✓									✓		
✓			✓							✓		
✓												✓
✓	✓											✓
✓												✓
✓												✓
✓												✓
✓										✓		
✓										✓		
✓					✓					✓		
✓										✓		
✓												✓
✓	✓											✓
✓										✓		
✓										✓		
✓												✓
✓												✓
✓										✓		
✓												✓

Good to know

	⏱ Time	★ Difficulty	🌿	🌿•	🌿	🌾	🌾•
Fat Thursday							
Pączki (145)	~4 h	★★★	✓				
Oponki (151)	~1 h	★★	✓				
Faworki (155)	~1 h 15 min	★★	✓				
Easter							
Easter *Żurek* (163)	1 h	★★					
Sałatka Jarzynowa (Polish Vegetable Salad) (167)	~2 h	★	✓				✓
Stuffed Eggs with Sundried Tomatoes, Garlic and Feta Cheese (171)	~30 min	★	✓			✓	
Stuffed Eggs with Mushrooms (174)	~40 min	★	✓			✓	
Stuffed Eggs with Tuna (176)	~30 min	★				✓	
Stuffed Eggs with Ham and Cheese (178)	~30 min	★		✓		✓	
Easter *Babka* (181)	2 h	★★	✓				
Easter Keks (185)	2 h 40 min	★★	✓				
Makowiec (Poppy Seed Roll) (189)	~3 h 30 min	★★	✓				
Christmas							
Christmas Eve Red Borscht with *Uszka* (197)							
Beetroot *Zakwas* (199)	7-10 days	★	✓		✓		
Soured Red Borscht (203)	~1 h 30 min	★	✓		✓	✓	
Uszka Filling (207)	2 h 30 min	★★	✓				
Uszka Dough (211)	40 min	★	✓				
Uszka (215)	2 h 30 min	★★	✓				
Christmas Eve Fried Fish (221)	~1,5 days	★★					✓
Christmas Eve Sauerkraut with Mushrooms (225)	~1 h 45 min	★	✓				
Makowiec with Walnut Cream and Chocolate Glaze (229)	~5 h	★★★	✓				
Christmas Gingerbread Cake (235)	2 days 5 h	★★★	✓				
Traditional Christmas Gingerbread Biscuits (241)	2 days 2 h 30 min	★★	✓				
Mulled Wine (245)	~20 min	★	✓			✓	

	🥛	🌾	🍄	🍷	🍷⊕	🐟	🐟⊕	🐄	🐄⊕	🥜	🌡	❄	🫙
	✓			✓	✓								✓
	✓			✓	✓								✓
	✓												✓
	✓					✓		✓			✓		
											✓		
	✓												
			✓										
										✓			
	✓					✓	✓						
													✓
	✓	✓											✓
	✓	✓											✓
											✓		
			✓								✓	✓	
	✓		✓										
	✓		✓								✓	✓	
	✓									✓	✓		
	✓		✓								✓		
	✓	✓				✓					✓		
	✓												✓
	✓												✓
				✓									

Good to know

Pantry	🕐	👨‍🍳	🌿	🌿	🌿	🌾	🌾
Tea-Boiled Ham (251)	4 days	★★				✓	
Beef and Poultry *Pasztet* (255)	4 h 10 min	★★					
Ogórki Kiszone (Sour Gherkins) (259)	~1 h	★	✓		✓	✓	
Ogórki Konserwowe (Pickled Gherkins) (263)	~1 h	★	✓		✓	✓	
Tomato Purée (267)	~1 h	★	✓		✓	✓	
Pickled Beetroot (271)	~2 h 10 min	★★	✓		✓	✓	
Pickled Peppers (275)	~1 h 10 min	★	✓		✓	✓	
Seasoned Red Cabbage (279)	~2 h	★★	✓		✓	✓	
Cucumber and Carrot Salad (283)	~14 h 30 min	★★	✓		✓	✓	
Pickled Vegetable Salad (287)	~1 h 20 min	★	✓		✓	✓	
Courgette *Leczo* (291)	~4 h	★★	✓		✓	✓	
Raspberry Juice (295)	~1 h 30 min	★	✓		✓	✓	
Strawberry Syrup (299)	~12 h 40 min	★	✓		✓	✓	
Sweet Cherry *Kompot* (301)	40 min	★	✓		✓	✓	
Pear *Kompot* (304)	40 min	★	✓		✓	✓	
Preserved Apple Slices (307)	~13 h	★	✓		✓	✓	
Apple Sauce (309)	~2 h	★	✓		✓	✓	
Raspberry Jam (313)	~1 h	★★	✓		✓	✓	
Powidła śliwkowe (Plum Jam) (317)	~4 h 30 min	★★	✓		✓	✓	
Candied Orange Peel (321)	~2 h 45 min	★★	✓		✓	✓	

🥛	🌾	🍄	🍷	🍾	🐄	🐄⚕	🐑	🐑⚕	🐟	🌡	❄	🫙
					✓					✓		
✓							✓			✓	✓	
										✓		✓
										✓		✓
										✓		✓
										✓		✓
										✓		✓
										✓		✓
										✓		✓
										✓		✓
												✓
										✓		✓
										✓		✓
										✓		✓
										✓		✓
										✓		✓
										✓		✓
										✓		✓
										✓		✓
											✓	✓

POLISH PRONUNCIATION

The recipes in this book will guide you step by step through the preparation of the dishes. Not all names can be translated, so to make it easier for you, I have prepared a helpful guide to the Polish alphabet below.

In Polish, each letter represents one specific sound.

Polish alphabet

A	a	**a**pple	M	m	**m**ixer
B	b	**b**ake	N	n	**n**uts
C	c	bi**ts**	O	o	**o**melette
D	d	**d**issolve	P	p	**p**epper
E	e	**e**gg	R	r	**r**adish
F	f	**f**lour	S	s	**s**poon
G	g	**g**arlic	T	t	**t**ender
H	h	**h**ummus	U	u	f**oo**d
I	i	**i**nstant	W	w	**v**inegar
J	j	**y**east	Y	y	t**u**rnip
K	k	**k**iwi	Z	z	**z**est
L	l	**l**id			

Additional letters in Polish alphabet

Ą	ą	teleph**on**e
Ć	ć	**ch**ip
Ę	ę	like **ą** but start as if to say **e**
Ł	ł	**w**hisk
Ń	ń	on**i**on
Ó	ó	f**oo**d (= U u)
Ś	ś	**sh**ip
Ź	ź	vi**si**on
Ż	ż	mira**ge**

Borrowed letters

Letters that do not appear in the Polish alphabet but are used in foreign words.

Q	q	**qu**arter
V	v	**v**inegar
X	x	bo**x**

Connected letters with a new sound
The following letters when put together in one word will create a new sound.

dz	ha**ds**
dź	**g**ym
dż	**j**elly
sz	wa**sh**
cz	**ch**erry

Connected letters with the same sound as existing letters
Two or three letters joined together will often represent existing sounds of letters in the Polish alphabet.

ci	=	ć
ch	=	h
dzi	=	dź
ni	=	ń
si	=	ś
zi	=	ź
rz	=	ż

Examples

żurek
ż   u   r   e   k
mira**ge** | f**oo**d | **r**adish | **e**gg | **k**iwi

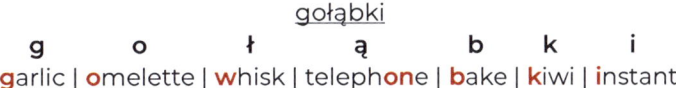
gołąbki
g   o   ł   ą   b   k   i
garlic | **o**melette | **wh**isk | teleph**on**e | **b**ake | **k**iwi | **i**nstant

kiełbasa
k   i   e   ł   b   a   s   a
kiwi | **i**nstant | **e**gg | **wh**isk | **b**ake | **a**pple | **s**poon | **a**pple

Polish pronunciation

Original title: *Przytulny smak Polski. Przepisy na pamiątkę. Tom 2*

Copyright © Wacław Jankiewicz, 2025

Editor of the Polish version: Ewa Cat Mędrzecka - https://www.instagram.com/catvloguje/

Translation: Natalia Mętrak-Ruda

Proofreading of the English version: Jamie James

Photos: Wacław Jankiewicz
Photo on page 8: Archiwum rodzinne
Photo on page 10: Roksana Głowińska - https://liryka.net/
Photos on pages 83, 173, 213, 325, 339: Bartłomiej Jankiewicz

Illustrations: Copyright © Wacław Jankiewicz

Graphic design: Copyright © Wacław Jankiewicz

All rights reserved.
No part of this publication may be reproduced or transmitted in any form or by any means, electronic or mechanical, including photocopy, recording or any other information storage and retrieval system, without the prior written permission of the copyright owner.

First edition

ISBN: 978-1-913986-31-5

https://cosytastes.com/

Printed in Great Britain
by Amazon

211081d4-0e07-4757-9728-a8f031eae0efR01